STUMPS AND SOVEREIGNTY

South Asian Cricket from Empire to the Digital Age

BY

SUFGHAN SARWAR KHAN

ISBN: 979-8-89571-186-6(paperback)
First Edition, 2025

Written by Sufghan Sarwar Khan
Edited by Ashley Emma and Editorial Team

For permissions, inquiries, and author contact:
Sufghan@gmail.com

Acknowledgements

The journey of writing this book has been both solitary and expansive — solitary in its research and reflection, but expansive in its engagement with ideas, histories, and the evolving landscape of global sport.

I am deeply grateful to Ashley Emma and her editorial team, whose meticulous attention, editorial sensitivity, and thoughtful suggestions helped sharpen the prose and elevate the final manuscript. Their contributions ensured that the narrative remained clear, compelling, and accessible to a wide readership.

Beyond this, the research, writing, structuring, and conceptual vision of the book were carried out independently — a process that, while demanding, proved intellectually rewarding and creatively fulfilling. Every chapter reflects a sustained engagement with cricket not just as a sport, but as a cultural archive and a lens through which to view broader questions of power, identity, and change.

To all those unnamed readers, historians, players, and thinkers — past and present — who have shaped how we understand cricket and its meanings: this work stands on your shoulders.

Dedication

To my maternal grandfather, Chaudhry Iqbal, who served with distinction in the British East Indian Railways before Partition and introduced cricket to his ancestral village, Buray Ke, Pasrur — embedding it into the cultural life of rural Punjab.

And to my paternal great-great-grandfather, Subedar Major Hashim Khan of the 58th Vaughan's Rifles, British Indian Army — who served under Field Marshal Lord Roberts in the Second Anglo-Afghan War (1878–1880) and under Sir Arthur Barrett in the Third (1919); and who, during the First World War (1914–1918), helped recruit over a thousand soldiers from his ancestral village, Rupo Chak, where he had introduced cricket in the late 19th century — planting its early seeds long before it became a sport of nations.

Preface

Cricket has always been more than a pastime. From the regimented fields of colonial cantonments to the high-definition arenas of global media capitalism, the game has long reflected—and at times helped reshape—the cultural, political, and economic rhythms of the world. Nowhere is this more vividly evident than in South Asia, where cricket has transcended its imperial imprint to become a site of identity, ambition, commerce, and postcolonial expression.

The impetus for this work arose not from nostalgia but from urgency. The world is changing—rapidly and irreversibly. Climate disruptions, digital revolutions, demographic shifts, and geopolitical uncertainty are redrawing the contours of everyday life. Cricket, like other global institutions, cannot afford to drift passively through these transformations. It must engage, adapt, and, where necessary, reinvent itself. This project seeks to situate cricket not as an isolated sport but as a dynamic cultural and political phenomenon—one that has always carried deeper implications than the scorecard suggests.

Each century has brought its own evolutionary leap in cricket's structure. The nineteenth century gave us Test cricket: a format steeped in endurance, etiquette, and empire. The twentieth century introduced the One-Day International, aligning the game with the tempo of modern life and mass media. The twenty-first century has embraced T20—a hyper-compressed spectacle tailored for attention economies and algorithmic consumption. These transitions were never accidental; they were responses to technological, social, and economic shifts. As the twenty-second century looms, new possibilities beckon.

Among them is the emergence of hybrid formats—compressed red-ball matches over three days, or adaptive scheduling that merges the narrative depth of Test cricket with the urgency of limited overs. Such innovations, while preserving tradition, could help the game remain relevant across diverse viewing publics and time constraints. Moreover, the integration of AI in strategy, officiating, and injury prevention is not just a technical upgrade—it signals a deeper reconfiguration of how sport and data co-evolve.

In this context, it is plausible—perhaps even inevitable—that human-machine collaboration will enter elite cricket. The concept of a Robo-Human Premier League, where biomechanically enhanced athletes compete under regulated conditions, may sound futuristic, but its logic is rooted in current trajectories across medicine, defense, and performance science. This is not speculative indulgence; it is anticipatory realism.

Yet, the story of cricket's transformation is not only technological. It is also social and geopolitical. Cricket has often found a second life in conditions of rupture. For communities in exile—whether Afghan refugees in Pakistan or displaced players in the Gulf—cricket has served as both continuity and aspiration. The Pakistan team's decade-long exile from home venues, reflect how the game can travel with people, offering dignity and direction during difficult times. Cricket's strength, in many ways, lies in its ability to adapt across terrains—political, digital, and emotional.

This book also closely examines one of the most underappreciated but vital engines of cricketing transformation: innovative captaincy. From the strategic brilliance of Don Bradman and the cultural revolution of Arjuna Ranatunga to the fearless aggression of Sourav Ganguly and the tactical maturity of Pat Cummins—this volume traces how leadership has often redefined the identity and trajectory of entire teams and eras. Imran Khan's statesmanlike leadership, blending charisma, political instinct, and visionary team building, not only delivered Pakistan its first World Cup in 1992 but also instilled a lasting ethos of self-belief. Mike Brearley's psychologically astute and empathetic leadership, most notably during England's Ashes revival in 1981, remains a model of how intellect and emotional intelligence can outmaneuver raw skill. Mark Taylor's revolutionary and innovative approach—helped Australia transition into its golden era with confidence and grace. In the contemporary landscape, Ben Stokes' era of "Bazball"—a high-octane, risk-embracing philosophy developed with coach Brendon McCullum—has disrupted orthodoxies, revitalized Test cricket's tempo, and electrified audiences, even as it continues to grapple with its own tactical limitations.

The globalization of cricket is another central axis of this study. Beyond the established powerhouses of South Asia and the Commonwealth, the book explores the unrealized potential of cricket in new frontiers—China, South Korea, Japan, the USA, Canada, and South America. These are not fanciful markets, but logical extensions of cricket's cultural and commercial trajectory. As with any global product, success in the 21st and 22nd centuries will depend not on heritage alone but on inclusion, imagination, and infrastructure. As the game migrates into these uncharted territories, it raises urgent questions about who gets to play, who gets to profit, and how the rules of the game might evolve in new geographies.

This volume seeks to chart that complex evolution. Rather than offering a linear history, it traces the game's shifting roles—from an imperial pastime to a postcolonial idiom, from a tool of soft power to a node in the platform economy. South Asia remains the gravitational center of this analysis—not only for its historical contribution, but for its continuing reinvention of cricket's commercial, aesthetic, and political meanings.

At the same time, the study moves beyond national boundaries to examine emerging and overlooked spaces. It considers how cricket is shaped by digital fan labor, streaming economies, climate anxieties, and speculative projections. As the sport enters new markets—from the

Gulf to the U.S., from Africa to virtual platforms—questions of governance, inclusion, and sustainability take on renewed importance.

Crucially, the book argues that the future of cricket will depend on its ability to manage contradiction: between innovation and heritage, market forces and equitable access, commercial spectacle and ethical responsibility. Its survival lies not in resisting change but in absorbing and reframing it. In that sense, cricket is not unique—but it is especially well-suited for the task, precisely because of its historical layering and cultural plasticity.

What began as a colonial game for elites has become a global narrative written in many dialects. It is now played in refugee camps and fantasy leagues, streamed to billions and debated in parliamentary chambers. It has entered blockchain economies and, potentially, extra-terrestrial imaginations. And yet, through all of this, it retains the intimacy of a child's first bat, the weight of a stadium's silence, and the memory of histories long contested.

This book follows cricket not only through its past and present but into its possible futures. It does so with critical affection: challenging, questioning, and occasionally unsettling—but always rooted in the belief that the game is worth understanding more deeply. Because in telling the story of cricket, we often tell stories of the world—and perhaps even of where we are going next.

A special tribute is due to Sir Geoffrey Boycott, whose unwavering dedication to the game of cricket has inspired me for decades. More than just a legendary opening batsman, he has been a voice of clarity, critique, and cricketing intellect, prompting me to study the sport not just as a spectacle, but as a layered cultural phenomenon. His passion for the game, both on and off the field, has profoundly shaped how I view cricket's deeper narratives. I extend my warmest wishes for his continued health and strength, with deep appreciation for all he has contributed to the game and to generations of cricket thinkers.

Table of Contents

Part I – The English Foundations

Chapter 1 – Origins and Early Growth

1.1 Elizabethan Roots: The Birth of Cricket

The history of cricket begins not in palaces or chronicles of state but in the quiet greens of rural England, before the Wars of the Roses in the 1400s, children in English villages were already playing basic wooden stick and ball games on open fields. These simple pastimes were the early roots from which cricket later developed. To understand the evolution of this game, one must return to the bloodied fifteenth century, when England was torn apart by dynastic strife. The Wars of the Roses (1455–1487) set York against Lancaster in a generation long struggle for the crown. Armies clashed at Towton, Barnet, and Tewkesbury; noble families were extinguished; and the common people endured decades of uncertainty. Only in 1485, when Henry Tudor triumphed at Bosworth and was crowned Henry VII, did the conflict finally end. His marriage to Elizabeth of York united red and white roses, offering stability at last. Historians generally agree that the conclusion of the Wars of the Roses also marked the end of medieval England. The medieval order of feudal lords and dynastic strife gave way to a more centralized monarchy under the Tudors, one that emphasized governance, law, and stability over private warfare.

The culmination of medieval England left the nation with two enduring legacies: a resilient crown that could command loyalty beyond noble factions, and a cultural foundation—of parish life, rural custom, and common law—that would later allow new forms of leisure, including games like cricket, to take root and flourish.

The Tudors, a Welsh descended family that rose from relative obscurity, would go on to rule England for more than a century. Their dynasty brought strong monarchs, who expanded England's influence, strengthened its navy, and encouraged culture. In binding the kingdom together, the Tudors also created conditions in which cricket, unnoticed but alive, could take root.

Henry VII ruled cautiously, preoccupied with survival and treasury. His son, Henry VIII, turned sport into spectacle: vast, energetic, and imposing, he hunted, jousted, shot bows, and played tennis at Hampton and Whitehall. Sport at court was ritual, a performance of dominance that reinforced monarchy itself. Yet while the king broke lances in tiltyards and entertained ambassadors with lavish tournaments, in the countryside shepherd boys in Kent and Surrey struck balls of wool or leather with crooked sticks; village children marked wickets on barn doors and sheep pens. Henry never noticed, but the shoots of cricket were already emerging in the overlooked corners of his realm.

His tumultuous reign also reshaped England's religious and social order. His break with Rome to marry Anne Boleyn the Reformation, leading to the dissolution of monasteries and the removal of feast days from the calendar. Yet the hunger for festivity remained, and games stepped into the spaces once filled by church ritual: bowls, stool-ball, football, cudgel-play, and cricket. Villagers sought amusement not just to pass idle time but to reinforce bonds of fellowship in communities newly stripped of monastic festivals. After Henry came Edward VI, frail and Protestant, then Mary I, his Catholic half-sister, remembered for her marriage to Philip II of Spain and her persecution of Protestants. Few believed England's future held promise in those years of religious upheaval. Yet her half-sister Elizabeth, daughter of Anne Boleyn, transformed the kingdom.

Elizabeth I reigned from 1558 to 1603, presiding over an age remembered as England's golden era. She restored the Protestant settlement, fostered a flowering of English drama, and guided the nation to naval triumph with the defeat of the Spanish Armada in 1588. Her reign gave England confidence, language, and vision. It was also during her rule that cricket first entered the written record. There are early hints of bat and ball games, a record from 1300 mentions Prince Edward playing a game called *creag* at Newenden in Kent, though historians are unsure if it was truly cricket. The first indisputable evidence came in 1597, when John Derrick, a 59-year-old witness in a Guildford court case, testified that as a schoolboy in the 1550s he had played "creckett." That passing remark, born of legal necessity, anchors cricket's origins in Tudor England and provides the first fixed point in its chronology.

In Elizabeth's time, cricket looked very different from today. The ball was bowled *underarm*, rolled or skimmed along the ground, and players used curved bats like shepherds' crooks to sweep it away. Wickets were just two stakes with a crossbar, not the three stumps we know now. Runs came from dashing between wickets, marked by notches on sticks. Some records from the early 1600s show men being fined for skipping church to play, proof that cricket had already moved beyond children's play and had become part of community life.

In the sixteenth century, sport was tied to law, religion, and community. Men were required by statute to practice archery, while village greens saw violent football games. Wrestling, cudgel-fighting, bowls, bearbaiting, and cockfighting were common; nobles hunted deer or falcons. Cricket was different, it needed little space or money, involved no cruelty, and could be enjoyed by both children and adults. Its simplicity became its strength.

The early years of cricket in England coincided with the age of Shakespeare, when both games and theatre shaped community life. Cricket's first steps unfolded in the same England that staged Shakespeare's plays. Although Shakespeare never mentioned cricket by name, his plays reflect the spirit of games. In Henry VI he refers to "the base," a rustic ball game. His comedies often show country contests that entertained crowds.

Elizabeth's reign was also about more than plays and games. Beneath its glitter, her ministers built the foundations of naval power. The Armada's defeat in 1588 secured not only survival but maritime promise. With this came exploration into new lands. In December 1600, Elizabeth granted a charter to the East India Company, a group of merchants determined to challenge the trade of the Portuguese and Dutch. At first, the Company was small, its future uncertain. Yet its ships carried more than cloth and spices: they carried English habits. Cricket travelled overseas with English sailors and officials, who played the game in ports like Madras and Calcutta.

Elizabeth's later years were marked by pride and anxiety. In March 1603, she died at Richmond, marking the end of the Tudor dynasty begun by Henry VII at the Battle of Bosworth. The crown passed to James VI of Scotland, who became James I of England, uniting the crowns and inheriting a more stable and outward-looking realm than any of the Tudors before him. Cricket, humble as it was, endured. Played on the greens of Kent, Surrey, and Sussex, it outlasted monarchs and reformations, embedding in rural life.

Gambling also found its way into matches, with wagers placed on which side might prevail, or which bowler could topple the wicket. Though modest in scale, these early bets foreshadowed cricket's later and more complex relationship with money—a shadow that would follow the game not only in England but also in India and other parts of South Asia.

While cricket lingered in English villages, another story was unfolding across the Indian Ocean, the rise of the Mughal Empire. In 1556, 13-year-old Akbar inherited a fragile throne after his father, Humayun, died suddenly. That same year, General Hemu marched to expel the Mughals. The armies met at Panipat; Akbar's regent, Bairam Khan, led his forces. When an arrow struck Hemu in the eye, his troops panicked, and the Mughal victory was decisive. Had Hemu triumphed, the dynasty might have ended; Akbar, then a boy, might have been erased from history. Without Akbar, there would be no Jahangir to welcome English merchants; the East India Company's charter might have been useless. Cricket's later journey to India depended, indirectly, on this outcome. The Mughal Empire traced its roots to Central Asia, founded by Babur of Ferghana Valley after his victory at Panipat in 1526. His son Humayun briefly lost the throne but regained it in 1555, paving the way for Babur's grandson, Akbar, to consolidate power. Under Akbar, the empire flourished across much of India.

Akbar's reign (1556–1605) was expansive and innovative. He consolidated Mughal power, abolished the jizya tax, promoted tolerance, and built an empire renowned for culture and debate. Elizabeth and Akbar even exchanged letters, early signs of diplomatic outreach across the oceans. Though they never met, their two realms, England and Mughal India were edging toward contact. When Akbar died in 1605, his son Jahangir inherited the throne. In 1613, Jahangir granted the East India Company its first trading rights at Surat, merchants who had once requested Elizabeth for a charter now negotiated in Mughal courts. Company men carried with them their food, ale, and games, cricket was among them. Not yet India's sport, it was nonetheless planted in Mughal soil.

The company's presence in India during these years was tentative and precarious. English factors lived in walled compounds, surrounded by heat, disease, and suspicion. To survive, they clung to rituals of home: prayers in English chapels, familiar foods when available, and games that reminded them of green fields left behind. Cricket, requiring only a bat and ball, could be played on any patch of ground. It was not merely diversion; it was continuity, an assertion of Englishness in an alien land. In this way, the game's survival in distant settlements foreshadowed the vast cultural exchanges and tensions of the empire.

By the 1620s, cricket remained on village greens in Kent and Sussex, yet its destiny was no longer purely English. It was tied now to ships, merchants, emperors, and empires. Its following chapters would be written across oceans as much as in England's shires. What began as a diversion for boys had, within a few decades, acquired the trappings of an adult pastime: risk, rivalry, and the shadow of the law. For East India Company officials abroad, it became a marker of power for Indians, eventually becoming a symbol of mastery.

1.2 – Stuart England: Cricket Through Turmoil and Restoration

Elizabeth's death in 1603 brought James VI of Scotland to the English throne as James I, opening the Stuart century. It was a period of civil war, regicide, dictatorship, restoration, and revolution—yet through it all, cricket endured. What began as a rustic diversion quietly grew into the pastime of men, proving its resilience in an age of upheaval.

James himself cared little for games beyond hunting and hawking, but in the countryside cricket continued. Records from Kent, Sussex, and Surrey show parishioners fined for playing on Sundays—evidence that adult men now played seriously enough to risk punishment. Authorities tried to curb it, yet the repeated fines show that cricket was not fading but spreading.

At court, politics and religion dominated. Cricket was ignored by nobles, but this indifference helped the game survive. Other sports could be taxed or banned, while cricket, modest and local, slipped beneath notice and endured through ordinary enthusiasm.

Charles I's troubled reign deepened tensions. Taxes, religious disputes, and finally civil war fractured the kingdom. Armies trampled fields, churches were occupied, and leisure shrank. Still, cricket lingered: soldiers between campaigns sometimes played, and village boys too young for muskets still carved wickets on greens. The game's survival owed much to its simplicity—no horses or expensive gear were needed, only a ball and bat.

After the king's execution in 1649, Cromwell's Puritan Commonwealth imposed stern repression. Festivals, theatres, and sports were curtailed, Sunday play punished. Yet even in this climate, records show men still charged for playing cricket. To take up bat and ball in those years was a small act of defiance, proof the game refused to vanish.

The Restoration of Charles II in 1660 revived both monarchy and merriment. Theatres reopened, taverns thrived, and sport flourished again. Cricket reemerged in fuller daylight. Local pride sharpened contests, small wagers added urgency, and disputes over stakes spurred the first need for rules. Audiences grew as parish teams faced rivals, with alehouses sponsoring sides. Gambling, once hidden, now gave cricket a competitive edge.

By the 1670s and 1680s, references to cricket increased in records and lawsuits. Matches expanded beyond villages, drawing crowds from surrounding areas. Wealthier patrons began to back sides, lending money and prestige. The outlines of organized cricket were forming contests that mattered, rules that were argued, and rivalries that drew spectators.

Meanwhile, England's expanding navy and the East India Company carried the game abroad. Sailors struck balls on decks, factors played in forts along India's coast. Cricket was still rustic, but already it was leaving English soil.

The Glorious Revolution of 1688 stabilized England under William and Mary. With political confidence came leisure, and with leisure, cricket had space to grow. By 1700, the game still looked crude—underarm bowling, curved bats, two-stump wickets—but its essence was established. Teams competed, runs were tallied, wagers raised the stakes, and onlookers cared who won.

Through a century of storm and recovery, cricket survived not by royal decree but by local stubbornness. Villagers risked fines, boys carved notches, and neighbours placed bets. By the end of the Stuart age, cricket was no longer fragile. It had endured its trial by fire and was ready for the next stage: to step beyond village greens and claim its place as England's national sport.

English Dynasties & Monarchs

Wars of the Roses (1455–1487): *Civil wars in England between the House of Lancaster (red rose) and the House of York (white rose) for the throne. Ended when Henry Tudor defeated Richard III at the Battle of Bosworth in 1485.*

Medieval England (c. 1066–1485) *– The period stretching from the Norman Conquest to the end of the Wars of the Roses, marked by feudalism, castles, and the rise of Parliament. It ended with the Tudor victory at Bosworth (1485), often seen as the transition to early modern England.*

House of Tudor (1485–1603): *Welsh-descended dynasty that ruled England.*

Henry VII (1485–1509): *Founder of Tudor dynasty, cautious and financially careful.*

Henry VIII (1509–1547): *Famous for six marriages, break with the Catholic Church, created the Church of England, loved sport and spectacle.*

Edward VI (1547–1553): *Henry's son, frail, Protestant, died young.*

Mary I (1553–1558): *Catholic, married Philip II of Spain, persecuted Protestants ("Bloody Mary").*

Elizabeth I (1558–1603): *Last Tudor monarch, oversaw England's "Golden Age," Shakespeare's plays, defeat of Spanish Armada (1588). Cricket first recorded during her reign.*

House of Stuart (1603–1714): *Scottish family that succeeded the Tudors.*

James I (1603–1625): *Formerly James VI of Scotland, united crowns of England & Scotland.*

Charles I (1625–1649): *Executed after Civil War.*

Commonwealth & Oliver Cromwell (1649–1660): *England became a republic, sports and festivities were restricted.*

Charles II (1660–1685): *Restored monarchy, allowed theatre, sport, and gambling to flourish again.*

James II (1685–1688): *Deposed in the Glorious Revolution.*

William III & Mary II (1689–1702): *Rulers after James II, stabilized monarchy.*

Mughal Emperors of India

Babur (1526–1530): *Founder of Mughal dynasty, Central Asian ruler who won at the Battle of Panipat (1526).*

Humayun (1530–1540, restored 1555–1556): *Lost empire, then regained it shortly before his death.*

Akbar the Great (1556–1605): *Expanded Mughal Empire, promoted religious tolerance, abolished jizya tax, built strong administration. Contemporary of Elizabeth I.*

Jahangir (1605–1627): *Akbar's son, patron of art, granted East India Company rights at Surat in 1613.*

Shah Jahan (1628–1658): *Builder of the Taj Mahal.*

Aurangzeb (1658–1707): *Expanded empire to its largest extent but enforced stricter Islamic laws; after him, Mughal power declined.*

Cricket Terms (Early & Modern)

Bat: *Originally curved like a shepherd's staff; now a flat wooden blade used to hit the ball.*

Ball: *Early balls were made of wool or leather; today, a hard leather sphere with a stitched seam.*

Wickets: *In early cricket, two stakes with a crossbar; modern cricket uses three wooden stumps with two bails on top.*

Bowling: *Delivering the ball towards the batter.*

Underarm bowling: *The ball was rolled or skimmed along the ground in early cricket (like bowling in tenpin).*

Roundarm bowling: *Emerged in the early 19th century, arm raised partway.*

Overarm bowling: *Allowed from 1864; bowler's arm goes over the shoulder, used in modern cricket.*

Runs: *Scored by batters running between wickets after hitting the ball. Early players used tally sticks to record runs.*

John Derrick (1597): *Schoolboy in Guildford during the 1550s who testified in a court case that he had played "creckett." His statement is the earliest definite evidence of cricket.*

Wagers*: Bets placed on cricket matches, especially in the 18th century, which drove aristocratic interest and shaped early professional play. Sums were often immense, influencing tactics and the need for standardized rules.*

Bowled*: One of cricket's oldest methods of dismissal, where the bowler delivers the ball and it hits the stumps, dislodging the bails. Considered the most definitive way to dismiss a batsman.*

Chapter 2 – Gambling, Gentlemen, and Clubs

2.1 The Game of Wagers and Gentlemen: Cricket in the Eighteenth Century

By the dawn of the eighteenth century, cricket had already survived a turbulent Stuart century marked by war, recession, Puritan repression, and the uncertainties of the Restoration. What had once been little more than a rustic diversion on village greens had begun to spread into something larger, something that carried with it not only the laughter of children but also the wagers of men with purses and influence. In this new age, cricket stepped onto a wider stage, no longer hidden in parish records or the fines of constables but present in the diaries of aristocrats, the notices of London newspapers, and the growing appetite for sport among England's gentry. The transformation that unfolded between 1700 and 1750 laid the foundations of the game as we know it.

The countryside remained the cradle, but the game was being lifted upward by patrons who saw in it both amusement and opportunity. Gambling played a significant role in shaping this transformation more than anything else. England in the early eighteenth century was a society of wagers. Gentlemen bet on horse races, cockfights, and prize fights with the same intensity that they later brought to cricket. Money gave a rural pastime sharper edges and higher stakes. Village contests that once ended with pride or laughter now concluded with coins exchanged, debts recorded, and reputations made or ruined. Gambling drew the gentry in, for they were men of leisure who required spectacles on which to place their bets. Cricket, adaptable and competitive, proved ideal.

The early decades of the eighteenth century saw aristocrats and landowners begin to sponsor village teams. They wagered on their tenants and laborers, sometimes even supplying equipment and coaching to secure victory. Some of the earliest recorded matches mention stakes of fifty guineas or more huge sums at the time, worth the equivalent of around $10,000 in today's money (2025). One famous contest in 1709, between teams from Kent and Surrey, is among the earliest known with a written record. Though details are scarce, it shows that counties—not just villages—were now fielding sides. Matches like these drew large crowds, for wherever serious money was at stake, excitement quickly followed.

By the 1720s and 1730s, London itself had become a center of cricketing attention, largely thanks to the Artillery Ground at Finsbury. This space, once used for militia practice, became the sport's premier venue. Here, gentlemen and commoners alike thronged to watch matches that were often advertised in newspapers. The *Daily Courant* and other sheets began printing notices of upcoming contests, listing wagers, locations, and sometimes even rules. Spectators came not only to see the game but to gamble themselves, for bookmakers prowled the crowd, offering odds on outcomes, totals, or the performance of players.

It was in the Artillery Ground that some of the most important developments of the early eighteenth century took place. The matches there were not casual affairs: they were highly organized, with umpires appointed and wagers enforced by honor and sometimes by law. Records mention contests such as the famous 1732 match between London and Surrey, which drew vast crowds and heavy betting. In 1739, a celebrated game saw Kent defeat All-England, with the great Kentish patron, the duke of Dorset, taking pride in his side's superiority. Dorset himself was a remarkable figure, often cited as one of cricket's first true aristocratic champions. He wagered vast sums on his Kentish teams and ensured that his tenants were trained and equipped to defend the county's honor.

Alongside Dorset were other patrons, including Sir William Gage, whose Sussex teams became formidable, and Frederick, prince of Wales, who occasionally attended matches. Patronage gave the game status, and wagers gave it urgency. Yet this union of money and sport demanded some measure of order. Rules, which had long been local and improvised, now had to be standardized, if only to prevent disputes that could ruin great bets. It was during this period that we first saw written "articles of agreement" before matches, setting out conditions such as the size of the wicket, the number of players, and the manner of dismissals.

In 1727, the duke of Richmond and Alan Brodrick, two noble patrons, drew up a set of articles for matches between their Sussex and Surrey sides. These documents, although not universal, represent some of the earliest attempts to codify cricket laws. They specified that the wickets should be twenty-two yards apart—the length that endures to this day—and described how the ball should be bowled underhand and how batsmen could be put out. They also established the role of umpires as arbiters whose decisions were final. Though simple, these articles were a critical step toward transforming cricket from a game of custom into a game of law.

The nature of play in these early decades was still rough by modern standards. Bowling remained strictly underarm, with the ball often rolled or skimmed along the ground. The bats were curved, more like hockey sticks than the flat willows of today, designed to meet balls that stayed low. Wickets consisted of two stumps with a single crosspiece, rather than the three-stump arrangement later introduced. Runs were counted, but they were not yet the essential measure they became; wagers often focused instead on whether a batsman would be bowled or how many outs a side could make within a set time. Matches could last all day, sometimes spilling into two, depending on the terms agreed beforehand.

Despite these rough edges, the game was growing in complexity and popularity. By the 1740s, large matches could attract thousands of spectators, some traveling from far afield. The Artillery Ground saw disorder at times, because the crowds were passionate and the sums wagered immensely. Riots occasionally broke out when disputes arose, and there were calls for tighter control. Yet this very chaos testifies to cricket's new place in English culture: it had become a public spectacle.

One of the most famous matches of the era occurred in 1744, when Kent faced an All-England XI at the Artillery Ground. This match is often associated with the publication of the first known printed laws of cricket, which appeared that same year. The 1744 Laws, drawn up by members of London clubs and patrons, codified many practices already in place. They confirmed the twenty-two-yard pitch, defined the size of the wicket, and laid down principles for scoring and dismissals. They also regulated the duties of umpires and established expectations for fair play. The very existence of such a document reflects the seriousness with which cricket had become taken. Disputes could now be judged not merely by custom but by reference to agreed law.

The 1744 Laws also mark the beginning of cricket's journey into respectability. While gambling remained its lifeblood, the existence of rules allowed gentlemen to argue that it was a game of order and fairness, not simply a vehicle for vice. Indeed, the lawmakers stressed that umpires' decisions must be accepted without dispute, an early nod to the idea that cricket is a moral as well as a physical contest. The tension between gambling and respectability would persist, but the balance was beginning to shift.

The mid-century also saw the rise of players whose names became known beyond their villages. Men like Richard Newland of Slindon, a batsman of formidable ability, drew crowds and patronage. Slindon's team, supported by the duke of Richmond, gained renown, defeating even London sides on occasion. Such stars gave cricket faces and reputations, further fueling wagers and interest. For the first time, individual players could be discussed in coffeehouses and taverns, admired or criticized by those who had never set foot on their village green.

At the same time, cricket was beginning to spread geographically. Matches were reported not only in London and the southern counties but also in the Midlands and beyond. Newspaper reports from the 1740s note games as far afield as Nottingham and Sheffield, early signs of the north's embrace of sport. The spread was uneven, but it showed that cricket was no longer confined to a handful of southern shires. Records from 1745 mention women's cricket in Surrey.

Through these decades, the game also attracted criticism. Moralists condemned the gambling and disorder, while some clergy railed against matches held on Sundays. The government occasionally worried about crowds and wagers, fearing riots or the loss of productive labor. Yet suppression never came; the game had become too popular and too closely tied to the interests of the gentry. Cricket's survival through these controversies speaks to its resilience and its appeal across classes.

By 1750, cricket was no longer merely a rustic diversion. It was a sport that drew noble patrons, filled the Artillery Ground with thousands, generated printed laws, and produced players of regional fame. Its future lay not only in the wagers of dukes but in the growing sense that it was a game worth preserving for its own sake. The century still had decades to run, and greater transformations were ahead—the rise of Hambledon, the founding of the MCC, and the spread of the game abroad. But in the first half of the eighteenth century, cricket had crossed a threshold. It had left behind the obscurity of parish fines and rustic notches and entered a new world: one of money, crowds, and law.

This transformation was neither smooth nor inevitable. It was built on wagers that could as easily have bankrupted patrons as enriched them; on crowds that could as easily riot as cheer; on laws that might have been ignored had they not been upheld by honor. Yet it endured, because the game itself—simple, adaptable, compelling—offered something that spectators and players alike desired. Cricket gave men of leisure a spectacle, men of labor a chance at fame, and gamblers an endless opportunity for risk and reward. It was this mixture that allowed cricket not only to survive but to thrive in the crucible of eighteenth-century England.

2.2 – The Hambledon Era

By the middle of the eighteenth century, cricket was no longer a scattered diversion of parishes and villages, but something more organized, visible, and contested. The decades between the 1750s and 1780s are remembered as the age when Hambleden in Hampshire rose as the first great club, technically first dynasty in cricket. A hub where the rustic game became more structured and began to resemble the sport that would later be codified at Lord's. It was also an age when gambling ran through cricket like a restless current, drawing in aristocrats who wagered fortunes and professionals who played for both pride and livelihood. The growth of the game in this period was inseparable from the culture of betting. Yet, paradoxically, it was also inseparable from the love of the game itself, for the contests that filled the Hambledon ground were thrilling enough to be remembered long after the stakes had been forgotten.

The Hambledon Club's rise reflected both its geographical location and the circumstances of the time. Nestled in rural Hampshire, it was accessible to London yet far enough removed to keep its rustic air. From the late 1760s onwards, cricket began to be played there with intensity and regularity unmatched elsewhere. Gentlemen patrons, many of whom were landed aristocrats, supported the club, while skilled local players added to the quality of the matches. For nearly three decades, Hambledon became, as later writers liked to put it, the "cradle of cricket," a place where rules were discussed, tactics debated, and crowds gathered. The sense of the village green remained, but the atmosphere was different: here, contests were organized, scores tallied carefully, and wagers placed openly. The club embodied the transition from pastime to proto-professional sport.

Even before Hambledon, schools and aristocratic sides were already giving cricket visibility. Although bat-and-ball games had been part of school life earlier, it was in the mid-18th century that more formal inter-school contests began to be recorded. In 1760, Winchester defeated Eton on Port Meadow at Oxford, a contest that proved the game had spread deeply into the world of education. Just a few years later, in 1763, cricket was recorded for the first time in Wales at Pembroke. By 1771, Sheffield was playing Nottingham, demonstrating the game's reach as far north as Yorkshire and Durham. Matches like these hinted at cricket's future as a truly national sport, no longer confined to the southern shires.

The Hambledon era also introduced crucial technical developments. The bat underwent significant changes during these decades. Earlier in the century, it still resembled a curved shepherd's crook, suited to balls bowled low along the ground. But as bowlers began to pitch the ball with more flight in the 1740s and 1750s, batsmen needed a new instrument. The curve gave way to a straighter blade, flat in front, better able to meet a rising ball. By the 1760s, the bat had assumed much of its current shape. Advertisements confirm this: in 1774, William Staples of Sevenoaks offered bats for sale, indicating a commercial trade was already in place. Surviving examples from the period, characterized by their heaviness and straight blades, testify to the game's technical evolution.

The ball was also changing. What had once been a lump of stitched leather wrapped unevenly around a core now became more standardized. The duke's family, who had been making balls for generations, presented in 1780 a six-seamed ball to the prince of Wales, later George IV, cementing their place in cricket lore. The new seam made grip easier and movement more pronounced, giving bowlers greater variety and ensuring that the duel between bat and ball remained balanced.

The wicket underwent its most famous transformation during this period. For much of the game's early life, it consisted of two stumps with a single crossbar, which left much room for the ball to pass through untouched. But in 1771, during a Hambledon match, Thomas White of Chertsey arrived at the crease, wielding an enormous bat as wide as the wicket itself, provoking outrage. The absurdity of a bat covering the entire wicket highlighted the inadequacy of the two-stump system. Soon after, a third stump was added, narrowing the batsman's advantage and bringing the game closer to fairness. This small moment became one of cricket's defining innovations, cemented in practice across the country by the 1770s.

Public interest in cricket during the Hambledon years was intense. The Artillery Ground in London had long hosted major contests, but the club added something distinctive: a blend of rustic festivity with organized, high-level play. Matches drew crowds of villagers and aristocrats alike. Naturally, even long before the 1770s, people kept tally of who won and lost—victories and defeats were remembered in local pride, gossip, and wagers—but detailed numerical scoring was often inconsistent or quickly lost. What changed at Hambledon was the effort to preserve results in a permanent, statistical form. The earliest known printed scorecards date back to 1776, produced by William Pratt of Sevenoaks. These were rudimentary, but they marked a new seriousness about recording cricket. By 1777, bowlers were even credited for catches taken off their bowling, another step toward the statistical culture that would later define the game.

Some matches stand out as landmarks. In 1769, John Minshull scored 107 for the duke of Dorset's XI against Wrotham, the first recorded century in cricket history. This achievement thrilled spectators and set a precedent for the batting milestones that remain central to the sport. In 1772, Hambledon played All-England in what is often described as the first great match to have its full score recorded at the fall of each wicket, an innovation in record-keeping that reflected a growing seriousness about the sport. Around the same time, a painting depicted boys playing cricket at Harrow School, providing visual proof that the game was becoming an integral part of England's educational elite.

The players of Hambledon became legends. Richard Nyren, who captained and later chronicled the club, John Small, famed for his batting prowess, and Thomas Brett, known for his pace bowling, gave the club a reputation for excellence. Nyren's reminiscences, published later in 1833, immortalized these figures and offered glimpses into the world of eighteenth-century cricket—the camaraderie, wagers, the rustic humor, and the intensity of play. For the first time, cricket had heroes whose names survived beyond the village.

The social dynamics of this era were fascinating. Gentlemen patrons, such as the duke of Dorset, funded teams and staked vast sums on the results, but local professionals provided the backbone of skill. In an era when English society was rigidly stratified, cricket created a space, however limited, where artisans and aristocrats mingled on relatively equal terms. That equality did not extend beyond the boundary, but within it, talent mattered as much as lineage.

Money drew players to perfect their skills, drew crowds to attend matches, and drew newspapers to report results. Critics decried the ruinous sums lost, but without gambling, cricket might have remained a rustic diversion. With it, the game grew into a national pastime.

By the 1780s, the center of gravity was shifting. The famous Hampshire club remained strong, but London's cricketing circles were stirring. In

1787, Thomas Lord opened his first ground at Dorset Square, staging Middlesex versus Essex, a match that marked the rise of Lord's as cricket's future home. The rural powerhouse that had once dominated now began to yield to the Marylebone Cricket Club, which was preparing to take up the role of guardian of the laws and organizer of the game. Yet its legacy endured: it had hosted matches that shaped equipment, rules, and culture; it had nurtured players whose reputations spread across the country; and it had given cricket a seriousness that could carry it into the national and eventually imperial stage.

The equipment innovations of this period illustrate how the sport was finding balance. The straight bat allowed batsmen to defend against more varied bowling; the improved, six-seamed ball gave bowlers better purchase; the three-stump wicket narrowed the contest fairly. Printed scorecards and systematic tallies created continuity, giving cricket a sense of memory and history. The public perception shifted, too: no longer only a rustic diversion, cricket was now a spectacle reported in newspapers, debated in clubs, and immortalized in anecdotes.

When Hambledon finally declined in the late 1780s and early 1790s, giving way to Lord's and the MCC, it left behind more than nostalgia. It left a culture of organized play, innovations in equipment that permanently altered the game's balance, and a spirit of fraternity—however imperfect—between classes. Most of all, it left stories: of Minshull's century, of Thomas White's oversized bat, of scorecards printed in Sevenoaks, of boys at Harrow with their crooked sticks. These tales became sport's lore, carried forward as part of cricket's identity.

For those who had watched its great matches, the memory was enduring. They had seen bats straighten and balls fly truer, wickets grow taller and narrower, scores recorded with care, and contests fought with passion. They had seen crowds cheer, wagers laid, reputations made and broken. They had seen cricket become more than a pastime. In the fields of Hampshire, amid the rolling downs and chalky soil, a village club had shaped the future of a game that would soon command nations. Brief though its era was, it burned brightly— and its light carried forward into every age that followed.

Reader's Notes

Cricket Innovations & Milestones

Artillery Ground (London, early 1700s): *Premier venue for cricket matches, known for large crowds and heavy gambling.*

1727 Articles of Agreement: *Early codified rules by the Duke of Richmond & Alan Brodrick (Sussex vs Surrey). Confirmed 22-yard pitch and umpire authority.*

1744 Laws of Cricket: *First printed laws; standardized wickets, pitch length, and umpire duties.*

Wickets: *Two stumps with a single crosspiece until the 1770s. Third stump added after 1771 (Thomas White's oversized bat incident).*

Bat evolution: *From curved (like a hockey stick) to straight blade in 1760s as bowlers pitched the ball higher.*

Ball evolution: *Standardized six-seam leather ball introduced in 1780 by the Duke's family.*

Scorecards: *First printed in 1776 at Sevenoaks; marks the start of cricket statistics.*

First Century: *John Minshull scored 107 in 1769 for the Duke of Dorset's XI – earliest recorded hundred.*

Patrons & Key Figures

Duke of Dorset (1720s–1780s): *Major patron of Kent cricket, backed teams heavily with wagers.*

Sir William Gage: *Sussex patron who raised powerful county sides.*

Frederick, Prince of Wales (1707–1751): *Son of George II, attended matches and boosted cricket's aristocratic appeal.*

Richard Newland (1713–1778): *Famous Slindon batsman, among cricket's first "stars."*

Richard Nyren (1734–1797): *Hambledon captain and chronicler, remembered as an early strategist.*

John Small (1737–1826): Legendary Hambledon batsman, central to the straight bat era.

Thomas Brett (1747–1809): Known for fast bowling at Hambledon.

Social & Cultural Context

Gambling: Integral to cricket's growth. Matches often involved wagers of 50 guineas or more (huge sums at the time).

Class Interaction: Aristocrats funded teams, while village professionals supplied the skill.

Criticism: Clergy and moralists condemned Sunday play, gambling, and disorder at matches.

Women's Cricket (1745): First recorded women's match played in Surrey.

Geography & Spread

London (Artillery Ground): The sport's hub for much of the early 1700s.

Kent, Surrey, Sussex: Early County strongholds.

Northward Spread: By 1770s, matches in Sheffield, Nottingham, and beyond marked cricket's expansion.

Wales: First recorded match in 1763 at Pembroke.

Hambledon Club (c. 1760s–1780s)

Regarded as cricket's **"cradle"** before Lord's and the MCC. Club was based in Hambleden, a rural village in Hampshire, England. It rose to prominence in the 1760s and 1770s, becoming the first great organized cricket club.

Innovations: three-stump wicket, straight bat, standardised ball, early scorecards.

Blended aristocratic patronage with local talent.

Declined by 1787 as **Lord's Ground** *and the* **Marylebone Cricket Club (MCC)** *rose to prominence.*

Key Documents in Early Cricket

Articles of Agreement (1727)

Drawn up by the Duke of Richmond and Alan Brodrick for Sussex vs Surrey matches.

Confirmed the **22-yard pitch length** *(still standard today).*

Required **two umpires***, one nominated by each side, whose decisions were final.*

Specified that the ball must be bowled **underarm** *along the ground.*

Set terms for dismissals (bowled, caught).

Aimed to avoid disputes, since heavy wagers were at stake.

Laws of Cricket (1744)

First printed "laws" circulated in London cricket clubs.

Fixed the **wicket dimensions***: two stumps, 22 inches high, with a 6-inch bail.*

Restated the **22-yard pitch** *distance.*

Clarified methods of dismissal: bowled, caught, stumped, or run out.

Gave umpires full authority and insisted their rulings must be accepted without argument.

Emphasized fair play, showing cricket's shift from rustic pastime to a **gentlemanly contest with order and respectability.**

2.3 Lord's and the Laws: The Birth of Marylebone Cricket Club

By the late 1780s, cricket's centre was moving decisively to London, Dorset square. The venue's first major contest, between Middlesex and Essex, marked not just another match but the beginning of a new era—Lord's as the emerging stage of English cricket.

The move was driven by the White Conduit Club, a group of gentlemen dissatisfied with the cramped conditions of their old field in Islington. In relocating, they not only secured a more exclusive venue but also created something far more enduring: the Marylebone Cricket Club (MCC). From its inception, MCC set itself apart—not merely another club for play and wagers, but an institution intent on order, fairness, and authority over the game.

By May 1788, this ambition took shape in the club's first codified Laws of Cricket. Those laws gave the game a backbone it had never truly possessed. They set the pitch at twenty-two yards—a distance that has endured untouched to the present day. They adjusted the ball's weight to be between five and a half and five and three-quarters ounces, and its circumference to be between eight and three-quarters and nine inches. They limited the bat to 38 inches in length and four and a quarter in width, preventing the ridiculous contrivances that had once mocked bowlers. Most importantly, they established three stumps rather than two, making the target more honest and the bowler's task fairer. The leg before wicket law was clarified, ensuring that batsmen could not simply thrust their pads forward and turn themselves into immovable walls. Overs were set at four balls apiece shorter than the eight or six of later times, but a move toward structure, nonetheless. These were not suggestions but standards, and from this moment, cricket ceased to be a purely local or improvisational affair. It was a game with rules, anchored by a club that would soon call itself the game's guardian.

The impact was immediate. Matches at Lord's attracted attention not only because of the quality of play but also because of their regularity. MCC members sponsored games, recruited top professionals, and began to maintain reliable records of play. In 1791, Samuel Britcher, MCC's first scorer, published the earliest printed record of match scores. These small booklets became annual, chronicling cricket year by year until 1805. For the first time, spectators and players alike could track averages, totals, and dismissals. The idea of statistics—so inseparable from cricket today—had entered the game.

The spread of organized matches in this period can be glimpsed through small but telling references. In 1794, Charterhouse and Westminster played one of the earliest school matches at Lord's. Two years later, in 1796, a contest between Eton and Westminster was staged at Hounslow Heath, against the orders of Dr. Heath, Eton's headmaster. The boys were flogged on their return for disobedience, but the precedent was set. Cricket had found a place in the culture of England's great schools, the breeding ground of the ruling class. Soon, school rivalries like Eton v. Harrow would become annual rituals at Lord's itself. What had once been the preserve of villagers and tavern-keepers was now embraced by the elite, even at the cost of corporal punishment.

The public appetite for cricket grew as matches became more organized. Gambling had not disappeared; indeed, wagers continued to color contests. Yet the presence of MCC and the standardization of the game helped reduce the chaos of the betting culture that had tarnished earlier decades. Patrons could now bet with clearer expectations, confident that the stumps were the same size in Surrey as they were in London, that the pitch length in Hampshire matched the one at Lord's. This consistency made cricket not only fairer but also more appealing to those who sought entertainment without quarrels and riots.

Equipment, too, began to evolve. The duke's family, ball-makers of Penshurst in Kent, supplied the first six-seamed ball in 1780 to the prince of Wales, later George IV. By the 1790s, their craft had become the standard for the best matches. A cricket ball was no longer a makeshift lump of leather and wool; it was a precision object, stitched to hold its shape, its seam designed to aid the bowler. Bats, too, followed the shape dictated by law, straighter and broader than the curved clubs of earlier times, adapted to meet the rising deliveries bowlers increasingly sent down. Stumps, with the third added by MCC's ruling, made the wicket both wider and fairer. The game looked more like modern cricket than it ever had before.

Cricket's growing seriousness invited its first attempts at theory. In 1800, Thomas Boxall published one of the earliest books on cricket technique. It laid out advice for batting, bowling, and fielding, reflecting the sense that cricket was no longer just learned through play but could also be studied and even taught. Manuals like this revealed that the game was deeply embedded in culture, inspiring instruction, codification, and self-improvement. A boy in a northern town or a village in Kent could, in theory, learn from the same printed words as a professional at Lord's. The game was slowly becoming national.

The 1790s were also years of political storm across Europe. The French Revolution in 1789 shook the continent, and war would soon pit England against revolutionary France. In this climate, the continuity of cricket was remarkable. While armies clashed abroad, in London the MCC held matches at Lord's, published scores, and revised laws. It was as if cricket, humble as it might seem beside politics, was becoming a quiet anchor of English identity. To play cricket in an age of upheaval was to insist on tradition, on order, on something peculiarly English that stood firm against chaos.

Not every development was smooth. In 1796, an extraordinary match at Lord's ended in a tie, one of the earliest recorded in history. The rarity of the result only heightened the sense that this was a game of drama, capable of tension and balance equal to any contest of war or theatre. Who could have imagined that 223 years later, in the summer of 2019, Lord's would witness another tie—this time in the World Cup Final, watched by more than a billion people across the globe, as England and New Zealand battled in one of cricket's most unforgettable matches.

The fact that such matches could be recorded, remembered, and discussed proved that cricket was no longer ephemeral. Its outcomes mattered, and they were written down.

By the turn of the century, from its Dorset Square beginnings, the ground would move twice more—to St. John's Wood in 1814, where it remains—but already the association was fixed. To play at Lord's was to play on the game's most important stage.

The MCC's early laws, many of which remain the foundation of cricket today, did more than resolve disputes about bats and balls. They turned cricket into a sport that could be transported across counties and eventually across oceans. A game with precise measurements, defined equipment, and recorded outcomes could travel in ways that stool-ball or cudgel-play never could. Sailors, merchants, and soldiers could take it abroad knowing that a wicket in Madras was the same as a wicket in Middlesex. That universality, born of MCC's ink on parchment in 1788, made cricket not only England's pastime but soon the empires.

As the century ended, cricket stood poised on the edge of modernity. Matches at Lord's were watched by London crowds, their results printed by Britcher, their rules overseen by MCC. Schools were producing new generations of players. Aristocrats still wagered, professionals still played for pay, and the game still carried its old countryside joy. But now it was enshrined in laws, supported by institutions, and imbued with a sense of permanence. The gentlemen of Marylebone, with their laws and their lords, gave it a future.

Reader's Notes

Thomas Lord *(1755–1832):* Yorkshire-born professional cricketer and entrepreneur. Founded the first Lord's ground at Dorset Square in 1787, laying the foundation for what became cricket's most famous venue.

Marylebone Cricket Club (MCC): Established in 1787 by members of the White Conduit Club, MCC became the official guardian of cricket's Laws. Its authority shaped the game's development across England and, eventually, the world.

Samuel Britcher *(active 1790s–1805):* MCC's first official scorer. Published annual booklets of cricket scores, marking the start of systematic statistical record-keeping in the game.

Thomas Boxall *(fl. 1800):* Author of one of the earliest cricket manuals, which formalized techniques of batting, bowling, and fielding, reflecting cricket's growing seriousness as a national sport.

1796 Lord's Tie: One of the earliest documented tied matches in cricket. Its rarity symbolized cricket's capacity for drama. Remarkably echoed centuries later at Lord's in the 2019 World Cup Final.

Six-seamed Ball: Standardized by the Duke family in the late 18th century, this design enhanced bowlers' grip and movement, cementing a balance between bat and ball that persists today.

LBW (Leg Before Wicket): *A batsman can be out if their leg or pad prevents the ball from hitting the stumps. Introduced in the 18th century, the law aimed to stop players from blocking the wicket with their body instead of the bat. Still one of cricket's most debated rules.*

Overs: *A unit of play in which a bowler delivers a fixed number of balls (originally four in the late 18th century, later standardized to six in most formats). Overs create structure in the game and mark tactical shifts, as teams rotate bowlers.*

Umpire: *The on-field official responsible for enforcing the Laws of Cricket, making decisions on dismissals, scoring, and conduct. In the 18th century, umpires were often chosen by each team, but MCC later formalized their authority.*

Innings: *A team's turn to bat. Each innings ends when all but one batsman are out, or when the allotted overs are completed. Early cricket often had two innings per side, a structure that continues in Test matches today.*

Methods of Dismissal (basic forms by the 18th century):

Bowled – the ball hits the stumps and dislodges the bails.

Caught – the batsman hits the ball and it is caught by a fielder without touching the ground.

Run Out – a batsman fails to make their ground before the stumps are broken while running.

Stumped – the wicketkeeper removes the bails while the batsman is out of their crease after missing the ball.

LBW – introduced later, a batsman can be given out if their leg blocks a ball destined to hit the stumps.
(Other dismissals like **"hit wicket**,*"* **"timed out**,*"* *and* **"obstructing the field"** *were codified much later.)*

Part II – Colonial Penetration and Early South Asian Encounters

Chapter 3– East India Company and Empire

3.1 The East India Company's World (1613–1707)

The story of cricket's journey to Asia cannot be told without first understanding the strange and precarious world of the East India Company during its first century in India. When the Mughal emperor Jahangir granted the English permission in 1613 to establish a trading post, or "factory," at Surat, it was no more than a cluster of warehouses, offices, and dormitories protected by a small guard of soldiers. The Company was still a merchant venture, chartered by Elizabeth I in 1600, competing against the far stronger Portuguese and Dutch. Its ambitions were simple: to buy spices, cotton cloth, saltpeter, and indigo cheaply in Asia and sell them at a profit in Europe. But from these modest beginnings, a way of life took shape—a colonial rhythm of trade, administration, survival, and leisure—in which cricket would eventually find a place.

At Surat, and later at Masulipatnam and Hugli, the Company's settlements were fragile enclaves, utterly dependent on the goodwill of local rulers. English merchants bowed before Mughal governors, presenting gifts and negotiating farmans, or imperial orders, that permitted trade. Ships unloaded at precarious wharves, while inland caravans brought bales of calico and sacks of pepper to the warehouses. In 1639, the English secured land from a local ruler near Madras to build Fort St. George. It began as a mud-walled fortification but soon evolved into a bustling town, with streets lined with merchants, soldiers, clerks, and Indian artisans. By 1661, Bombay, once a Portuguese holding, passed into English hands as part of Catherine of Braganza's dowry when she married Charles II. The Crown leased it to the Company in 1668 for a mere ten pounds a year, and Bombay soon developed into one of the most important harbors in India. In Bengal, the English built Fort William at Calcutta in the 1690s, completing its walls in 1696, giving the Company a stronghold on the banks of the Hooghly River. These three port cities—Madras, Bombay, and Calcutta—became the anchors of English power and trade in India.

Life inside these settlements was a mixture of drudgery and danger. The Company's hierarchy was rigid. At the bottom were "writers," young clerks sent out from England in their teens, often the sons of minor gentry or merchants who paid for the appointment. A newly recruited "writer" on £5–£10 a year was earning the rough equivalent of £1,000–£2,000 today, barely subsistence even for a teenager abroad. By comparison, most Indian laborers in the 1600s survived on a fraction of that—perhaps £2–£3 annually in modern terms—showing both the low pay of junior Company men and the even harsher realities for locals. Above them were "factors" and "junior merchants," who managed accounts and correspondence. Senior merchants, after years of service, might preside over trade negotiations, supervise warehouses, and command respect from Indian brokers. At the top were governors or presidents, who ruled Company towns like petty kings. Fort St. George had its Council chamber, where disputes were resolved and orders issued, and Bombay developed its own governor's residence and court system. In these miniature societies, the Company exercised not only commercial but also judicial and military power.

Salaries were meager, and the real lure of service lay in "private trade." Although technically restricted, Company servants bought and sold goods on their own account, enriching themselves through side deals. Diamonds, saltpeter, and fine muslins passed through their hands. Some became fabulously wealthy "nabobs," returning to England with fortunes that astonished contemporaries. Others died penniless in India, undone by bad luck, disease, or debt. Corruption was endemic, but it was also tacitly tolerated, for the official pay was so low that without private trade, men could hardly survive. This culture of opportunity and risk defined Company life, and it shaped the social world in which leisure pursuits, including games, were prized.

The daily routine of Company men was governed by the rhythms of trade and climate. Business began early in the morning, before the worst heat set in. Writers copied letters and balanced ledgers; factors bargained with Indian merchants; soldiers drilled in the courtyards of forts. By afternoon, the heat drove indoors. Dinners of salted beef, rice, and ale were taken in communal halls, though over time, European staples mingled with Indian dishes. Curries, pilau rice, and local fruits found their way to English tables, adapted to colonial tastes. Evenings were for socializing, with activities such as cards, dice, music, and sometimes amateur theatricals. At Fort St. George, records show plays performed by Company servants, including Shakespeare's works, staged before small but appreciative audiences. Leisure was not just entertainment; it was a way of maintaining identity. In a foreign land, threatened by disease and distance, Englishmen clung to their customs.

Disease was the constant shadow. Malaria, dysentery, cholera, and fevers carried thousands. In Surat, mortality was so high that many new arrivals never survived for three years. The cemeteries beside every factory tell the story in stone: rows of young men cut down in their twenties, women dead in childbirth, children who never reached maturity. Aurangzeb himself mocked the Company's weakness, remarking that the English "come here as traders and die like sheep." In such a world, survival itself was a victory, and leisure took on new urgency. Cards and music, horse racing and hunting, and increasingly cricket became not frivolities but necessities, helping men preserve morale against the ever-present fear of death.

The first stirrings of cricket in India emerged quietly within this colonial leisure economy. English sailors had long played games aboard ship to pass the months between London and Surat, striking balls across the deck or bowling along planks. In the ports of India, they sometimes carried this habit ashore. Soldiers garrisoned at Madras or Bombay would often improvise games in open spaces near their barracks particularly during winter or spring. Company officials, eager for diversion, may have introduced cricket informally among their late afternoon pastimes, alongside bowls or cards. Though no record survives of matches before the eighteenth century, the cultural soil was prepared: a society of Englishmen isolated in a foreign land, clinging to familiar customs.

By the late seventeenth century, the three presidencies—Madras, Bombay, and Calcutta—had developed distinct characters. Madras, with Fort St. George, became a hub of the textile trade, exporting calicos and chintzes that flooded the English market. Bombay, protected by its fine natural harbor, grew into a naval base as well as a trading center. Calcutta, at the mouth of the Hooghly, became the gateway to Bengal's riches in silk and opium. In each, the Company's power rested on fragile negotiations with local rulers, defended by small garrisons of soldiers and the walls of forts. Yet within these enclaves, the English built replicas of their homeland: churches for Sunday service, taverns for ale, assembly halls for dances, and open fields where the games of England might be played.

Aurangzeb's reign (1658–1707) cast a long shadow over this period. Stern, pious, and warlike, he viewed European traders with suspicion but tolerated them if they paid tribute and caused no disturbance. His endless campaigns against the Marathas drained the empire's strength. By the time of his death in 1707, the Mughal Empire, once so formidable, was fraying. For the East India Company, this moment marked a turning point. With imperial authority weakened, regional rulers began to assert independence, and the Company, already entrenched in fortified ports, was positioned to expand its influence. What started as a trading corporation was becoming a political power. Alongside warehouses and forts, there were parade grounds and gardens, and in those spaces, cricket could take root.

The century between 1613 and 1707 was thus the Company's apprenticeship in India. It learned to trade, to govern, to survive and learned local languages for business deals. Its servants endured disease, adapted to the climate, and built lives in alien lands. They earned little but schemed a lot, creating fortunes through private trade. They lived in barracks, dined in communal halls, attended Sunday service, staged plays, gambled at cards, and sought diversion in sport. The very act of playing, whether with dice or bat and ball, was a way of asserting that they remained English even at the edge of empire. By the dawn of the eighteenth century, cricket had not yet become India's game, but the English who carried it were firmly embedded in Indian soil. With Aurangzeb's death, the great Mughal umbrella splintered, and the Company, hardened by a century of survival, stood ready to seize its chance. In its forts and settlements, the echo of bat and ball could already be heard, a faint prelude to the game that would one day dominate the fields of the subcontinent.

3.2 From Aurangzeb to Plassey Cricket's First Shadows in India (1707–1757)

Aurangzeb left behind an empire stretched to its limits, brittle at the edges, and governed more by memory than authority. Aurangzeb's relentless Deccan campaigns consumed enormous revenues on armies and fortresses, while his strict religious policies alienated allies; by the time of his death, decades of war had emptied the treasury and left the empire overextended and unstable. Old foes—Marathas, Sikhs, Rajputs—rose with renewed energy. Within a generation, the once-mighty empire fractured into competing powers: Hyderabad, Bengal, Awadh, Mysore, each claiming semi-independence while the emperor in Delhi became little more than a figurehead. In 1739, the Mughal Empire suffered one of its most devastating blows when Nadir Shah of Persia swept into Delhi, defeated the imperial army, and looted the capital. His forces carried away unimaginable wealth, including the

Peacock Throne and the Koh-i-Noor diamond—while tens of thousands of civilians were massacred. The plunder shattered the aura of Mughal invincibility and left the treasury empty. In the decades that followed, as the empire weakened under the weight of this catastrophe, the East India Company would steadily exploit the vacuum of authority to extend its own power. It was into this world of fading imperial grandeur and rising regional states that the English East India Company advanced rapidly, still nominally merchants but increasingly soldiers, rulers, and tax-collectors.

For the Company, post Aurangzeb period was a turning point. Under his iron watch, the English had been tolerated but hemmed in, their trading posts dependent on imperial license and local favor. Now, amid political uncertainty, governors and princes sought allies, gold, and guns. The Company offered all three. Its fortified factories at Calcutta, Madras, and Bombay became more than warehouses; they were islands of English culture, defended by walls, cannon, and the discipline of drilled European troops. Inside those walls, another life unfolded—one part mercantile, one part military, and increasingly, one part English domestic routine transplanted to tropical soil.

The men who staffed the Company in the early 1700s were often very young. Many were "writers," clerks barely in their teens when they sailed from Gravesend, apprenticed to counting-houses where they learned double-entry bookkeeping and the subtle arts of barter. Others were factors, seasoned traders who managed warehouses of silk, indigo, pepper, or saltpeter. Above them were merchants and senior officials with decades of experience in Asia, and at the top were the governors of each Presidency—Calcutta, Madras, and Bombay. It has been mentioned earlier that salaries were indeed modest, often too low to tempt men to risk the voyage, but the real lure lay in private trade and opportunity. It was no secret that Company servants enriched themselves by sideline ventures, smuggling, or partnership with local brokers. By the mid-eighteenth century, "nabobs"—Company men returning from India with sudden fortunes—would become both admired and despised in England.

Daily life in the settlements blended monotony with bursts of danger. The heat was oppressive; the air was often heavy with disease. Malaria, dysentery, and smallpox killed more Englishmen than rival armies. Letters at home are filled with laments about fevers and funerals. Yet amid the hardships, the English created bubbles of familiarity. The architecture itself was part of the transplant: houses with whitewashed walls, pillared verandas, and gardens where roses struggled alongside palms; dining rooms where roast beef was served when possible, and Madeira wine washed down spicy local fare. Sundays were marked by services in improvised chapels, sermons railing against both heathen temptations and the Company's own corruption. Afternoons offered a different sort of relief: games of cards, amateur theatricals, billiards, and, increasingly, sport in the open air.

Cricket belonged to this world of leisure and identity. For the young men who came out from England, it was the game of their boyhoods, played on greens at Eton, Harrow, or village fields in Kent and Surrey. To mark runs in notches on sticks or to defend a wicket, however primitive, was to feel for a moment at home in a land that seemed intent on stripping identity away. The Company's fortified towns offered spaces where cricket could take root. In Madras, the open esplanade outside Fort St. George provided a ground where clerks and soldiers could gather; in Bombay, the maidan before the walls offered a similar field; in Calcutta, the wide stretches by the Hooghly River, though humid and rough, served well enough. Although cricket was surely played informally in Company settlements before mid-century, the first recorded reference comes from 1721, when British sailors are said to have played a match near Cambay (in present-day Gujarat). Historians debate the reliability of this account, but it remains the earliest documented glimpse of cricket on Indian soil—a faint but significant milestone in the game's long journey east.

In the taverns of Sevenoaks or the grounds of Hambledon, the game acquired rules, technique, and fame. The company recruited individuals who were shipped eastward, carrying those changes with them. They described matches in letters, ordered new bats or balls in cargo manifests, and explained to puzzled locals why the striking of leather on willow mattered so much.

The hierarchy of the Company mirrored itself in sport. Young writers, dismissed from their ledgers for an afternoon, formed the bulk of players; factors and junior merchants sometimes joined in, though more often they wagered from the sidelines. Officers of the Company's private armies, drilled in musket and cannon, brought their own competitiveness to bat and ball. Governors and senior merchants, rarely seen wielding a bat, nonetheless encouraged the games as healthy diversions for restless youth. In this way, cricket became an integral part of the social economy of the settlements, binding men together, easing tensions, and providing a ritual of familiarity.

There were challenges. The climate made long games punishing; monsoons drenched fields; the soil was often too hard or uneven for true pitches. Yet improvisation prevailed. Bats were carved locally when imports were scarce, balls were stitched by native craftsmen followed English design, and wickets could be knocked together from bamboo or teak. As mentioned earlier no records survive of scores or players in this period, but the persistence of anecdote, diary, and later recollection confirms that cricket was present, if only in shadow. By mid-century, it had become a fixture of Company life, a quiet inheritance carried across seas.

Meanwhile, the political landscape around the settlements underwent a dramatic shift. In Bengal, the Nawabs grew increasingly independent, balancing the interests of Delhi, local elites, and European traders. In the Deccan, the Nizam asserted autonomy. The Marathas pressed northward, challenging Mughal claims. Amid this fragmentation, the English and French companies maneuvered for favor and footholds, fortifying their positions and raising sepoy armies. The rivalry that would culminate at Plassey and beyond was already visible. Yet within the walls, life went on—warehouses opened at dawn, ships unloaded spices and cotton, clerks scribbled accounts, and in the evenings, young men took to the field with bat and ball.

To Indian onlookers, the sight of Englishmen playing cricket must have seemed odd—grown men sprinting between stakes, shouting in a foreign tongue, and celebrating the fall of wooden stumps with exaggerated delight. At first it was little more than a spectacle of curiosity, but gradually servants, interpreters, and local allies lingered to watch, some even imitating the play. These early encounters were not structured lessons but acts of quiet observation, through which the game's strange rhythms began to take root. The seed of cricket in India was planted long before it would truly blossom in later generations.

The Company's reach expanded steadily. By the 1730s and 1740s, it had evolved from a merchant body to a military power. Its armies, half European and half Indian sepoys, marched in step to defend factories and allies. Governors negotiated not just trade but territory. Fort William at Calcutta, rebuilt after disasters and sieges, stood as a symbol of the Company's will to permanence. The settlements were now towns, with streets, taverns, shops, and a rhythm of daily life that was recognizably English in structure but Indian in setting. And within that rhythm, cricket found a place: not yet celebrated, not yet shared widely, but practiced, remembered, and passed on.

The connection to England was constant. Ships sailed twice a year, bearing cargo and correspondence. The East India Company's shipping patterns before 1757 were shaped by distance, monsoons, and limited resources. A round trip from London to Bombay, Madras, or Calcutta often took 12–18 months, depending on winds and stopovers at the Cape of Good Hope. Because ships had to time their departure with the monsoon winds of the Indian Ocean, most fleets left England only once or twice a year in convoy, heavily armed against pirates or rival

European powers. In the trunks were packed not only letters and ledgers, but also bats, balls, and scorebooks. Recruits arrived with fresh tales of cricketing feats at home; old hands, preparing to return as "nabobs," carried with them memories of matches under tropical suns. Just as Company commerce was a bridge between continents, so too cricket became a bridge of culture, carried silently yet enduringly across oceans.

By 1757, when Clive faced Siraj-ud-Daulah at Plassey, the East India Company had transformed. It was no longer one merchant among many but a force capable of toppling rulers. That battle, decided by intrigue as much as arms, marked the beginning of British dominion in India. And though cricket was far from the minds of Clive's sepoys as they marched through the Bengal countryside, the game was already there, tucked into the daily lives of Company servants. As the empire was born on the fields of Bengal, cricket too was finding its first soil on the banks of the Hooghly and the shores of Madras and Bombay.

The years between Aurangzeb's death and the Battle of Plassey were thus formative for both the empire and the sport. The Mughal sun was setting, regional powers jostled for supremacy, and the English East India Company turned from merchant to master. Amid this great upheaval, a quieter story unfolded—of young clerks and soldiers striking balls with crooked bats, of games played on humid late afternoons and early evenings in sight of trees and minarets, of a pastime that gave comfort to strangers in a strange land. It was modest, improvised, and easily overlooked. Yet from these first shadows, cricket in India began.

Readers Notes

East India Company *(chartered 1600)* – A joint-stock trading company established by Elizabeth I, initially focused on spices and cloth. By 1757, it had become a military and political power in India.

Factory – Term used for Company trading posts or settlements (e.g., Surat, Madras, Calcutta), which were fortified warehouses with living quarters.

Writer – The lowest rank in the Company hierarchy; young clerks sent to India, earning £5–£10 annually. Equivalent today: £1,000–£2,000, meager even abroad.

Factor – A mid-level merchant or trader responsible for managing accounts and warehouses.

Nabob – A slang term for Company men who returned to England wealthy from private trade, often controversial figures.

Private Trade – The practice of Company servants conducting personal trade on the side, technically illegal but widespread and often lucrative.

Plassey *(1757)* – The decisive battle in Bengal where Robert Clive's East India Company forces defeated Siraj-ud-Daulah, marking the start of Company dominion in India.

Maidan – An open ground or field often near a fort; became natural playing grounds for cricket in Bombay, Calcutta, and Madras.

First Cricket in India *(1721)* – The earliest recorded reference is of English sailors playing near Cambay, Gujarat, though cricket likely appeared earlier informally in Company settlements.

Dismissals *(early cricket)* – Ways a batsman could be out: bowled (stumps hit), caught, run out, stumped, or leg-before-wicket (LBW). Many of these rules were evolving during this period.

Nadir Shah (1688–1747) – *Ruler of Persia (1736–1747), famed as a brilliant but ruthless conqueror. In 1739 he invaded India, defeated the Mughal army at Karnal, and sacked Delhi.*

Plunder of 1739 – *Often described as the most catastrophic event in Mughal history. Nadir Shah's troops massacred Delhi's citizens and carried away immense treasures, including the*

Peacock Throne *(symbol of Mughal grandeur) and the* **Koh-i-Noor diamond**. *The loss crippled the Mughal treasury and prestige.*

Peacock Throne – *A jewel-encrusted throne commissioned by Shah Jahan in the 17th century. After Nadir Shah's sack of Delhi, it was taken to Persia and later dismantled; fragments were dispersed across royal collections.*

Koh-i-Noor Diamond – *One of the world's most famous diamonds, seized by Nadir Shah in 1739. It passed through Persian, Afghan, and Sikh hands before being taken by the British in 1849. Today it rests in the British Crown Jewels, a symbol of contested imperial legacy.*

Chapter 4 – Consolidation and the First Indian Glimpses

4.1 Empire in the Balance – Cricket Between Plassey and Seringapatam (1757–1799)

The year 1757 marked a decisive shift in the fortunes of the East India Company and, indirectly, in the transplantation of cricket from English greens to Indian soil. The Battle of Plassey was as much a commercial coup as a military one. Robert Clive, commanding a small Company force, defeated the Nawab of Bengal, Siraj-ud-Daulah, and secured the immense revenues of Bengal. From this moment onward, the Company ceased to be merely a trading body and began its metamorphosis into a territorial power. Forts, garrisons, and administrative offices expanded across Bengal, and with them came the habits and amusements of Englishmen abroad. Cricket, already flourishing in England, now appeared in India not as a cultural mission but as part of the baggage of colonial life.

Company offices bustled with paperwork and human endurance. There were no typewriters, no electricity, no machines to ease the strain. Every letter, every tally, every entry in the accounts was copied by hand, and every duplicate bound and dispatched to London, taking a year or more to draw a reply. The working day was relentless: young recruits and clerks, called writers, were expected to rise before sunrise, and the offices opened by six o'clock in the morning to make use of the cooler hours. Work continued steadily until the midday heat became unbearable. Shutters were drawn, candles guttered in the gloom, and the settlement slowed to a pause. A short respite followed, when men slept, read, or sought shade, before returning to duty until evening. Only when the sun sank and the books of account were closed did leisure begin. In those pauses of late afternoon, and on occasional rest days during early evenings, cricket became a cherished release.

Life under the Company sun was harsh—heat, fever, and disease cut men down quickly—but routines of work and play kept them sane. In the evenings, cricket was improvised on maidans outside Calcutta, Bombay, and Madras became a permanent routine.

The matches were not grand spectacles. Stumps were fashioned crudely from bamboo, bats were hewn from local wood, and balls were sometimes improvised until shipments from England arrived. Yet the men played with energy and affection. Cricket was not just a pastime but a connection: it bound them to memories of home, soothed the monotony of office work, and built fraternity among men separated from families for years. A surviving letter from a young Company writer in the 1770s captures the novelty. He confessed that life in the fort was "tedious and most oppressively warm," but added that "some of us have contrived a ground upon the great plain, and there of an evening or in the afternoon recess we set our stumps and play at cricket until the sun sinks.

Indian servants stood and watched, marveling at the odd contrivance of bat and ball, while the sepoys later tried to copy our strokes with such laughter that it made us laugh in turn. Though they know not our rules, they swing their sticks with spirit, and I dare say in time they shall play as well as any lad in Kent." The words reveal how cricket in India began not through design, but through imitation—a spectacle gradually transformed into participation.

Indians in Company employ—sepoys, grooms, household boys—watched these games with curiosity. To them, cricket seemed alien and theatrical, a ritual of the rulers. Yet mimicry was natural. In barracks or village lanes, they replayed with what they had seen, using sticks and cloth balls, laughter echoing across the compounds. At first, it was nothing more than parody, but parody gradually evolved into practice, and practice eventually hinted at the earliest adoption. Cricket in India began not as a gift but as a sight, a curiosity that slowly crept into other hands.

By the 1780s, when the Marylebone Cricket Club was formed in London and laws were codified, the game had acquired permanence. For Company officers in India, such news arrived slowly in letters or gazettes, yet it mattered. Recruits brought fresh habits, spoke of new strokes and styles, and carried the evolving English game into the Indian setting. What was played on the Calcutta Maidan or the Bombay esplanade was never frozen; it grew with each shipload of men arriving from Portsmouth or Gravesend.

Hardened by wars against the French and victorious at Plassey in 1757 and Buxar in 1764, the Company began to entrench itself as a sovereign power. Bengal's revenues now sustained both commerce and armies, and with those armies came a tide of Englishmen—clerks, officers, and soldiers—who carried their culture with them in ever greater measure. By the 1770s, Governor-General Warren Hastings presided over an English presence that was no longer transient. Families arrived, children were born in India, and the culture of leisure clubs, gardens, amateur theatricals, and cricket became inseparable from colonial identity.

Cricket was not confined to the highest ranks. Junior clerks, poorly paid but ambitious, played matches against officers or sailors awaiting departure. Naval men in Bombay, accustomed to long stretches of idleness, brought their own energy to the game. Soldiers at Madras, after long drills and parades, turned to cricket in their respite. And everywhere, small wagers accompanied play: a round of ale, a supper for the victors, or a few rupees placed on a side. The habit of betting, deeply entwined with cricket in England, traveled naturally across the seas.

By the 1780s, records note cricket in Calcutta more explicitly. Company officials staged matches on the Maidan, where cows grazed and kites wheeled above. These games drew crowds of onlookers, both Indian and English, and the spectacle began to attract commentary. Cricket was becoming part of the colonial scene, a visible marker of Englishness. In Bombay and Madras, too, the habit spread. Matches were still small in scale, but there were unmistakable signs that the game had crossed oceans.

By the 1780s, cricket and empire were both entering new phases. The six-seamed ball of 1780, Thomas Lord's ground in 1787, and MCC's codified laws marked the game's maturity, even as the East India Company consolidated power in India. Sport and empire advanced in parallel, each gaining permanence and authority. At the same time, Britain had lost its American colonies, and though cricket had crossed the Atlantic, it gradually faded there during the new republic's rise. In India, however, the story was different: the game, carried east with empire, would endure and eventually flourish, becoming one of the most powerful legacies of British rule.

The decisive stroke came in 1799 at Seringapatam. Company armies defeated Tipu Sultan, the formidable ruler of Mysore, and secured southern India. With Tipu's fall, British dominance in the subcontinent was undeniable. Soldiers and officers, flushed with victory, turned once more to their routines of leisure—dinners, cards, and cricket. Accounts from the aftermath describe Englishmen playing the game on dusty clearings near cantonments, stumps hammered into alien soil that had just been won by cannon. Cricket was an assertion of identity in conquered territory.

For Indians, the game remained distant but visible. Boys who worked in English households carried balls and bats, fielded when ordered. Sepoys watched their officers play and sometimes bowled in practice. To most Indians, it was still a spectacle, but one they could not ignore. What was once the exclusive domain of rulers was becoming something shared, however unevenly.

By 1799, two parallel stories had reached new maturity. In England, cricket was celebrated as the national sport of its day—long before football's later dominance—complete with rules, clubs, and institutions, in India, it had passed from the novelty of shipboard amusement to a fixture of colonial life. The East India Company, which had evolved from a trading body into a ruling power, inadvertently introduced cricket to the heart of the subcontinent. Empire and sport had become inseparable, each reinforcing the other, and the trajectory was clear. What had begun as a pastime of clerks in afternoon recess was destined to become one of India's deepest passions.

Readers' notes

Battle of Plassey (1757): *A decisive victory where Robert Clive and the East India Company defeated Nawab Siraj-ud-Daulah of Bengal, largely through bribery and intrigue. It marked the beginning of Company rule in India and gave access to Bengal's immense revenues.*

Battle of Buxar (1764): *Fought against the combined forces of Bengal, Awadh, and the Mughal emperor, the Company's victory confirmed its dominance in northern India and secured the right to collect revenue (diwani) in Bengal.*

Warren Hastings (1732–1818): *The first Governor-General of India (1773–1785). Hastings consolidated Company authority, established administrative reforms, and presided over the cultural transplant of English institutions—including cricket—into Indian soil.*

Tipu Sultan (1751–1799): *The ruler of Mysore, famed for his resistance against the British and his alliance with the French. His defeat and death at the Siege of Seringapatam (1799) ended Mysore's independence and secured Company dominance in southern India.*

Seringapatam (1799): *The final battle where Tipu Sultan was killed. Seen as the symbolic moment when British military supremacy in India became undeniable.*

Cricket in India (18th century): *Before 1800, cricket was played mainly by Company clerks, soldiers, and sailors on maidans and esplanades in Calcutta, Madras, and Bombay. Matches were informal, equipment improvised, and records sparse, yet the game became part of colonial identity and routine leisure.*

Wagers in India: *Echoing English practice, even small matches in India carried wagers—whether rupees, ale, or dinners—showing that gambling was inseparable from cricket's early spread.*

Sepoys and Servants in Cricket: *Indian soldiers and household staff often watched Europeans play and sometimes joined informally. Their mimicry of strokes and improvisation with sticks and cloth balls marked the very earliest steps toward cricket's indigenization.*

4.2 Cricket under a Consolidated Empire (1800–1835)

The nineteenth century opened with the East India Company standing taller than ever before. The French, its most serious European rival in India, had been pushed to the margins after the fall of Tipu Sultan at Seringapatam in 1799. The once-proud Mughal Empire lingered only as a shadow in Delhi, more symbolic than sovereign. Long before, the Company had watched with interest the Third Battle of Panipat (1761), when Ahmad Shah Durrani's Afghan cavalry shattered the Marathas in one of the century's bloodiest encounters. The staggering losses fractured Maratha unity, and though they revived, their power never fully recovered—a weakness the Company would later exploit in its final triumph over the confederacy by 1818.

Three Anglo–Maratha wars, fought between 1775 and 1818, tested the Company's strength. By the end, the Peshwa, Baji Rao II, had been deposed, and the Company stood as the paramount power in India. Bengal, Mysore, and Maratha territories were now under its control, with only Ranjit Singh's Sikh kingdom holding independence in the north. Between 1800 and the 1830s, India was increasingly ruled not by princes but by clerks and generals answering to a joint-stock corporation in London. Within this expanding empire of bayonets and bureaucracy, cricket also took firmer root, woven into colonial life even as it evolved rapidly in England.

For Company men in Calcutta, Bombay, and Madras, daily life remained harsh and monotonous—quills and ledgers at dawn, long hours under the sun, evenings of cards, drink, and, when daylight allowed, cricket on maidans or esplanades. Matches were modest affairs with bamboo stumps or rag balls, but they offered camaraderie and a vital link to England. Indian sepoys and servants often watched curiously, sometimes joining informally as bowlers or fielders, the earliest stirrings of local participation.

Meanwhile, back in England, cricket was gaining new permanence. In 1806, Lord's staged the first *Gentlemen v Players* match, dramatizing the sport's deep social divide: wealthy amateurs against paid professionals. In 1817, William Lambert, one of the finest cricketers of his day, was expelled from Lord's after a betting scandal—his career ruined, and cricket's reputation scarred. From Lambert in 1817 to Hansie Cronje in 2000, the game has shown how gambling could repeatedly corrode its spirit.

The 1820s brought one of cricket's great technical controversies: the rise of round-arm bowling. Innovators like John Willes of Kent experimented with raising the arm for extra pace and bounce, sparking fierce disputes. The MCC's *Round-Arm Trial Matches* of 1827 at Lord's drew huge crowds and fierce debate. Though not immediately sanctioned, the style soon gained acceptance and paved the way for modern overarm bowling. Even in India, Company officers awkwardly attempted the new delivery, raising laughter among sepoys who watched their masters bowling in exaggerated fashion.

The 1830s produced a new star: Fuller Pilch, often hailed as the greatest batsman before W. G. Grace. His straight-bat defense and commanding 153 not out for Kent in 1833 became legend, and his fame traveled across the seas. For young officers in Calcutta or Bombay, reading of Pilch in old newspapers gave the game stature equal to statesmen and generals.

Cricket in India was still an overwhelmingly European pastime but growing in visibility. Matches between clerks, soldiers, and naval men were common in Calcutta, Bombay, and Madras, usually accompanied by modest wagers. Small though they were, these contests gave the sport permanence on Indian soil. By the 1830s, whispers of Indian clubs—particularly among Bombay's Parsi community—were beginning to stir, though still embryonic.

Beyond cricket, the Company was reshaping Indian society. After Maratha defeat, it reorganized territories, reformed taxation, and extended its courts. The most lasting cultural intervention came in 1835 with Thomas Babington Macaulay's *Minute on Indian Education*. He urged English to replace Persian as the medium of higher learning, aiming to train Indians "English in taste, in opinions, in morals, and in intellect." Though he never mentioned cricket, the schools and colleges established under his vision became nurseries of both literature and sport, planting the ground for Indian engagement with the game.

By 1835, cricket's story ran on two tracks. In England, it had matured into an organized sport—regulated by the MCC, marked by the drama of Gentlemen v Players, the disgrace of Lambert, the revolution of round-arm bowling, and the brilliance of Pilch. In India, it had become a fixture of colonial life, stitched into the rhythms of work and leisure, still foreign but increasingly familiar. The East India Company stood secure in power, but with English education spreading and Indian spectators edging closer to participation, cricket was already poised to slip beyond colonial hands. The seeds of a national passion had been sown.

Third Battle of Panipat (1761) – *A catastrophic clash between the Marathas and Ahmad Shah Durrani of Afghanistan. The Marathas were shattered, weakening their power and opening space for later British dominance.*

Baji Rao II (1775–1851) – *The last Peshwa of the Maratha Confederacy, defeated in 1818, marking the end of Maratha sovereignty.*

Gentlemen v Players (from 1806) – *Annual matches at Lord's between amateur "gentlemen" (wealthy, aristocratic) and professional "players" (working-class, paid cricketers). A fixture until 1962, it symbolized cricket's class divide.*

William Lambert (1779–1851) – *Brilliant all-rounder banned for life from Lord's in 1817 after a betting scandal, the first major fixing case in cricket history.*

Hansie Cronje (1969–2002) – *South African captain, banned for life in 2000 after admitting to match-fixing. His downfall echoed Lambert's scandal almost two centuries earlier.*

Round-Arm Bowling (1820s–1830s) – *A controversial new delivery style pioneered by John Willes, where the bowler's arm was raised higher than underarm. It led to fierce disputes but laid the foundation for modern overarm bowling.*

Fuller Pilch (1804–1870) – *Renowned English batsman, celebrated for his straight bat and defensive mastery; widely regarded as the finest batsman before W.G. Grace.*

Thomas Babington Macaulay (1800–1859) – *British historian and politician. His "Minute on Indian Education" (1835) advocated English as the medium of instruction, shaping Indian elites and indirectly fostering cricket through schools and colleges.*

Esplanade/Maidan Grounds – *Open parade fields in Calcutta, Bombay, and Madras, originally cleared for military drills but later doubling as early cricket pitches.*

Part III – Colonial Society, Politics, and Cricket

Chapter 5 – Cricket and Social Hierarchies

5.1 The Parsis – First Indian Pioneers (1830s–1880s)

By the early 19th century, cricket was no longer just a curiosity in India's port cities. In Bombay, European regiments played regularly on Bombay Green (later the Oval Maidan), and newspapers were already recording match notices by the 1820s. In Calcutta, the Calcutta Cricket Club (founded in 1792, and regarded as the oldest cricket club in India, and perhaps outside Britain itself) gave the game permanence among Company officials, staging matches on the Maidan near Fort William. These fragments marked cricket's transformation daily routine game. Out of that routine, an Indian response began to form—first in Bombay, and first among the Parsis.

The Parsis were well positioned to adopt the game. By the early 19th century, they were already a dynamic community, thriving in commerce, English education, and civic life. Cricket suited their ambitions: it was rule-bound, visible, and carried symbolic weight with colonial authority. By the 1840s, young Parsi boys lingered on maidans after European matches, copying stances, chalking wickets on walls, and experimenting with the bat. In 1848, they institutionalized their enthusiasm by forming the Oriental Cricket Club, the first Indian cricket club, establishing that the game would no longer be only watched but actively played.

Through the 1850s and 1860s, Parsi teams multiplied and began playing not only among themselves but also against European sides at the newly built Bombay Gymkhana. At first these contests were unequal— Europeans enjoyed resources, better coaching, and experience—but every wicket, boundary, or hard-fought draw inscribed the Parsis more securely into the city's sporting life. They understood that practice alone was not enough: English coaches were hired to teach batting technique, bowling action, and field placements, so that Parsi cricketers could master the game at its technical roots rather than merely imitate it.

By the 1870s, the Europeans vs. Parsis annual fixture had become Bombay's most symbolic contest. Though Europeans usually won, the Parsis steadily improved. Coaching, disciplined practice, and better equipment began to tell. Crowds gathered—no longer just idlers, but Parsi families under parasols, cheering their own boys. The construction of the Parsi Gymkhana at Marine Lines in the mid-1880s further cemented their place: with their own pavilion, turf, and facilities, they could no longer be dismissed as outsiders.

The Parsis also reached beyond India. The first Parsi tour of England in 1886 was earnest but underprepared, with Indian players struggling against English conditions—green wickets, fading light, and unfamiliar movement. They lost heavily but learned invaluable lessons about patience and technique. A second tour in 1888 was stronger, with sturdier performances that proved Indians could compete, however unevenly, on English grounds. For the first time, Indians had stepped onto Lord's and other English arenas, measured on the same twenty-two yards as their colonial rulers.

Meanwhile, Calcutta developed its own rhythm. Eden Gardens, laid out in the 1840s and opened to cricket in 1864, gave the sport a grand public stage. Europeans dominated early matches, but Indian schoolboys and clerks watched closely. With Macaulay's English education reforms feeding schools and colleges by mid-century, cricket entered curricula alongside grammar and literature. By the 1880s, Calcutta boasted Indian elevens who played with confidence on grounds that had once excluded them.

Newspapers amplified this change. By the 1870s, Indian readers eagerly followed reports of W. G. Grace, the bearded giant of English cricket.

His feats—such as scoring a *double hundred* (200 runs in a single innings, an extraordinary achievement of stamina and skill)—were retold in Indian papers, alongside tales of Arthur Shrewsbury's patience, Fred Spofforth's ferocious pace in the 1882 Ashes, and Charles Bannerman's century in the very first Test match of 1877 in Melbourne Cricket Ground. These reports connected Bombay and Calcutta boys to a global cricketing imagination, giving them heroes, models, and standards to aspire toward.

By the late 19th century, every decade had added a layer of normality: in the 1830s, Indians fetched balls; in the 1840s, they founded clubs; in the 1850s and 1860s, they contested Europeans; in the 1870s, annual fixtures fixed rivalries; and in the 1880s, Indians crossed the seas. Cricket had ceased to be only a colonial performance and had become an Indian activity.

The Parsis' achievement lay not in miracle but in method. They built clubs, practiced relentlessly, studied foreign reports, engaged English coaches, and endured defeats before returning stronger. Their progress inspired other communities—Hindus, Muslims, and later Christians— to form their own gymkhanas, leading to the Triangular, Quadrangular, and Pentangular tournaments of the next century. The Parsis had not only learned cricket; they had shown how to inhabit it with pride and purpose.

What began with a boy chalking wickets on a Bombay wall ended with Indians walking onto English grounds. The first fluent pages of Indian cricket were written in Gujarati surnames and Parsi Gymkhanas, and the rest of the subcontinent would soon learn to read—and to answer—in kind.

The decades between the 1860s and 1880s were not just formative for Indian cricket but also for the Indian nation-to-be. These were the years when Mahatma Gandhi (b. 1869), Muhammad Ali Jinnah (b. 1876), and Jawaharlal Nehru (b. 1889) were born leaders who would later reshape the destiny of South Asia. Their births coincided with a period when Parsis were assimilating into colonial institutions, when Indian communities first claimed cricket as their own, and when British engagement in India deepened across politics, education, and culture. The generation born in this era inherited not just the colonial state but also its games—and they would one day wield both politics and sport as tools of identity and nationhood.

Calcutta Cricket Club (CCC) – Established in 1792, it is considered the oldest cricket club in India and among the oldest outside Britain, symbolizing the early European institutionalization of the sport in the subcontinent.

Oriental Cricket Club (OCC) – Founded in 1848 in Bombay by Parsis, it was the first Indian cricket club, marking the beginning of organized Indian participation in the game.

Gymkhana – A social and sporting club, often built by Europeans in colonial India, providing facilities for games like cricket, tennis, and polo. The Parsi Gymkhana (1880s) gave Indian cricketers their own pavilion and turf, allowing them to play on equal terms.

Century & Double Century – A century is when a batsman scores 100 runs in a single innings—a benchmark of excellence. A double century (200 runs) is rarer still, demanding stamina, patience, and immense skill.

W. G. Grace – England's most famous cricketer of the 19th century, whose batting dominance and iconic beard made him the first global cricket celebrity.

Fred Spofforth – Nicknamed the "Demon Bowler", he was the Australian fast bowler who inspired Australia's first Ashes victory in 1882 by dismantling England at The Oval.

The Ashes – The England–Australia Test rivalry, originating in 1882 when Australia's victory at The Oval was mockingly described in the press as the "death of English cricket," whose "ashes" would be taken to Australia. It remains one of cricket's greatest contests.

The Generation of Change – *The late 19th century not only saw Indians like the Parsis take to cricket but also witnessed the birth of leaders who would reshape the subcontinent: Mahatma Gandhi (1869), Muhammad Ali Jinnah (1876), and Jawaharlal Nehru (1889). Their emergence coincided with the period when cricket was becoming embedded in Indian civic life, a reminder that political and sporting awakenings were unfolding side by side.*

5.2 Princes, Palaces, and Class Lines (1857–1914)

The Indian Mutiny of 1857 was not only a political and military upheaval but also a cultural watershed. The British Crown, assuming direct control from the East India Company in its aftermath, imposed a firmer administrative structure, an expanded military presence, and a more deliberate program of cultural influence. Cricket, already seeded among Company officials, now grew in the soil of a colonial society that had shifted from mercantile dominance to imperial authority. The game would become a subtle yet powerful instrument of both British prestige and Indian aspiration in the years that followed.

The rebellion's suppression left scars across northern India, but it also convinced the British that their permanence on the subcontinent depended not only on bayonets but also on institutions. Schools, universities, and civil service examinations were expanded. English education became a ladder for ambitious Indians. From these new schools—Calcutta, Bombay, Madras, and later Lahore—emerged a generation of "brown sahibs" familiar with Shakespeare, Macaulay's essays, and the language of the empire. They also inherited the games of their masters, and none more so than cricket.

In the 1860s and 1870s, princely states began to embrace the game as a badge of modernity. Maharajas of Patiala and Baroda laid out private grounds within palace walls. The Nizam of Hyderabad, the rulers of Rajkot, and, above all, the Jam Sahib of Nawanagar, Ranjitsinhji, would later have their names indelibly tied to cricket's story. For princes, cricket was a means of showing sophistication to their British overlords while displaying patronage and generosity to their subjects. Palaces echoed with the crack of bat on ball, and visiting English teams found themselves hosted not only in cantonments and clubs but also in royal courts.

Cricket in Bombay also reflected the city's social divisions. Excluded from European gymkhanas, Indians built their own—first the Parsis, then Hindus and Muslims. These clubs later gave rise to communal tournaments like the Quadrangular, where sport and society's divides played side by side.

For sepoys and Indian recruits in the British Indian Army, cricket also became a common diversion. Soldiers drilled at dawn and marched through the heat, but in the evenings or on Sundays they took bat and ball. What had once been a curious spectacle of English officers now became a regular pastime of sepoy regiments. During leave, many carried the game back to their villages, where crude versions of the sport became part of rural amusements. Entire villages gathered to watch, children learned the strokes, and cricket began to spread beyond cantonments and palaces into the broader fabric of Indian life.

Education, military drill, and royal patronage collectively established cricket's foothold in the latter nineteenth century. Meanwhile, the wider cricketing world was also entering a new era. The first international cricket match had technically been staged as early as 1844 between the United States and Canada, but the game never flourished in North America, where post-revolutionary culture turned toward baseball instead. True international cricket took shape only in the 1870s, when England and Australia began playing official Test matches, giving the sport a new global dimension. By the 1880s, the Ashes rivalry was born after Australia's famous victory at The Oval in 1882, and cricket in England was advancing rapidly with growing crowds, newspapers chronicling every contest, and heroes who became household names. Reports of these developments filtered into India, where educated elites increasingly saw cricket as more than amusement—it was a stage on which they might one day prove equality with their colonial rulers.

By the early twentieth century, cricket had become the most visible sport in colonial India. Princely states sponsored teams, gymkhanas anchored it in cities, and sepoys carried it into the countryside. Yet the game remained divided: Europeans, Parsis, Hindus, and Muslims played in separate tournaments, and caste boundaries often shaped who could represent a side. Could one caste rise above its own? Remarkably, cricket sometimes allowed it. The most striking case was Palwankar Baloo, a Dalit spinner who broke barriers by playing for the Hindu team in the early 1900s. Though he faced discrimination off the field— denied entry to pavilions or dining tables—his skill with the ball earned him respect across communities. Victories by Parsi elevens over Europeans in the 1890s, and Baloo's rise soon after, showed that cricket could become a stage where Indians glimpsed equality and dignity otherwise denied in society.

The years between the Mutiny and the First World War were thus formative. Cricket became the most important bridge between ruler and ruled, palace and barracks, village and metropolis. It was played in princely estates and dusty maidans, in gymkhanas and regimental squares, by English officers and Indian sepoys, by princes in silks and peasants in simple cotton. By 1914, the game had become unmistakably part of Indian life—still colonial in its structures, still divided by race and religion, but already claimed by Indians as their own. It was no longer a spectacle of the rulers; it was becoming a sport of the people.

5.3 From Mutiny to Modernity: Overarm Bowling and Cricket Before the Great War

The Raj that emerged after the great uprising of 1857 reshaped India in drill and discipline: cantonments laid out with geometric precision, railways binding provinces, and administration moving by clock and file. Within this order, cricket became less a novelty and more a routine. Soldiers played it as naturally as they paraded—mornings for drill, midday for clerical duty, afternoons for nets and inter-company matches before the light failed. Sundays, pay days, and regimental holidays turned fields into theatres of bat and ball.

Two changes gave this discipline fresh direction. In England, the Marylebone Cricket Club legalized overarm bowling in 1864, revolutionizing the sport. Bowlers found bounce and movement, batsmen reshaped their stance and technique, and the forward defensive became the grammar of survival. Coaching manuals and match reports carrying these lessons arrived by steamer, and within a few seasons overarm deliveries were the norm not only at Lord's but also on maidans from Peshawar to Madras.

The other change was administrative: regiments treated cricket like drill. Kits were kept in stores, scorebooks maintained, and matches scheduled with military neatness. Quartermasters issued bats and balls as carefully as ammunition. Soldiers absorbed the game's habits and carried them home on leave, marking out pitches in villages, teaching boys to bowl a length, and slowly weaving cricket into the rhythms of rural life.

In my ancestral village of Rupochak, this process took vivid form. My great-great-grandfather, Subedar Major Hashim Khan of the 58th Vaughan's Rifles, served under Field Marshal Lord Roberts from 1878 to 1918. Rising to one of the highest ranks available to Indian soldiers, he brought cricket back from the regiment to his village. Matches he organized drew entire crowds: children watching in wonder, elders debating strokes under trees, and soldiers recalling their barrack-square training. He also recruited hundreds of men from the region who later served in the Great War. For Rupochak, cricket became more than diversion; it became entwined with service, pride, and identity. Hashim Khan was honoured with the Medal of Gallantry and lifelong service—yet his quieter legacy was the bat and ball that turned a village into a team.

Beyond the cantonments, urban India built its own stages. Presidency towns set aside maidans where Europeans ran clubs, while Indian communities began forming their own institutions. Matches once polite became contested, their scorecards printed in newspapers with the precision of shipping manifests. Crowds learned the etiquette of applause, and bazaars buzzed with post-match analysis. Cricket had crossed the line from colonial curiosity to public conversation.

By the turn of the century, cricket in India stood on three strong legs: the regimental culture that drilled technique and discipline, the civic institutions that scheduled and reported fixtures, and the villages that adapted the game as their own. Princes and patrons helped with pavilions and coaches, but the real spread came from soldiers, clerks, and schoolboys who played it daily.

By 1914, as the world moved towards war, cricket in India was no longer a colonial courtesy. It had become habit, identity, and aspiration—a game still marked by divisions of class and community, yet firmly planted in Indian soil.

Readers notes

Indian Mutiny of 1857 – *Also called the First War of Independence, this uprising marked the end of East India Company rule and the beginning of direct Crown control. It reshaped the British presence in India, embedding military regiments and institutions that later carried cricket into wider society.*

Overarm Bowling (Legalized 1864) – *A revolutionary change in cricket laws by the MCC that permitted bowlers to deliver the ball with a raised arm. This innovation gave rise to pace, bounce, and swing, transforming batting technique and making the forward defensive a cornerstone of play.*

Gentlemen v Players Matches – *Initiated in 1806 and continuing into the late 19th century, these contests pitted wealthy amateurs (Gentlemen) against professional cricketers (Players). They symbolized England's class divide, but also became popular reference points for regimental and club cricket in India.*

William Lambert & Gambling Scandals *(1817) – Lambert, a leading English batsman, was banned for alleged match-fixing. His downfall remained a cautionary tale, resurfacing in Indian cricket where wagering at gymkhanas and cantonments was common. A reminder that cricket's spirit has often been tested by money.*

Fuller Pilch (1804–1870) – *Known as the "greatest batsman before W.G. Grace," his defensive play and celebrated 153 not out in 1833 at Tunbridge Wells shaped batting orthodoxy. His technique was cited in coaching manuals that reached regiments in India.*

County Championship (formalized in 1890) – *The competitive structure of English cricket, providing regular high-level play between counties. Reports of county rivalries, particularly Yorkshire v Lancashire ("The Roses Match"), were avidly followed in India, feeding the imaginations of both soldiers and clerks.*

First Test Match (1877) – *England v Australia at Melbourne, widely regarded as the birth of international cricket. It gave the sport a global stage just as India was beginning to internalize the game.*

Palwankar Baloo (1876–1955) – *A Dalit cricketer who rose to prominence as a left-arm spinner for the Hindu Gymkhana. His skill challenged entrenched caste prejudices, showing that cricket could sometimes transcend rigid Indian social hierarchies, even if inequality persisted off the field.*

Princely Patronage – *Maharajas such as the rulers of Patiala, Baroda, and Nawanagar (notably Ranjitsinhji) invested in cricket grounds, equipment, and professional coaching. Their* *involvement elevated cricket from cantonments into palaces and schools, making it a mark of prestige and modernity.*

Hashim Khan of Rupochak (1857–1927) – *Subedar Major in the 58th Vaughan's Rifles who served under Field Marshal Lord Roberts (1878–1918). He introduced cricket to his ancestral village Rupochak, now in Narowal district, Punjab. A decorated soldier awarded the Medal of Gallantry, he recruited over a thousand men for service in the Great War. Beyond the battlefield, his legacy was cultural: cricket in Rupochak became a local institution, linking village life with regimental pride.*

Rupochak (Narowal District) – *A small village in current Pakistani Punjab that produced senior officers of the British Indian Army from the Sulheria Rajput clan. After 1947, the same clan played a significant political role in Pakistan, serving in government and public life for over five decades. Rupochak's story symbolizes how villages at the margins of empire could become unlikely cradles of both military distinction and cricketing culture.*

58th Vaughan's Rifles (Frontier Force) – *A distinguished infantry regiment of the British Indian Army, raised in the mid-19th century as part of the Punjab Frontier Force. Known for its service on the North-West Frontier and later in overseas campaigns, it became a key unit where many Indian Subedars and Jemadars rose to prominence.*

Field Marshal Lord Roberts (1832–1914) – *One of Britain's most celebrated military commanders, Roberts served extensively in India and Afghanistan before becoming Commander-in-Chief of the Indian Army (1885–1893). A Victoria Cross recipient, he embodied the martial values the Raj sought to instill, and under his leadership regiments like the 58th Vaughan's Rifles gained both discipline and prestige.*

Chapter 6 – The World Wars and Partition

6.1 Wars, Tests, and the Partition of Empire (1914–1947)

The summer of 1914 opened with the familiar rhythm of English county cricket—crowds at Lord's, The Oval, Old Trafford, and Headingley—but the outbreak of the First World War silenced the game. Grounds became parade squares and hospitals, players traded flannels for khaki, and many never returned. Kent's Colin Blythe, one of the great spinners of his era, fell on the Western Front in 1917, a symbol of how cricket's ranks were thinned by war. Across the Empire, Indian sepoys and officers carried memories of the game into trenches in France and Mesopotamia, even as fixtures at home faltered and the Bombay Quadrangular dwindled during the war years.

When peace returned in 1918, cricket revived quickly. In England, Jack Hobbs and Herbert Sutcliffe became the batting pair that reassured a nation emerging from trauma. In Australia, the 1930s belonged to Donald Bradman, whose astonishing run-scoring feats turned him into the first truly global cricket celebrity. Indian readers in Bombay and Calcutta followed his double centuries with awe, learning that cricket could elevate a man into myth.

In India, the 1920s and 1930s brought transformation. The Quadrangular tournament resumed, its communal divisions intensifying rivalries but also drawing vast crowds. Princely patrons—Maharajas of Patiala, Nawanagar, and Holkar—funded grounds and teams, entwining cricket with politics and prestige.

The decisive breakthrough came in 1932, when India was granted Test status. That summer, an Indian team traveled to England for its first official Test at Lord's (25–28 June 1932). Nominally captained by the Maharaja of Porbandar but effectively led on the field by C. K. Nayudu, the team faced an England side under Douglas Jardine—the same Jardine who, within a year, would become infamous for the *Bodyline* tactics in Australia.

The match itself was memorable far beyond the result. England, vastly more experienced, won by 158 runs, but the contest contained flashes of Indian resilience. Bowling first, India dismissed England for 259, with medium-pacer Mohammad Nissar making history as India's first Test wicket-taker. His pace surprised the English batsmen, and he finished with 5 for 93, a remarkable debut that established India's capacity for fast bowling. Amar Singh, India's other paceman, also impressed with swing and accuracy.

India's batting was less secure against England's established attack. In the first innings, India managed only 189, Nayudu top-scoring with a fighting 40. Jardine, alongside his star all-rounder Wally Hammond, pressed England forward in the second innings, setting India a daunting target after declaring at 275 for 8. Once again, Nissar and Amar Singh were the standout performers, taking wickets and earning praise in the English press.

Chasing 346 to win, India showed flashes of resistance. The debutant Nazir Ali played with spirit, and Amar Singh hit some bold strokes. Yet England's attack, led by Bill Bowes and Walter Robins, proved too strong. India was bowled out for 187, leaving England victors, but not without admiration for the newcomers' courage.

What resonated most was the quality of India's fast bowlers. English commentators admitted surprise that the tourists, imagined as a team of spinners and stroke makers, had unleashed genuine pace at Lord's. The *Times* noted that Nissar would have "walked into any county side."

Nayudu, though not prolific with the bat, impressed spectators with his fearless hitting, famously striking Hedley Verity back over his head and drawing a roar from the Lord's crowd.

Though defeat was clear, the symbolism was powerful. For the first time, India had walked onto the hallowed turf of Lord's as equals, their names on the scorecard beside England's best. Indian newspapers treated the result as a triumph of recognition. One Calcutta paper declared, *"England has taken centuries to master the game; India has begun the struggle today."*

Ironically, Jardine—the opposing captain who shook hands with Indian debutants—would just months later become infamous in the Bodyline series (1932–33), instructing Harold Larwood and Bill Voce to bowl short-pitched at Bradman's body. To Indian readers, who had celebrated their first Test, the Bodyline storm revealed cricket's double edge: it was a stage for pride and equality, but also a theatre of imperial ruthlessness.

The 1932 Test thus stood at a crossroads: India's initiation into Test cricket and Jardine's last polite gesture before the most notorious controversy in cricket's interwar years. For India, it was less about the scoreline and more about legitimacy. A new nation-in-waiting had announced itself on cricket's grandest stage.

India's progress continued with the Ranji Trophy in 1934, a domestic championship named after the great Ranjitsinhji. It created a national ladder of competition, feeding directly into Test selection. New stars appeared: Vijay Merchant, whose flawless technique made him India's finest batsman of the decade, and Lala Amarnath, who in 1933 became the first Indian to score a Test century against England.

That same season, India hosted England for its first official Test series on home soil (1933–34). Matches were staged in Bombay, Calcutta, and Madras, drawing immense crowds that confirmed cricket's growing grip on Indian imagination. Though England, captained by Douglas Jardine of Bodyline fame, won the series 2–0, the highlight came at Bombay's Gymkhana Ground, where Lala Amarnath's brilliant 118 became India's first Test century. His innings was celebrated across the country as a symbolic triumph, proof that Indians could excel against their rulers not only abroad but on their own grounds.

These achievements made cricket more than a pastime; it became a stage where Indians could challenge their rulers on equal terms, at least within the twenty-two yards.

Globally, the interwar years saw cricket grow in stature. England and Australia's duels, especially *Bodyline*, attracted worldwide coverage. By the late 1930s, Test cricket included not only England and Australia but also South Africa, the West Indies, New Zealand, and now India. Cricket was no longer parochial—it was unmistakably international.

The outbreak of the Second World War in 1939 disrupted the game again. Players joined the armed forces: Denis Compton and Bill Edrich in Britain, Keith Miller flying fighters for Australia, his later quip becoming legend— "pressure is a Messerschmitt up your arse, not playing at Lord's." Matches continued only as charity exhibitions or morale-boosters in barracks and prisoner-of-war camps. In India, wartime politics overshadowed sport, but cricket persisted in fragments: the Bombay Pentangular still drew large crowds in the early 1940s, even as the Quit India movement shook the Raj.

By 1945, as peace returned, cricket was among the first cultural activities to rebound. Crowds thronged to grounds in England and Australia, starved for leisure after years of rationing. In India, the game surged again, driven by Merchant, Amarnath, and younger talents. But politics pressed closer. The Pentangular communal divisions mirrored the very fractures of society, and by 1947, Partition would tear apart not only nations but also cricketing institutions. Players shifted allegiances overnight: those in Lahore became Pakistan's nucleus, while those in Bombay or Calcutta stayed with India.

By the late 1940s, cricket had passed through two world wars, acquired global reach, and survived Partition. It had been scarred but not broken—played in trenches, POW camps, palaces, maidans, and cantonments. The end of the Second World War left Britain victorious but exhausted. The war had drained its treasury, shattered its economy, and exposed the limits of imperial power. Once the "workshop of the world," Britain was now reliant on American loans and struggling with debt and rationing at home. The Royal Navy no longer ruled unchallenged seas, and the empire that had once spanned continents now appeared an unsustainable burden. Within this climate of decline, India's long struggle for freedom entered its decisive phase.

At the forefront of freedom struggle were three towering figures— Mahatma Gandhi, Jawaharlal Nehru, and Muhammad Ali Jinnah—each embodying distinct visions of India's future. Gandhi, already the spiritual leader of the independence movement, continued to preach non-violence, mass mobilization, and civil disobedience. His Quit India campaign of 1942 had shown the depth of Indian resistance, even as it was brutally suppressed. After the war, Gandhi remained a moral compass, urging reconciliation between Hindus and Muslims even as communal divisions deepened.

Nehru, the charismatic leader of the Indian National Congress, represented the modernist, secular vision of an independent India. Steeped in Fabian socialism and inspired by internationalism, Nehru argued that India must not only win freedom but also build a democratic, industrial, and scientific state. His leadership during the waning years of British rule positioned him as India's first prime minister-in-waiting, embodying the aspirations of millions who looked beyond colonial subjugation to a new republic.

Opposite Nehru stood Jinnah, the charismatic barrister who transformed himself into the Qaid-e-Azam, leader of the Muslim League. Jinnah's demand for Pakistan—an independent homeland for Muslims—reshaped the final act of the independence struggle. Once a nationalist who shared platforms with Congress leaders, Jinnah emerged after the war as the uncompromising voice of Muslim political identity. The 1940 Lahore Resolution, demanding separate states, had seemed distant at the time, but by 1946–47, amid communal violence and political deadlock, it became the defining reality.

In London, these currents coincided with seismic political change. Winston Churchill, the war leader lionized for defying Hitler, was unexpectedly defeated in the 1945 general election. His fall shocked the world but revealed Britain's exhaustion with war and desire for domestic reform. The new Labour government under Clement Attlee had little appetite or capacity to maintain the empire at its old strength. Attlee's ministers, pragmatic and financially constrained, resolved to accelerate India's independence. By 1947, Britain would leave the subcontinent, not from magnanimity but from necessity.

The years 1946–47 were indeed decisive. Communal riots scarred Calcutta, Lahore, and Noakhali; the naval mutiny in Bombay exposed deep fissures within the colonial military apparatus; and the Cabinet Mission failed to reconcile Congress and League visions. Partition became inevitable, leaving independence inseparable from division. On 14-15 August 1947, Pakistan and India gained independence respectively. The summer of 1947 unleashed one of the largest human migrations in recorded history. An estimated 12–15 million people crossed the new borders, as Hindus and Sikhs fled from West Punjab, Sindh, and the North-West Frontier Province into India, while Muslims moved in vast numbers from Punjab, Delhi, Uttar Pradesh, Bihar, and Bengal into Pakistan. The violence that accompanied this exchange claimed up to one million lives, with countless others uprooted, widowed, or orphaned. East Bengal, with its Muslim majority, became East Pakistan (later Bangladesh in 1971), while West Bengal and Assam remained with India. Punjab, the great heartland of northern India, was split between East Punjab (India) and West Punjab (Pakistan), dividing cities, families, and centuries of shared culture. Sindh, with Karachi as its capital, stayed with Pakistan, while Kashmir's fate remained contested, igniting wars and rivalries that would last decades. What emerged from the carnage were two new nations—India and Pakistan—whose borders were born in haste and violence, but whose futures would also be tied by cultural continuities, none more visible than cricket.

Cricket, though seemingly peripheral, was swept into these upheavals. The communal lines of the Bombay Pentangular foreshadowed the division of cricketing loyalties along national borders. Players who had once shared dressing rooms—such as Abdul Hafeez Kardar, who played for India in the 1946 tour of England but later became Pakistan's first captain—now found themselves symbols of separate nations. The founding of Pakistan's cricket board in 1947, alongside the reconstitution of India's Board of Control for Cricket in India (BCCI) as the guardian of a sovereign nation's game, signaled how cricket, like politics, was redrawn by Partition. In India, the BCCI now represented not just a colony's pastime but the sporting identity of a free nation. In Pakistan, the creation of its own governing body laid the foundation for a new cricketing tradition, one that would soon seek international recognition and legitimacy. Just as ministries, armies, and institutions were divided, so too cricket was reshaped—its boards became symbols of national pride and instruments through which both countries projected themselves onto the global stage.

Thus, the legacies of Nehru, Jinnah, and Gandhi extended far beyond politics. Their competing visions shaped the nations that would also field their own cricket teams, each carrying with it the memory of shared history and painful separation. Britain's decline, Churchill's fall, and Attlee's pragmatism created the conditions for independence, but the turmoil of 1946–47 ensured that cricket in South Asia would forever be intertwined with the narratives of identity, rivalry, and nationhood. The rivalries first born in those years—India versus Pakistan, later joined by Sri Lanka, Afghanistan and Bangladesh—remain some of the most charged encounters in the game today, proof that the events of those years still echo on the cricket field.

6.2 Cricket's Ghost Nations: Forgotten Teams of a Vanishing Empire

As the British Empire unraveled in the mid-20th century, so too did several cricketing identities that had once flourished within its borders. These "ghost nations" of cricket—teams formed by colonial officers, military regiments, civil services, and princely states—represented the imperial structure more than any national allegiance. With the political earthquakes of war, independence, and Partition, they vanished almost overnight, leaving behind only scorecards and fading photographs.

In pre-1947 India, sides such as the "Europeans XI" and "Viceroy's XI" were staples of the cricketing calendar. Composed largely of British officials and settlers, they played first-class matches and commanded home grounds, trophies, and even loyal spectators. These teams were more than recreational—they reflected the social order of the Raj. Yet, following independence, they disappeared entirely. Their institutional support dissolved, their purpose voided by sovereignty. What remained were archival records of matches played, but no enduring legacy—no flag, anthem, or successor.

Beyond India, other imperial formations followed similar trajectories. The "Malaya XI," "Burma XI," and "Federated Malay States" competed against visiting English teams and regional rivals under colonial patronage. In many ways, they functioned like proto-national sides within British frameworks. But after decolonization, these teams fragmented, their players folded into the emerging nations of Malaysia and Myanmar. Often, the cricketing momentum was lost altogether.

In East Africa, too, colonial multi-ethnic sides flourished under British administration. Teams based in Nairobi or Kampala brought together players from different racial and ethnic communities—Europeans, Indians, and Africans—united by empire, not nation. Once independence arrived, eligibility rules, local politics, and shifting identities redefined what it meant to represent a team.

These ghost teams remind us that cricket's global history is not only about nationhood—it is also about institutions that no longer exist. The sport once served as a stage for imperial unity, played under flags that no longer fly. Their disappearance invites deeper reflection: When political borders dissolve, what becomes of the sporting identities they carried? And how do we remember cricketers who played not for countries, but for empires that have been folded into history?

Readers notes

Colin Blythe (1879–1917) – *Brilliant left-arm spinner for Kent who took over 2,000 first-class wickets. He was killed on the Western Front in World War I, symbolizing cricket's human cost during the Great War.*

First World War (1914–1918) – *A global conflict that halted organized cricket in England and India. Many grounds were turned into military facilities, and hundreds of players enlisted, with many never returning.*

Sir Jack Hobbs (1882–1963) – *Legendary English opener, nicknamed the "Master." Alongside Herbert Sutcliffe, he gave interwar England reassurance with his consistency and grace.*

Herbert Sutcliffe (1894–1978) – *Yorkshire opener whose stoicism symbolized post-war resilience. His partnerships with Hobbs became classics of English cricket.*

Sir Donald Bradman (1908–2001) – *Australian batsman whose astonishing average of 99.94 made him cricket's greatest icon. Emerging in the late 1920s, he carried Depression-era Australia's hopes and became a global celebrity, inspiring even Indian fans who read of his feats in newspapers.*

Douglas Jardine (1900–1958) – *England captain notorious for the Bodyline series (1932–33) against Australia, where his bowlers targeted Bradman's body with short-pitched deliveries. Ironically, he captained England against India in their first Test at Lord's in 1932, shaking hands with Indian debutants just months before his most infamous controversy.*

Bodyline (1932–33) – *England's controversial tactic in Australia under Jardine's captaincy, involving fast leg-theory bowling aimed at the batsman's body with a packed leg-side field. Effective but widely condemned as unsporting.*

Mohammad Nissar (1910–1963) – *India's first genuine fast bowler. In the 1932 Lord's Test, he stunned England by taking 5 for 93 in the first innings. Widely praised in the English press as "good enough for any county side."*

Amar Singh (1910–1940) – *India's second great pace bowler of the early years, partner to Nissar, noted for his swing, seam, and stylish batting cameos.*

C. K. Nayudu (1895–1967) – *India's first Test captain in practice (though nominally under Porbandar), famous for his aggressive batting. His bold strokes in 1932 earned applause at Lord's.*

97

Maharaja of Porbandar (Natwarsinhji Bhavsinhji, 1901–1979) – *Official captain of India's 1932 Test side. His limited cricketing skills meant Nayudu led on the field, but his presence symbolized princely patronage of Indian cricket.*

India's First Test Match (1932) – *Played at Lord's from 25–28 June 1932. England won by 158 runs, but India's spirited bowling impressed. This debut marked India's official entry into Test cricket.*

Ranji Trophy (est. 1934) – *India's premier domestic championship, named after Prince Ranjitsinhji, designed to provide a structured pathway for regional teams and future Test players.*

Lala Amarnath (1911–2000) – *The first Indian to score a Test century (1933 against England at Bombay). He became a national hero and a symbol of Indian cricketing pride.*

Wally Hammond (1903–1965) – *England batsman and all-rounder of the 1930s, rival to Bradman in stature, known for his powerful batting and prolific run-making.*

Bombay Quadrangular / Pentangular – *Annual communal tournaments dividing teams by community (Europeans, Parsis, Hindus, Muslims, and later "The Rest"). Hugely popular but also controversial, as they mirrored communal divisions in colonial India.*

Second World War (1939–1945) – *Again disrupted cricket globally. Many players enlisted: Denis Compton and Bill Edrich in Britain, Keith Miller as a fighter pilot for Australia. Cricket survived in charity matches, barracks, POW camps, and overseas garrisons.*

Keith Miller (1919–2004) – *Charismatic Australian all-rounder whose wartime service as a fighter pilot shaped his famous quip: "Pressure is a Messerschmitt up your arse, not playing at Lord's."*

Winston Churchill (1874–1965) – *British wartime Prime Minister (1940–45), lionized for defying Hitler but unexpectedly defeated in the 1945 general election. Famously resistant to Indian independence, contrasting with his successor's pragmatism.*

Clement Attlee (1883–1967) – *Labour Prime Minister (1945–51) whose government, facing economic exhaustion and declining imperial power, resolved to accelerate Indian independence.*

Quit India Movement (1942) – *Mass civil disobedience campaign launched by Gandhi demanding immediate British withdrawal. Though suppressed, it intensified nationalist momentum during WWII.*

Mahatma Gandhi (1869–1948) – *Spiritual leader of the independence movement, advocate of non-violence and communal harmony. Urged reconciliation even as Partition drew near.*

Jawaharlal Nehru (1889–1964) – *Leader of the Indian National Congress and India's first Prime Minister. Advocated a modern, secular, socialist democracy.*

Muhammad Ali Jinnah (1876–1948) – *Founder of Pakistan, leader of the Muslim League. His call for a separate homeland for Muslims culminated in Partition.*

Partition of 1947 – *Division of British India into India and Pakistan, accompanied by mass migration of 12–15 million people and up to a million deaths. Punjab was split between East (India) and West (Pakistan); Bengal between India and East Pakistan (later Bangladesh). Sindh, NWFP, and Baluchistan went to Pakistan.*

Abdul Hafeez Kardar (1925–1996) – *Played for India in the 1946 England tour but became Pakistan's first Test captain after Partition, symbolizing cricket's realignment with new national borders.*

Board of Control for Cricket in India (BCCI) – *Founded in 1928, it was reconstituted after independence as the governing body of Indian cricket, symbolizing sovereignty.*

Pakistan Cricket Board (PCB) – *Established in 1947 following Partition. Initially fragile, it sought Test recognition and quickly became a platform for national pride.*

Part IV – Post-Independence South Asian Cricket

Chapter 7 – Indian Cricket After Independence and Rise as a Superpower

7.1 Early Years of Independence (1947–1959)

When India achieved independence in 1947, its cricketing story entered a new chapter. The Board of Control for Cricket in India (BCCI), though modest in resources, now represented a sovereign nation rather than a colony. The tricolour was raised not just in politics but also on the cricket field, and the decade that followed saw India searching for its place among established Test powers.

India's first major outing as an independent nation was the historic 1947–48 tour of Australia, where Don Bradman's side overwhelmed the visitors 4–0 in a five-Test series. Bradman's brilliance was unanswerable, but India earned admiration for flashes of resilience—Vijay Hazare scoring twin centuries in Adelaide remains one of the tour's most celebrated feats. Though defeats were heavy, the symbolism of an Indian team touring Australia so soon after independence carried weight: India was no longer just a participant in empire cricket, but a nation seeking identity on the world stage.

The following season brought India's first home Test series since independence, against the West Indies in 1948/49. In a five-Test series, West Indies prevailed 1–0, but crowds flocked in record numbers to Bombay, Calcutta, and Madras, affirming cricket's new role as a national theatre.

India's first brush with victory came in 1951/52 at home against England, when the series was drawn 1–1 after India secured a historic first Test win at Madras. That same year saw another milestone: India's first Test series against Pakistan (1952/53). In a contest loaded with political and emotional meaning, India won 2–1, Lala Amarnath's leadership and the bowling of Vinoo Mankad becoming defining features. This victory gave cricket an early role in shaping post-Partition identity.

Results through the 1950s were mixed. India drew a hard-fought series in Pakistan in 1954/55 but endured heavy losses abroad, including a 3–0 defeat in England (1952) and a 5–0 whitewash in England (1959). At home, fortunes were steadier: India defeated New Zealand 2–0 in 1955/56, its first series win against non-Asian opposition, though losses to Australia (1956/57) and West Indies (1958/59) reminded all of the gulf with cricket's strongest powers.

The decade's pattern was clear: at home, on spinning tracks and in front of passionate crowds, India could hold its own; abroad, the team struggled. Yet the 1947–59 period was about more than results—it was about planting cricket in the soil of independent India. Heroes like Hazare, Amarnath, and Mankad gave the public figures to believe in, while victories against Pakistan and England proved that Indian cricket could triumph on its own terms.

These formative years did not bring glory in numbers, but they brought something more lasting: legitimacy, confidence, and the foundations on which future triumphs would stand.

Reader's notes

Vinoo Mankad (1917–1978) – *Legendary Indian all-rounder, remembered for his left-arm spin and gritty batting. His 413-run opening stand with Pankaj Roy in 1956 stood as a world record for nearly 52 years.*

Polly Umrigar (1926–2006) – *India's most reliable batsman of the 1950s, known for his calm temperament and powerful strokes. He scored 3,631 Test runs, a national record at the time.*

Subhash Gupte (1929–2002) – *Celebrated leg-spinner hailed by many as India's finest before Anil Kumble. He took 149 Test wickets with mesmerizing control and variation.*

1952 Madras Test Victory – *India's first-ever Test win, defeating England by an innings and 8 runs. Vinoo Mankad starred with 12 wickets, etching his name into cricketing folklore.*

1947–48 Australia Tour – *India's first major Test series abroad after independence, led by Lala Amarnath. They faced Don Bradman's Australia and lost 4–0, but the tour marked India's entry as a sovereign Test nation.*

7.2 The Tiger Pataudi Era and the 1960s

In the 1960s, India was still a young republic, its economy slowly restructuring after independence. The country was focused on industrialization and nation-building, but resources for sport remained scarce. Unlike the wealthier boards such as the England and Wales Cricket Board (ECB) or the Australian Cricket Board (ACB), the BCCI operated on limited budgets. India lacked both financial muscle and political weight in the corridors of international cricket, often accepting tours on terms dictated by richer boards.

Into this backdrop emerged Mansoor Ali Khan "Tiger" Pataudi, one of Indian cricket's most charismatic leaders. Born into princely privilege, educated at Oxford, and tragically losing an eye in a car accident in 1961, Pataudi redefined courage on the cricket field. Appointed captain at just 21 after Nari Contractor's injury, he became India's youngest-ever Test skipper. His leadership style brought fresh confidence to a side that had long been timid abroad.

The decade produced a mixed bag of results. India began with a cautious drawn home series against Pakistan in 1960/61, after which political tensions led to a long suspension of cricketing ties—a pattern that has repeated throughout Indo-Pak relations. A 2–0 win over England in 1961/62 showed promise at home, but the same winter India was humbled 5–0 in the West Indies, as Garfield Sobers's team dominated. Subsequent years brought both highlights and disappointments: a drawn home series against Australia in 1964/65, victory over New Zealand in the same season, but crushing defeats abroad—3–0 in England (1967) and 4–0 in Australia (1967/68). Yet the tour of New Zealand that winter brought a historic achievement: India's first overseas Test series win, clinched 3–1, a milestone that lifted national morale.

Pataudi's personal aura mattered as much as results. His bold field settings, insistence on professionalism, and faith in Indian spinners gave the team self-belief. His marriage to actress Sharmila Tagore in 1969 was another first: the early blending of cricket and Bollywood, a connection that would later define much of India's cricketing culture.

The wider context shaped cricket too. The Sino-Indian War of 1962, the death of Jawaharlal Nehru in 1964, and the Indo-Pak war of 1965 all impacted national life, with sport often seen as a morale-builder. Television was in its infancy—only a handful of sets existed in Delhi in the 1960s—so most Indians still followed cricket through radio commentary and newspapers. Till mid 60's, India was a hockey powerhouse, winning Olympic golds, while cricket remained a developing passion.

The 1960s were thus not an age of dominance but of direction. Under Pataudi, Indian cricket discovered self-confidence and tactical sharpness. Even in defeat, the seeds of future triumphs were planted.

Reader's notes

Mansoor Ali Khan "Tiger" Pataudi (1941–2011) – *India's youngest Test captain at 21, who led despite losing vision in one eye. His bold leadership, attacking field placements, and faith in spinners transformed India's cricketing mindset.*

First Overseas Test Series Win (1967/68) – *India defeated New Zealand 3–1 to secure their first-ever Test series triumph abroad, a landmark in cricketing self-confidence.*

Sharmila Tagore – *Leading Bollywood actress who married Pataudi in 1969, marking the first high-profile union of Indian cricket and film, later a recurring cultural trend.*

Sino-Indian War (1962) – *Short but devastating conflict with China that shocked India's political establishment and strained national morale.*

Jawaharlal Nehru (1889–1964) – *India's first Prime Minister, who died in 1964; his passing coincided with a period of uncertainty in national politics and sport.*

Indo-Pak War (1965) – *Armed conflict between India and Pakistan that froze cricketing ties after the 1960/61 Test series, a pattern of interruptions that persists in bilateral cricket.*

Doordarshan (est. 1959) – *India's state television broadcaster, in its infancy during the 1960s, with limited reach. Cricket was still followed primarily via radio commentary and newspapers.*

India's Hockey Supremacy (1928–1964) – *India won six consecutive Olympic gold medals in field hockey (1928–1956), remaining a global powerhouse while cricket was still developing.*

7.3 The 1970s – Gavaskar and India's First Golden Phase

The 1970s marked India's first golden era in cricket, when the team broke out of its colonial shadow and began to command respect on the world stage. At the heart of this transformation was Ajit Wadekar's leadership, Sunil Gavaskar's meteoric rise, and a band of spinners whose artistry defined Indian cricket for a generation.

The breakthrough came in 1970/71, when India stunned the cricketing world by defeating the West Indies of Sir Gary Sobers in their own backyard. A young Sunil Gavaskar, making his debut, announced himself with 774 runs in the series, including four centuries, and became an instant national hero. The victory carried symbolic weight: India had overcome one of cricket's powerhouses on foreign soil. Soon after, in the summer of 1971, India sealed another landmark by defeating England 1–0 in a three-Test series. The victory at The Oval—immortalized by Indian fans releasing a painted elephant onto the ground—was India's first series win in England, a triumph that resonated far beyond the boundary ropes.

India's strength in this period rested heavily on its celebrated spin quartet: Bishan Singh Bedi, Erapalli Prasanna, Bhagwat Chandrasekhar, and Srinivas Venkataraghavan. Each brought a unique weapon—Bedi's flight and guile, Prasanna's loop, Chandra's unorthodox leg-spin, and Venkat's accuracy—together forming an arsenal that could trouble the best batting line-ups. On turning tracks in India, they were nearly unplayable, and abroad, they often delivered decisive breakthroughs when conditions allowed. Their craft gave India the confidence to compete even when batting faltered.

The decade, however, was not without drama. In the late 1970s, Bishan Bedi captained India during a controversial series in Australia (1977/78), where fiery encounters, disputed umpiring decisions, and aggressive tactics defined the contests. India lost 3–2, but the fight they showed in alien conditions was widely admired. The following year in

Pakistan (1978/79), India lost a three-Test series 2–0, with Bedi's captaincy questioned. Yet the return of Indo-Pak cricket after nearly two decades of political freeze was historic, drawing huge crowds and immense passion on both sides of the border.

The wider national backdrop added to cricket's resonance. The 1971 war with Pakistan, which led to the creation of Bangladesh, reshaped the subcontinent. India's economy, still in early phases of restructuring after independence, faced challenges of poverty, inflation, and slow industrial growth, yet cricket emerged as a powerful unifier. Hockey was gradually declining in India, but cricket was gaining ground rapidly as the game of aspiration and identity in 70's.

The 1970s also saw the emergence of a new generation. Amid the dominance of Gavaskar and the spinners, a rookie fast bowler from Haryana, Kapil Dev, debuted in 1978. With his athleticism, attacking batting, and genuine pace, he offered a glimpse of the future—a future where India would not rely solely on spin.

This decade was also marked by highs and lows. Famous home wins, such as the 1979/80 triumphs over Pakistan and Australia, stood alongside humiliating defeats: the 1974 tour of England where India collapsed for 42 at Lord's, and dismal Prudential World Cup campaigns in 1975 and 1979, including a shocking loss to Sri Lanka. Yet taken as a whole, the 1970s transformed India from perennial underdogs into genuine contenders.

By its end, India had heroes in Gavaskar, Wadekar, Bedi, Engineer, and the spin quartet, and hope in the rising Kapil Dev. The foundations for the World Cup glory of the 1980s had been laid—the 1970s were the decade India truly learned how to win.

Reader's Notes

Ajit Wadekar – *Indian captain who led India to historic overseas series wins in 1971 against the West Indies and England, changing global perceptions of Indian cricket.*

Sunil Gavaskar – *Prolific opener who debuted in 1971 with 774 runs in the West Indies; became the backbone of Indian batting through the 1970s.*

The Spin Quartet – *Bishan Singh Bedi, Erapalli Prasanna, Bhagwat Chandrasekhar, and Srinivas Venkataraghavan; India's famed spin unit whose variations and control terrorized batsmen worldwide.*

The Oval Elephant (1971) – *Symbolic moment during India's first-ever series win in England, when an elephant painted with Indian colours was paraded at The Oval after victory.*

Farokh Engineer – *Stylish wicketkeeper-batsman who played key roles in India's successes, equally known for his flamboyance and reliability behind the stumps.*

Kapil Dev (Debut 1978) – *Haryana all-rounder who burst onto the scene with pace bowling and fearless batting, marking India's turn toward fast bowling tradition.*

1974 "Summer of Disaster" – *India's tour of England where they lost 3–0, including being dismissed for 42 at Lord's, one of the lowest points in their Test history.*

Prudential World Cups (1975 & 1979) – *India's disappointing early World Cup campaigns, including a humiliating loss to Sri Lanka in 1979, reflecting the team's struggle in limited-overs cricket.*

1971 Indo-Pak War – *Geopolitical conflict leading to the birth of Bangladesh; cricket between India and Pakistan resumed only in 1978 after a 17-year hiatus.*

Bishan Singh Bedi's Captaincy – *Known for his artistry as a left-arm spinner but also for controversial decisions and heated encounters, especially in Australia (1977/78) and Pakistan (1978).*

Sir Garfield Sobers – *Legendary West Indian all-rounder, regarded as the greatest cricketer of his era, who captained the West Indies against India in the 1971 series that heralded India's first overseas triumph.*

7.4 The 1980s – Kapil Dev and miracle of 1983 World Cup victory

The 1980s stand as one of the most dramatic decades in Indian cricket — a blend of astonishing highs that permanently altered the nation's relationship with the sport, and sobering lows that reminded everyone of how fragile success could be.

India entered the decade still trying to shed its inconsistency. A drawn series in Australia (1980/81) was followed by defeats in New Zealand, England and Pakistan, reflecting the team's inability to string together results abroad. At home, India remained stronger, beating England in 1981/82, but the cracks soon showed. The 1983/84 home series against the West Indies, fresh on the heels of India's World Cup triumph, was billed as a test of credibility. Instead, it ended in a sobering 3–0 defeat, Viv Richards and Malcolm Marshall reminding Indian fans of the gulf between isolated glory and sustained dominance. Soon after, England under David Gower inflicted a 2–1 series defeat in 1984/85, proving that home advantage could no longer be taken for granted.

However, we must not forget that perception of cricket in India changed forever in June 1983.

The Prudential World Cup in England was expected to be another West Indian coronation. Lloyd's men had won in 1975 and 1979, and their mix of intimidating pace and flamboyant batting made them overwhelming favourites. India, by contrast, had won only a single World Cup match across the two previous editions. When they entered the group stage, expectations were minimal. But something clicked. A victory against the West Indies in the opening match sets the tone. The defining moment came against Zimbabwe at Tunbridge Wells, when Kapil Dev, walking in with India reeling at 17 for 5, played what remains one of the most famous innings in World Cup history after

Glen Maxwell's 201* vs Afghanistan in Mumbai 2023 World Cup. His unbeaten 175 not only rescued India but also gave the side belief that miracles were possible.

At Old Trafford, Amarnath and Binny strangled England in Semi Final, and on 25 June 1983 at Lord's, India defended 183 against the all-conquering West Indies. Kapil Dev's sprinting catch to dismiss Richards became a symbol of self-belief, and Amarnath's all-round brilliance sealed the triumph. India, overnight, had become world champions. That afternoon at Lord's is remembered as the turning point of Indian cricket, the day the sport became the heartbeat of a nation.

Momentum continued in 1985 at the Benson & Hedges World Championship of Cricket in Australia, where Sunil Gavaskar's men, playing in colored clothing under lights, beat Pakistan in the final at the MCG. Mohinder Amarnath again starred, and the victory confirmed that 1983 was no fluke — India had mastered the one-day game.

But cricket is never linear. By 1986, India tasted one of its most painful defeats: the Australasia Cup final in Sharjah, where Javed Miandad's last-ball six off Chetan Sharma became a permanent scar. That loss dented national morale and ushered in a period of Pakistani dominance. Later that year, Pakistan toured India and inflicted heavy defeats in both Tests and ODIs, including a 1–0 Test series win and 5-1 ODI series win on Indian soil (1986/87), a first for Pakistan. Imran Khan's team, brimming with Wasim Akram, Abdul Qadir, and Saleem Malik, became India's most formidable rival, a trend that haunted the late 1980s.

Still, India produced moments of resilience. In 1986, they achieved a rare 2–0 Test series win in England, with Dilip Vengsarkar excelling at Lord's. That same year, India and Australia fought out only the second tied Test in history at Madras, a match that encapsulated both the drama and endurance of Test cricket. Yet, despite such highs, defeats in

West Indies (1988/89) and draw in Pakistan (1989/90) revealed the limits of India's depth beyond their stalwarts.

The 1987 Reliance World Cup, the first to be staged outside England, brought cricket to Indian and Pakistani stadiums in front of massive crowds. Though India fell to England in the semi-final at Bombay, the fact that the final was staged at Eden Gardens in Calcutta and later at Lahore in 1996 World Cup symbolized that the subcontinent had become the epicentre of world cricket. Hosting the World Cup was more than logistics; it was acknowledgment that India had become a formidable cricketing power, even if results fluctuated.

The decade closed with both hope and heartbreak. In 1989, a packed Eden Gardens witnessed Imran Khan lifting Nehru Cup after beating West Indies in Final, another great tournament which India hosted, but the sheer scale of the event underlined the sport's cultural centrality. That same year, a 16-year-old schoolboy from Bombay named Sachin Tendulkar made his Test debut against Pakistan in Karachi. Facing Imran Khan, Wasim Akram, and Waqar Younis, Tendulkar's courage and compact strokeplay offered a glimpse of the future. The baton was being passed from the Gavaskar-Kapil-Amarnath generation to a new era.

The 1980s, then, were a paradox. On the one hand, India claimed its greatest triumphs: the 1983 World Cup, the 1985 World Championship, the Madras tied Test, and the 1986 win in England. On the other, the decade exposed vulnerabilities — home series defeats to West Indies, England and Pakistan's stranglehold post-1985 along with underwhelming performance in the 1987 World Cup and 1989 Nehru Cup. The lasting memory, however, is that of transformation. Lord's 1983 had ignited a fire that would never be extinguished. Cricket became India's identity, its obsession, and its stage to prove parity with the world. By the decade's end, as Tendulkar stepped into the arena, India was preparing for its next great chapter.

Readers' notes

Kapil Dev (1959–) – *India's iconic all-rounder and 1983 World Cup–winning captain. His 175* against Zimbabwe at Tunbridge Wells remains one of ODI cricket's greatest innings, while his catch to dismiss Viv Richards in the final at Lord's became a symbol of India's self-belief.*

Prudential World Cup 1983 – *The third edition of the Cricket World Cup, played in England and famously won by India. India defeated the West Indies in the final at Lord's on 25 June 1983, marking the definitive turning point in Indian cricket history.*

Mohinder Amarnath (1950–) – *The hero of both the 1983 World Cup semi-final and final. Known for his calm temperament and ability to deliver under pressure, Amarnath was named Man of the Match in both decisive matches.*

Benson & Hedges World Championship of Cricket (1985) – *A special one-day tournament hosted in Australia to celebrate 150 years of Victoria's founding. India won the final against Pakistan at the MCG, reinforcing their growing dominance in limited-overs cricket.*

Australasia Cup Final, Sharjah 1986 – *Pakistan defeated India in the final when Javed Miandad hit a last-ball six off Chetan Sharma. It remains one of the most famous (and painful) finishes in ODI history and symbolized Pakistan's rising supremacy over India in the late 1980s.*

Tied Test (Madras, 1986) – *Only the second tied Test in cricket history, played between India and Australia at Chepauk. Dean Jones scored 210 for Australia, while India, chasing 348, were bowled out with the scores level. Sunil Gavaskar's men fought valiantly, but the match ended dramatically in a tie.*

Sunil Gavaskar (1949–) – *India's greatest opener of the 1970s and 1980s, who became the first batsman to reach 10,000 Test runs. He retired in 1987, symbolizing the end of an era, just as Sachin Tendulkar's career was beginning.*

Reliance World Cup 1987 – *The first World Cup to be held outside England, jointly hosted by India and Pakistan. Though India lost in the semi-final to England, the event itself marked the subcontinent's arrival as the new center of global cricket.*

Nehru Cup 1989 – *A high profile multi-nation ODI tournament held at Eden Gardens, Calcutta, in commemoration of Jawaharlal Nehru's birth centenary. It was won by Pakistan.*

Sachin Tendulkar (1973–) – *Made his Test debut at the age of 16 against Pakistan in 1989. His courage against the pace of Imran Khan, Wasim Akram, and Waqar Younis signalled the rise of India's greatest batsman, who would dominate world cricket for two decades.*

7.5 The 1990s to 2000s – Sachin Tendulkar and the Era of New Icons

The 1990s opened a new chapter for Indian cricket, a decade when the game mirrored the nation's own transformation. Politically and economically, India was moving away from its semi-socialist framework: the 1991 economic liberalization under Prime Minister P. V. Narasimha Rao and Finance Minister Manmohan Singh brought sweeping reforms. Foreign investment, satellite television, and consumer markets poured into the country. Dish antennas appeared on rooftops across India and Pakistan, giving millions direct access to live cricket broadcasts. For the first time, cricket was not just a sport of stadiums and radio commentary; it was a prime-time spectacle in every household. Television advertising flooded the game, and the Board of Control for Cricket in India (BCCI), once a modest body with limited means, began to grow into a financial giant. The stage was set for cricket to become the defining cultural and commercial force in Indian society.

The Hero Cup of 1993 is often remembered as the dress rehearsal for the Wills World Cup that followed three years later. Played in India to mark the Cricket Association of Bengal's diamond jubilee, it showcased the subcontinent's capacity to stage cricket on a grand scale, with over 100,000 fans packing Eden Gardens in Kolkata for the final. India's triumph over the West Indies in that decider was one-sided, thanks largely to Anil Kumble's sensational 6 for 12, which dismantled the Caribbean batting order. Yet the defining memory of the tournament came earlier, in the semi-final against South Africa, when an unlikely hero emerged. With South Africa needing six runs off the last over and India out of frontline options, Sachin Tendulkar took the ball. Mixing guile and composure beyond his years, he conceded just three runs, sealing a famous win in a finish that remains one of Indian cricket's most replayed moments. While the absence of powerhouses like Pakistan, Australia, and England meant the competition lacked full global weight, the Hero Cup still provided drama, spectacle, and the sense of a new era beginning—where Indian crowds, television audiences, and cricketing heroes would increasingly define the game's future.

At the heart of this era was the rise of Sachin Tendulkar, the "Little Master." Having debuted in 1989 as a 16-year-old in Karachi, by the mid-1990s Sachin was no longer a prodigy but the face of Indian cricket. His straight drive off the front foot became the symbol of India's confidence. In Sharjah, his twin centuries against Australia in 1998 during the "Desert Storm" series elevated him from national hero to global icon. Sachin was not merely admired; he was revered, embodying the dreams of a young India ready to assert itself in the world. He was joined by a strong supporting cast—Anil Kumble, the tireless leg-spinner who in 1999 claimed all ten wickets in an innings against Pakistan in Delhi; Javagal Srinath, the spearhead of India's pace attack; and experienced batsmen like Azharuddin, Sanjay Manjrekar, and later Rahul Dravid and Sourav Ganguly.

The 1996 World Cup, co-hosted by India, Pakistan, and Sri Lanka, symbolized the subcontinent's emergence as cricket's commercial hub. For the second time, the tournament was dominated by colourful imagery, corporate sponsorships, and packed stadiums across South Asia. India's 1996 World Cup journey began with the weight of expectation as co-hosts, and the campaign quickly turned into a theatre of highs and heartbreaks. Their most intense group-stage clash came against Mark Taylor's Australia at the Wankhede Stadium in Bombay. In front of a packed and expectant crowd, Sachin Tendulkar stood tall with a sparkling 90, carrying India's chase with sublime strokeplay. Yet the day belonged to Mark Waugh, whose elegant century showcased his authority as one of the finest one-day batsmen of the era. His timing and placement were immaculate, and despite Tendulkar's heroics, India fell short by 16 runs in a thriller that reminded fans that this World Cup would be no easy ride.

India responded with a spirited win over the West Indies, reasserting their credentials, but their next major test came against Sri Lanka in

Delhi. It was here that Sanath Jayasuriya changed the rhythm of one-day cricket forever. Unleashing a brutal assault on Manoj Prabhakar in the early overs, Jayasuriya struck with ferocity rarely seen before in the Powerplay, dismantling India's opening bowling plans. Kaluwitharana joined the charge, and the usually economical Prabhakar was forced out of the attack, his career effectively finished that day. Though India again showed resistance, Sri Lanka's revolutionary batting approach overwhelmed them, handing India another group-stage defeat that exposed the changing dynamics of limited-overs cricket.

The quarter-final against Pakistan in Bangalore on 9 March 1996 became one of the most emotionally charged contests in India's cricket history. Batting first, India were buoyed by Navjot Sidhu's composed 93, but it was Ajay Jadeja who turned the game on its head. In the final overs, Jadeja tore into Waqar Younis, producing an audacious blitz that sent the Chinnaswamy crowd into delirium. His fearless hitting provided India with late momentum, lifting them to 287 for 8. Pakistan's reply began with Aamir Sohail playing with swagger, at one point gesturing provocatively towards Venkatesh Prasad after dispatching him for four. The very next ball, Prasad struck back, sending Sohail's stumps cartwheeling and delivering a glare that remains etched in Indo-Pak cricket folklore. That dismissal turned the tide. Despite spirited batting, Pakistan's chase faltered, and India sealed a famous 39-run win, sparking nationwide celebration.

The semi-final at Eden Gardens, Kolkata, was meant to be India's crowning moment, but instead it descended into tragedy. Facing Arjuna Ranatunga's confident Sri Lankan side, India began steadily while chasing a competitive target, but the dismissal of Sachin Tendulkar triggered a dramatic collapse. From 98 for 1, India slumped to 120 for 8 against the wiles of Muralitharan and Jayasuriya. In front of over 100,000 fans, the atmosphere soured as bottles were thrown, and fires lit in the stands. Match officials halted play, and eventually the game was awarded to Sri Lanka. The sight of Indian players walking off a hostile

Eden Gardens summed up a campaign that had promised glory but ended in disillusionment.

The decade, however, was not without shadows. The late 1990s brought the specter of match-fixing, with the global scandal triggered by Hansie Cronje's revelations in 2000. Several Indian cricketers were banned for life in its aftermath. The scandal shook the public's faith in the integrity of the game, though the passion of fans ensured that cricket survived the blow. Diplomatically, Indian cricket kept commentary restrained, but the episode forced administrators to tighten governance. Out of crisis emerged a sense of resilience that would serve Indian cricket in the new millennium.

On the field, India oscillated between brilliance and heartbreak. Home dominance remained a hallmark—England, Sri Lanka, and South Africa fell in the early-to-mid 1990s, highlighted by Kumble's spin webs. But abroad, India struggled, particularly in Australia (4–0 defeat in 1991–92) and South Africa (2–0 in 1996–97). The nadir came in Chennai, 1999, when Sachin Tendulkar's heroic fourth-innings century against Pakistan nearly won India the Test, only for the visitors to snatch victory by 12 runs—a heartbreak etched in memory. Few weeks later, in the Asian Test Championship at Eden Gardens, Shoaib Akhtar's searing pace dismissed Dravid and Tendulkar in successive balls, an image that embodied Pakistan's dominance over India in Tests and ODIs during the decade. Barring ICC tournaments, where India regularly prevailed, Pakistan generally held the upper hand in bilateral contests.

Still, India produced stirring highs. The 1998 Independence Cup in Dhaka saw India triumph over Pakistan in a pulsating decisive final, cementing the subcontinent's obsession with their rivalry. At home, Tendulkar's dismantling of Shane Warne in the 1998 Border–Gavaskar Trophy electrified fans, as India beat Australia 2–1. In Tests, India remained formidable at home, with a near-unbroken streak stretching back to the late1980s—until Hansie Cronje's South Africans stunned them 2–0 in 2000, ending an era of fortress-like supremacy.

The 1990s were also the years of Mohammad Azharuddin's captaincy, marked by elegance at the crease but inconsistency in results. His era gave way to the emergence of Sourav Ganguly at the turn of the millennium. Ganguly, fiery and unapologetic, represented a new generation that would stand toe-to-toe with the best. Alongside him, the "Wall" Rahul Dravid and the artistry of VVS Laxman provided the balance that would carry Indian cricket into the 2000s.

By the end of the decade, the BCCI was no longer a junior partner in the cricketing world. Its revenues from sponsorship and television rights began to eclipse those of traditional boards like the ECB and ACB. With South Asia established as cricket's commercial heartland, India's role in shaping the global game had become undeniable. The 1996 World Cup, the rise of Tendulkar, and the television revolution ensured that cricket in India was no longer merely a sport—it was an industry, a theatre of national identity, and a promise of power to come.

Readers' notes

Sachin Tendulkar (1973–) – The *"Little Master"* of Indian cricket, Tendulkar debuted in 1989 at age 16 and became the sport's most prolific batsman. Known for his technical perfection and stroke-making across all conditions, he symbolized India's cricketing rise in the 1990s and 2000s.

Anil Kumble (1970–) – India's legendary leg-spinner, renowned for accuracy and persistence rather than extravagant spin. His career highlight came in 1999, when he claimed all 10 wickets in an innings against Pakistan at Delhi, only the second bowler in history to achieve the feat.

Mohammad Azharuddin (1963–) – Stylish batsman and Indian captain through much of the 1990s. His wristy stroke-play was admired worldwide. His captaincy era combined success at home with struggles abroad, but it ended amid controversy during the match-fixing scandals of 2000.

Sourav Ganguly (1972–) – Left-handed batsman and future captain, Ganguly emerged in the mid-1990s and led India from 2000. Known as the *"Prince of Calcutta,"* he was instrumental in instilling self-belief and aggression in Indian cricket, laying foundations for the team's dominance in the 2000s.

Venkatesh Prasad (1969–) – Indian medium-pacer, remembered most vividly for his fiery send-off of Aamir Sohail in the 1996 World Cup quarter-final at Bangalore, a symbolic moment of India–Pakistan rivalry.

Ajay Jadeja (1971–) – Indian middle-order batsman, famous for his explosive batting against Waqar Younis in the 1996 Bangalore quarter-final. Later embroiled in controversies, but remains remembered for his flair in limited-overs cricket.

Hansie Cronje (1969–2002) – South African captain admired for his leadership but disgraced in 2000 after admitting to involvement in match-fixing. His confession exposed the global scale of corruption in cricket and led to lifetime bans for players worldwide.

1996 Cricket World Cup – Hosted jointly by India, Pakistan, and Sri Lanka, this tournament showcased South Asia as cricket's commercial hub. India's campaign featured highs (Bangalore win over Pakistan) and heartbreak (semi-final loss to Sri Lanka at Eden Gardens).

1999 Chennai Test (India vs Pakistan) – A heartbreaking defeat where Sachin Tendulkar's heroic fourth-innings century almost pulled off victory for India, but Pakistan won by 12 runs. Still remembered for its sporting spirit, as Chennai crowds applauded Pakistan's triumph.

Asian Test Championship (1999) – A one-off triangular Test event between India, Pakistan, and Sri Lanka. At Eden Gardens, Shoaib Akhtar's fiery pace dismantled India's top order, a defining image of Pakistan's dominance in the 1990s.

Jagmohan Dalmiya (1940–2015) – *Indian cricket administrator who played a pivotal role in turning the BCCI into a global financial powerhouse during the 1990s. Instrumental in bringing the 1996 World Cup to South Asia.*

7.6 The Ganguly–Dravid-Dhoni Era (2000–2010): India's Turning Point Decade

The first decade of the 21st century marked the most decisive turning point in the history of Indian cricket. It was the decade when Indian cricket shook off its reputation as inconsistent fighters and emerged as a force capable of challenging anyone, anywhere. Sourav Ganguly symbolized this era.

At the heart of this transformative decade stood Sourav Ganguly, whose impact extended far beyond mere statistics or match results. Known as the "Prince of Calcutta," Ganguly assumed leadership at a time when Indian cricket was bruised by scandals and burdened by inconsistency. India had not reached the final of an ICC tournament since the historic 1983 World Cup triumph, nor had it lifted any global silverware since — a drought Ganguly began to reverse. Under his stewardship, India reached the final of the ICC Champions Trophy in 2000, though India lost the final to New Zealand, Ganguly had planted the seeds of a team built on self-belief and fearless cricket.

The following year, Ganguly's men etched another chapter of folklore at Lord's. In the NatWest Series Final of 2002, chasing 325 against England, India's chase faltered before two youngsters, Mohammad Kaif and Yuvraj Singh, pulled off a stunning win. Ganguly's shirt-waving celebration from the balcony became an enduring image of a new, aggressive India unwilling to be overshadowed.

Under his leadership India won the shared ICC Champions Trophy in autumn of 2002 (after a rain-abandoned final against Sri Lanka).

Another unforgettable highlight came at the 2003 World Cup in South Africa. India lost the final to Ricky Ponting's Australia; the journey itself was heroic. Ganguly's team reached the main World Cup final, breaking a 20-year jinx, with memorable victories along the way. Chief among them was the group-stage match against Pakistan in Centurion, where Sachin Tendulkar's blazing 98 off 75 balls dismantled Wasim Akram, Waqar Younis, and Shoaib Akhtar. That innings, capped with Sachin's uppercut for six off Shoaib, became a symbol of India's dominance over Pakistan in ICC tournaments, a trend that continues.

His rise was not merely symbolic — it was deeply substantive. Ganguly's fearlessness was evident much earlier, notably in the 1997 Sahara Cup against Pakistan in Toronto, where he single-handedly won matches with both bat and ball and was named Player of the Series. A year later, in the 1998 Independence Cup final in Dhaka, he produced a match-winning 124 against Pakistan under intense pressure. Yet, it was not only his personal brilliance that mattered — it was the culture he cultivated. Ganguly demanded intensity, loyalty, and belief from his players. He backed emerging stars like Sehwag, Yuvraj, Harbhajan, Kaif and Zaheer when others hesitated. In Test arena the defining moment of this new spirit arrived at Eden Gardens in 2001. Facing Steve Waugh's all-conquering Australian side, unbeaten in 16 consecutive Tests, India were forced to follow on. What followed became one of cricket's greatest comebacks. V. V. S. Laxman's 281 and Rahul Dravid's 180 turned the match around, while Harbhajan Singh's 13 wickets sealed an improbable victory. India went on to win the series 2–1, breaking Australia's aura of invincibility. For many, this was the day Indian cricket stopped being merely competitive and started believing in greatness.

Ganguly taught India not just how to compete — but how to win with intent, with grit, and with aggression. Two decades later, many hallmarks of the modern Indian team — its self-belief, boldness abroad, and no-fear attitude — can be traced directly to the template Ganguly laid down.

The mid-2000s brought milestones long thought impossible. The decade also saw India finally shed their long-standing struggles in Pakistan. In 2004, they not only won a Test series in Pakistan but also an ODI series. Under Rahul Dravid's leadership but still with Ganguly's aggressive spirit, India achieved their first-ever Test series win in Pakistan by 2–1. For 52 years, no Indian team had managed this feat. It was sweet revenge for decades of close contests and near-misses. India also started performing better overseas. In 2003–04, they drew 1–1 in Australia, with Dravid's epic 233 at Adelaide securing a rare away win. Though they lost controversially in Australia again in 2007–08 by 2–1, the fiery Sydney Test remembered for the Harbhajan–Symonds incident and umpiring controversies showed India were no longer pushovers abroad. Perhaps the most emotional win came in 2002 at Headingley against England, when India piled 628 for 8 with centuries from Dravid, Tendulkar, and Ganguly, before spinners sealed an innings victory. This was a glimpse of a balanced Indian side capable of dominating even overseas.

If Ganguly laid the foundations of India's fearless cricket, Dhoni transformed it into trophies. His rise was sudden and stunning. In 2007, India, under a young Dhoni, entered the inaugural ICC T20 World Cup in South Africa with little expectation. By the end, Dhoni's calm leadership and daring tactics had brought home the trophy. The final against Pakistan in Johannesburg became instant folklore. Chasing 157, Pakistan fell agonizingly short when Misbah-ul-Haq attempted a scoop shot over short fine-leg, only to hand the catch to Sreesanth. India won by five runs, and Dhoni, with his long hair and unflappable demeanor, became a national hero overnight. For Indian fans, the image was symbolic: if Javed Miandad's last-ball six in Sharjah in 1986 had haunted India for decades, Misbah's scoop in 2007 finally exorcised that ghost with reverse fortunes.

Under Ganguly and then Dhoni, India consistently featured in ICC finals. This consistency marked India as a rising global power. In Tests, India achieved another landmark by reaching the No. 1 ICC Test ranking in 2009 under Dhoni's leadership. Memorable series included the 2008 home win over Australia by 2–0, which ended the era of Ricky Ponting's dominance, and overseas victories such as the 2007 series in England, India's first in 21 years was truly iconic. Asia Cup wins further boosted India's stature as regional leaders.

If one had to pick two matches that encapsulated India's transformation, it would be the 2001 Kolkata Test and the 2002 NatWest Final at Lord's. The former proved India could topple the strongest team in the world from an impossible position, the latter showed they could chase down the biggest totals on the biggest stages. These games created a psychological shift. India was no longer content being gallant losers; they expected to win.

The decade ended with perhaps the most influential development in cricket history: the birth of the Indian Premier League in 2008. Backed by the BCCI's growing financial might, the IPL blended cricket with Bollywood glamour, global superstars, and unprecedented money. For India, it was both a commercial and cultural revolution, cementing their dominance in world cricket economics. Players like Chris Gayle, Shane Warne, and AB de Villiers became household names in India, while young Indian cricketers like Virat Kohli, Rohit Sharma, and Ravindra Jadeja used the platform to launch stellar careers. The IPL's success was also symbolic. India was no longer following cricket's trends, it was setting them.

There were, however, some setbacks amidst the triumphs. The 2007 ODI World Cup in the Caribbean turned into a national heartbreak when India, expected to reach the latter stages, was knocked out in the group phase after a stunning defeat to Bangladesh and a loss to Sri Lanka. The early exit shocked the nation and triggered widespread criticism of the team's inconsistency. Later, poor performances in the 2009 ICC Champions Trophy in South Africa and early eliminations from successive ICC T20 World Cups 2009 and 2010 exposed that India, despite its rising stature, occasionally struggled to balance formats and cope with pressure in global tournaments. The Test series defeat against Pakistan in early 2006, following the high point of India's historic 2004 win across the border, was also seen as a bitter disappointment and highlighted and served as a reminder that the journey to dominance was not without its flaws.

From Ganguly's shirtless defiance at Lord's in 2002 to Dhoni's ice-cool triumph in Johannesburg in 2007, from Laxman and Dravid's miracle at Eden in 2001 to India reaching number one in Tests in 2009, the first decade of the 21st century was Indian cricket's coming of age. It was a period of three consecutive ICC finals between 2000 and 2003, a historic World T20 win, and a foundation for the 2011 World Cup triumph that followed. This era deserves to be remembered as the Ganguly–Dhoni decade, an era when Indian cricket transformed from hopeful challengers into the heartbeat of the global game.

Sourav Ganguly (1972–) – *One of India's most influential captains, Ganguly instilled self-belief in a young team. Under his leadership, India won overseas Tests in England, Australia, and Pakistan, reached the final of the 2003 World Cup, and shared the 2002 ICC Champions Trophy. His aggressive style marked a new chapter in Indian cricket.*

Rahul Dravid (1973–) – *Nicknamed The Wall, Dravid epitomized grit and resilience. His epic innings at Eden Gardens in 2001, alongside V. V. S. Laxman, remains one of the greatest comebacks in Test history. He also captained India during a transitional phase.*

V. V. S. Laxman (1974–) – *Known for his artistry and calm under pressure, Laxman's 281 against Australia in 2001 is regarded as one of the finest innings ever played in Tests, turning the Kolkata Test and the series on its head.*

Anil Kumble (1970–) – *India's greatest match-winning bowler of the era, with a never-say-die attitude. His 10-wicket haul against Pakistan in 1999 and later captaincy in 2007–08 reflected his stature as a true giant of Indian cricket.*

MS Dhoni (1981–) – *Emerging in the mid-2000s, Dhoni's calm leadership and finishing ability with the bat transformed India's limited-overs cricket. He led India to victory in the inaugural 2007 T20 World Cup, followed by the historic 2011 ODI World Cup on home soil, and the 2013 ICC Champions Trophy, making him the only captain to win all three major limited overs ICC tournaments—a symbolic turning point in India's cricketing journey.*

Yuvraj Singh (1981–) – *A flamboyant left-hander and one of India's greatest match-winners in ODIs. His debut heroics in the 2000 Champions Trophy and his six sixes in an over during the 2007 T20 World Cup cemented his legend.*

India–Pakistan Rivalry – *In this decade, the rivalry reached fever pitch. India won its first Test series in Pakistan in 2004 but lost at home in 2006. Pakistan's last-ball victory in the 1986 Australasia Cup had haunted India, but Dhoni's team reversed that script by defeating Pakistan in the 2007 T20 World Cup final.*

BCCI's Commercial Rise – *By the late 2000s, the BCCI had become the financial superpower of world cricket, with India's massive television audience and sponsorships dictating global cricket schedules. The launch of the Indian Premier League (IPL) in 2008 showcased this economic dominance.*

2001 Eden Gardens Test – *Widely regarded as India's greatest Test comeback. Following on, Dravid and Laxman's epic stand and Harbhajan Singh's off-spin brilliance broke Australia's 16-Test winning streak.*

2007 ODI World Cup Shock – *India's first-round exit after a loss to Bangladesh remains one of its darkest moments, triggering a major rethink of team strategies and leading to Dhoni's eventual captaincy in shorter formats.*

2007 T20 World Cup Final – *India's win against Pakistan in Johannesburg under Dhoni marked the birth of a new era, establishing India as a powerhouse in T20 cricket and setting the stage for the IPL.*

7.7 Dhoni's Magic: The 2011 World Cup and 2013 Champions Trophy Triumphs

Dhoni's calm aura and unflinching confidence reached its greatest expression in 2011, when India hosted the ICC Cricket World Cup for the first time since 1996. The nation's mood was electric: India's economy under Prime Minister Manmohan Singh was rapidly growing, the IPL had become a cultural and commercial juggernaut, and anticipation surrounded the "last dance" of Sachin Tendulkar, who, despite a glittering career, had yet to lift a World Cup trophy. The squad reflected both continuity and renewal. Veterans such as Tendulkar, Virender Sehwag, Yuvraj Singh, Zaheer Khan, and Harbhajan Singh were joined by stars of the newer IPL age like Gautam Gambhir, Yusuf Pathan, and a young Virat Kohli. For India, the 2011 tournament was more than sport—it was a test of a rising power's self-belief.

The group stages brought solid performances, but it was in the knockouts that India captured the nation's imagination. The quarter-final at Ahmedabad against defending champions Australia was billed as a clash of generations: the fading aura of Ricky Ponting's giants against a hungry Indian side. Yuvraj Singh's unbeaten 57 and Zaheer Khan's incisive spells turned the contest, as India ended Australia's 12-year reign as World Cup holders. The semi-final at Mohali against Pakistan was far more than cricket. In front of both prime ministers—Manmohan Singh and Yousuf Raza Gilani—it became a diplomatic and emotional high-voltage spectacle. Pakistan's misfields and missed chances handed India the edge, while Sachin, reprieved multiple times, ground his way to 85. As Misbah-ul-Haq and Younis Khan struggled to accelerate, Indian spinners applied the squeeze. India won by 29 runs, maintaining their perfect World Cup record against Pakistan, and celebrations echoed the euphoria of the 1996 Bangalore quarter-final.

The final at Mumbai's Wankhede Stadium against Sri Lanka was the ultimate stage. Mahela Jayawardene's graceful century threatened heartbreak, but Gambhir's steely 97 steadied India's chase. Then, in one of cricket's most iconic moments, Dhoni—promoting himself up the order—finished with a majestic six over long-on, sealing India's second World Cup. The image of Dhoni's bat swing lit up the night sky, reminiscent in symbolic weight of Kapil Dev's catch in 1983. For Tendulkar, carried around the ground by teammates in tears of joy, it was the perfect farewell to his World Cup journey. For Kohli, making his first World Cup mark, it was the beginning of his ascent as India's new talisman.

Yet Dhoni's leadership was tested in the years immediately after. India suffered heavy away defeats in England (4–0 in 2011) and Australia (4–0 in 2011–12), and even a rare home Test series loss to England in 2012. Still, Dhoni's popularity endured, sustained by the memory of 2011 and his unshaken authority in the dressing room. Redemption came in 2013 at the ICC Champions Trophy in England. In a rain-curtailed final at Edgbaston against the hosts, Dhoni marshalled his bowlers brilliantly, and India edged home by five runs. It was India's third ICC trophy under his captaincy, making him the only man in history to win the T20 World Cup, ODI World Cup, and Champions Trophy.

By the time Tendulkar retired in 2013 after the West Indies series at home, India had transitioned into a new era. Dhoni was firmly entrenched as India's greatest limited-overs captain, while Kohli was becoming the heir apparent with the bat. The period from 2011 to 2013 symbolized not only India's dominance but also cricket's integration into the broader story of a confident, rising nation.

At the same time, the global cricketing landscape was undergoing a power shift. This was the period when the so-called "Big Three" — England, Australia, and India — consolidated their stranglehold over international cricket's financial and administrative structures. Revenues, broadcast rights, and ICC governance were increasingly centered on these three boards, giving them disproportionate influence in scheduling and tournament planning. Older powers such as the West Indies, Pakistan, and even Sri Lanka, which had once shaped cricket's global storylines, began to experience a gradual decline in clout. Their domestic struggles and financial constraints mirrored their reduced voice at ICC tables, reinforcing the sense that the game's future was being scripted by the Big Three.

Readers' Notes

2011 ICC Cricket World Cup

Held across India, Sri Lanka, and Bangladesh. India defeated Pakistan in a tense semifinal at Mohali and beat Sri Lanka in the Mumbai final to claim their second World Cup. Gautam Gambhir's 97 and Dhoni's unbeaten 91* were decisive. It was Sachin Tendulkar's last World Cup and the only one he won.

2013 ICC Champions Trophy

Hosted in England and Wales, this was the last edition of the tournament. India, under Dhoni, defeated England in a rain-shortened final at Edgbaston by 5 runs. India remained unbeaten through the tournament, consolidating Dhoni's legacy as the only captain to win all three major ICC trophies.

Zaheer Khan (1978–)

Spearhead of India's pace attack in the 2011 World Cup, taking 21 wickets. His early breakthroughs and death-overs skill were pivotal to India's success.

Gautam Gambhir (1981–)

Key Indian opener who scored 97 runs in the 2011 World Cup final, providing the foundation for India's chase against Sri Lanka.

Virat Kohli (1988–)

Future captain who made his World Cup debut in 2011, contributing crucial runs in the final. Later became India's dominant batting force in the 2010s.

The Big Three *– Refers to the cricket boards of India (BCCI), Australia (CA), and England (ECB), which by the early 2010s consolidated financial and political dominance in the International Cricket Council (ICC). Their control over broadcasting rights, revenue distribution, and scheduling elevated their clout, while traditional powers like West Indies, Pakistan, and Sri Lanka saw their influence wane.*

7.8 The ICC Drought and Heartbreaks (2014–2024)

The mid-2010s marked the gradual decline of M. S. Dhoni's dominance as captain and the start of an era where India, despite boasting some of the greatest cricketers of their generation, earned the unwanted tag of "chokers" in ICC events. The sequence began with the 2014 T20 World Cup final in Dhaka, where India, after dominating most of the tournament, faltered against Sri Lanka. The following year, at the 2015 ODI World Cup in Australia, India surged to the semi-finals unbeaten, only to be undone in Sydney by a century from Steven Smith, as the hosts marched to the title.

The heartbreak continued home soil in the 2016 T20 World Cup. In front of a raucous Bombay crowd, India posted a commanding 192 against the West Indies, only to see Lendl Simmons and Andre Russell dismantle their attack in the semi-final. The inability to defend a huge total epitomized India's struggles in high-pressure knockout games.

Yet individually, Indian cricket was blessed with titanic batting figures. Virat Kohli, whose consistency in chases and unforgettable knocks against arch-rivals Pakistan elevated him to superstardom, became the heartbeat of the team. Alongside him, Rohit Sharma redefined ODI batting with his effortless Strokeplay, registering the highest ever individual ODI score — a monumental 264 — and becoming the "Hitman" whose hundreds regularly lifted India in bilateral contests.

But in ICC finals and semi-finals, the pain only grew. At the 2017 ICC Champions Trophy in London, a billion people tuned in to watch India face Pakistan at The Oval. For Pakistan, led by Sarfaraz Ahmed, it was redemption — a crushing 180-run victory that avenged their 2007 T20 final loss to India. For India, the defeat was a stunning blow to national pride.

Two years later, the 2019 ODI World Cup semi-final against New Zealand at Old Trafford stretched across two rain-affected days.

Despite a brilliant bowling effort, India's top order collapsed. Dhoni's late fight, cut short by a heartbreaking run-out, sealed their exit. That image of a dejected Dhoni walking back remained one of the most poignant in modern Indian cricket.

India's Test fortunes brought both glory and frustration. They reached back-to-back World Test Championship finals in 2021 and 2023, only to lose to New Zealand at Southampton and to Australia at The Oval. Yet in bilateral Test series, India touched historic heights — beating Australia in back-to-back away series, including the miraculous 2021 triumph at Brisbane, becoming the first Asian side to win twice in Australia. At home, they remained nearly invincible, defeating visiting sides in long unbeaten streaks. But in South Africa and England, the elusive away dominance slipped from their grasp.

Nothing, however, equaled the agony of the 2023 ODI World Cup final at Ahmedabad's Narendra Modi Stadium. In front of over 100,000 fans, India's unbeaten campaign ended in silence as Pat Cummins' Australia stunned them. The loss, with echoes of the West Indies' shock defeat to India in 1983, cut deeply. Just as Shoaib Akhtar's fiery spell at Eden Gardens in 1999 silenced Calcutta, Cummins did the same in 2023 — a cruel irony that highlighted cricket's symmetry of triumph and despair.

This period defined India's paradox. In bilateral cricket, they looked unstoppable, conquering Australia, dominating at home, and consistently producing world-class talents. Yet, when it came to the grand stage, the team stumbled repeatedly. The ICC drought from 2014 to 2024 remains one of the most frustrating sagas in Indian cricket history — an era where brilliance and heartbreak lived side by side.

Despite the absence of ICC trophies between 2014 and 2024, India's cricket and political stature only grew stronger. The Board of Control for Cricket in India (BCCI) emerged as the undisputed financial superpower of world cricket, dictating much of the global calendar through the IPL and dominating ICC decision-making. Economically, India surged under the BJP-led governments, rising into the world's top five economies, while its foreign policy tone grew harder than the softer approach of earlier Congress administrations. Cricket mirrored these changes: even without major silverware, India commanded unmatched influence through broadcasting, sponsorship, and governance.

At the same time, cricket's entanglement with geopolitics deepened. Since the 2008 Mumbai attacks, India and Pakistan have effectively frozen bilateral cricket, restricting engagements to ICC tournaments and Asia Cups. Flashpoints such as the 2019 Pulwama–Balakot episode, and more recently Operation Sindhoor in 2025, underscored how political skirmishes hardened positions on both sides. Test cricket between the two nations has not been played since 2007, with no clear indication of a softening in sight. Yet, whenever they meet in multilateral events, the matches remain among the most watched sporting spectacles in the world, a reminder that rivalry endures even without bilateral tours.

Readers' notes

Rohit Sharma (1987–)

Nicknamed the "Hitman," Rohit holds the record for the highest individual ODI score (264) and redefined modern opening batting with multiple double-centuries in ODIs. Later became India's captain.

2014 T20 World Cup Final

India lost to Sri Lanka in Dhaka, despite entering as favourites, marking the start of their ICC knockout woes in this era.

2015 ODI World Cup Semi-Final (Sydney)

India's unbeaten run ended when Steven Smith's century led Australia to victory.

2016 T20 World Cup Semi-Final (Bombay)

Despite posting 192, India lost to West Indies, highlighting defensive failures under pressure.

2017 ICC Champions Trophy Final

Played at The Oval, London, where Pakistan shocked India with a 180-run win. It was watched by over a billion viewers globally.

2019 ODI World Cup Semi-Final (Old Trafford)

A rain-affected thriller in which India's batting collapse and Dhoni's run-out sealed a shocking loss to New Zealand.

World Test Championship (2021 & 2023 Finals)

India reached two consecutive finals but lost to New Zealand at Southampton (2021) and Australia at The Oval (2023).

Border-Gavaskar Triumphs (2018/19 and 2020/21)

India won back-to-back Test series in Australia, including the dramatic Gabba victory in 2021, becoming the first Asian team to achieve this feat.

Pat Cummins (1993–)

Australian fast bowler and captain who silenced a 100,000-strong crowd in Ahmedabad during the 2023 World Cup final, symbolizing Australia's resilience.

Shoaib Akhtar (1975–)

Pakistan's "Rawalpindi Express," remembered for silencing Eden Gardens in 1999 — a parallel often drawn to Cummins' 2023 feat.

Ahmedabad 2023 World Cup Final

India's unbeaten campaign ended in a devastating loss to Australia in front of their home crowd, considered one of the biggest heartbreaks in Indian cricket history.

7.9 India's Back-to-Back ICC Triumphs (2024–2025)

After more than a decade of heartbreak in global tournaments, India finally ended its ICC drought in spectacular fashion by winning the 2024 T20 World Cup. Led by Rohit Sharma, India played the tournament with supreme authority, remaining unbeaten throughout. The final against South Africa evoked echoes of the inaugural 2007 clash, going down to the very last overs. Jasprit Bumrah delivered a magical spell under pressure, and Suryakumar Yadav's breathtaking boundary catch to dismiss David Miller turned the tide. India narrowly prevailed, and the victory unleashed scenes of jubilation rarely witnessed in modern sport. Over a million fans thronged the streets of Mumbai in a victory parade, hailing it as redemption not only for the team but especially for Rohit Sharma, who had endured years of criticism for failing to deliver ICC silverware despite his glittering domestic and bilateral record.

The momentum carried into 2025, where India clinched the ICC Champions Trophy in emphatic fashion. The tournament was marred by controversy from the outset—originally hosted by Pakistan, but due to political tensions India refused to tour. Matches were relocated to Dubai, which swiftly became a fortress for the Men in Blue. On pitches that suited their blend of batting depth and versatile bowling, India dominated every opponent. No side came close to matching their intensity, and Rohit Sharma lifted his second ICC trophy as captain. For India, it marked a remarkable back-to-back triumph, a feat last achieved by Australia in 2023, and it reinforced their reputation as the pre-eminent force in limited-overs cricket.

Yet this period of ODI and T20 success contrasted sharply with India's struggles in the Test arena. In late 2024, India suffered one of their most humbling setbacks at home, being whitewashed 3-0 by New Zealand. It was their first home Test series defeat since England in 2012 and the first clean sweep in India since Hansie Cronje's South Africa had stunned them in 2000. The loss sent shockwaves through Indian cricket, raising questions about their depth and adaptability in the longest format. Away results offered little solace—Australia triumphed 3-1 in a fiercely contested Border-Gavaskar Trophy, while India missed out on yet another World Test Championship final.

One highlight, however, came in England. The Anderson–Tendulkar Trophy of 2025 ended in a gripping 2-2 draw under new Test Captain Shubman Gill, the final Test at The Oval which India won by only 6 runs was especially memorable: Mohammed Siraj's fiery spell was poetic and remarkable. The missed opportunity to win that series symbolized India's paradox in this period—a world-beating white-ball side capable of dazzling triumphs, yet an inconsistent Test team unable to sustain dominance abroad or at home.

The period from early 2010s to mid-2020's also witnessed India producing two of the finest spin-bowling all-rounders in modern cricket: Ravichandran Ashwin and Ravindra Jadeja, who shaped countless Test victories at home and abroad. Alongside them, the rise of a formidable pace trio in Bumrah, Shami, and Siraj gave India an unprecedented fast-bowling arsenal. This blend of quality spinners and lethal pacers became the hallmark of Indian cricket in the 2010s and 2020s.

India's back-to-back ICC triumphs of 2024 and 2025 nevertheless stand as landmark moments. They not only restored faith among fans who had grown weary of near misses but also cemented Rohit Sharma's place among India's most successful leaders. If their Test fortunes wavered, the double crown in limited-overs cricket ensured that this era would be remembered for its glory, resilience, and the ability of Indian cricket to rebound from its darkest disappointments.

Jasprit Bumrah (1993–) – *India's pace spearhead, renowned for his deadly yorkers and calmness under pressure. His decisive spell in the 2024 T20 World Cup final against South Africa was a turning point that sealed India's triumph.*

Suryakumar Yadav (1990–) – *A modern T20 batting innovator with 360-degree stroke-play. His spectacular boundary catch in the 2024 World Cup final to dismiss David Miller became an iconic moment in Indian cricket history.*

Shubman Gill (1999–) – *Touted as the next batting superstar of Indian cricket, Gill emerged as a consistent run-scorer in all formats. In the mid-2020s, he was already seen as the natural heir to Virat Kohli, blending classical technique with modern flair.*

Mohammad Shami (1990–) – *One of India's most reliable fast bowlers, Shami combined pace with devastating reverse swing. He often delivered breakthroughs in critical matches, excelling particularly in World Cup knockouts.*

Mohammad Siraj (1994–) – *Rose from humble beginnings to become India's strike bowler in Tests and ODIs. Known for his fiery opening spells, his memorable burst at The Oval in the 2023 England Test series became one of his defining moments.*

Ravichandran Ashwin (1986–) – *One of the finest off-spinners of his generation, Ashwin became a match-winner in Tests with his variations and batting resilience. His dominance at home was pivotal in India's series wins through the 2010s and 2020s.*

Ravindra Jadeja (1988–) – *India's quintessential all-rounder of the modern era, Jadeja's left-arm spin and dynamic batting made him indispensable across formats. His sharp fielding and ability to turn games with both bat and ball became hallmarks of India's success.*

The IPL Revolution: India's Cricketing Super-League

Although this book has traced India's international journey through Tests, ODIs, and ICC tournaments, the Indian Premier League deserves its own special treatment. The IPL is not a chapter of India's national team story, but a parallel revolution that transformed cricket's economics, schedules, and global reach. Much like Kerry Packer's World Series in the 1970s, it sits outside the international record yet reshaped the very way the sport is played, consumed, and imagined.

When the Indian Premier League (IPL) was launched in 2008 under the stewardship of Lalit Modi, few anticipated the sheer magnitude of its impact. What began as an experiment in franchise T20 cricket has grown into the most lucrative and visible cricketing spectacle on the planet. The tournament fused cricket with Bollywood glamour, corporate money, and global star power, creating an entertainment product unlike anything the sport had seen before. Cheerleaders, floodlit matches, film stars as team owners, and cricketers auctioned like footballers gave the IPL an immediate cultural resonance.

The league's format — franchises representing major Indian cities — created fierce loyalties. Chennai Super Kings (CSK) under MS Dhoni and Mumbai Indians (MI) under Rohit Sharma emerged as the two dynasties, winning many titles and cultivating global fan bases. Their success stories added to the myth of the IPL as not merely a competition but an annual festival that Indians marked on their calendars as keenly as Diwali or Eid.

Yet the IPL's growth was not without turbulence. Early in its history, allegations of match-fixing and betting controversies rocked the tournament, leading to suspensions of players, team bans, and Lalit Modi's own exile from Indian cricket administration. Critics feared that the league's dazzling glamour concealed rotten foundations. Still, the Board of Control for Cricket in India (BCCI) moved swiftly to stabilize and professionalize the operation, ensuring its long-term survival. The controversies, instead of derailing the IPL, only heightened its mystique and made its resilience a story in itself.

At its core, the IPL redefined the economics of cricket. The auctions became global media events, with players fetching sums previously unimaginable in the sport. Overnight, cricketers from Afghanistan, the West Indies, and even associate nations found opportunities and paychecks that dwarfed what they earned in international cricket. For many, the IPL was a financial lifeline; for others, it was a platform to display their talent to the world. The sheer scale of money involved meant that the IPL came to feel like cricket's equivalent of Kerry Packer's World Series Cricket revolution in the 1970s — only bigger, louder, and more deeply embedded in the sport's official structures.

The league also forced international cricket to bend around it. The IPL's two-month window each year effectively froze global schedules, with national boards reluctant to clash with the behemoth. Players themselves prioritized IPL contracts, sometimes withdrawing from national duty to preserve fitness for the tournament. Purists lamented this distortion, arguing that Tests and ODIs were being sidelined, but there was no denying that the IPL had become the gravitational center of world cricket.

Culturally, the IPL transformed how Indians consumed cricket. Satellite TV, streaming platforms, fantasy leagues, and Bollywood-style marketing campaigns made it more than sport — it became spectacle. The sight of Shah Rukh Khan cheering from the stands, or Priety Zinta celebrating a last-ball win, reinforced the marriage between cinema and cricket, two of India's greatest passions.

By the mid-2010s, the IPL was no longer just a tournament but a symbol of India's rise as cricket's economic superpower. Its glitz, controversies, and sheer pulling power galvanized the sport globally, setting the template for leagues in Australia, the Caribbean, and beyond. Whether hailed as a carnival or criticized as commercialization gone too far, the IPL undeniably reshaped cricket's landscape, turning India's domestic league into cricket's most powerful brand.

Chapter 8 – Pakistan Cricket: From Kardar's Dream to Imran's Glory and Global Triumphs

8.1 Early Steps – From Independence to Test Recognition (1947–1952)

The partition of the Indian subcontinent in August 1947 was one of the most traumatic upheavals of the twentieth century. Out of the violence, migration, and administrative chaos was born a new nation, Pakistan, and with it the task of building institutions from scratch. Cricket, carried over from the colonial era, quickly became one of the few cultural arenas where the young country sought both legitimacy and identity. In the years between 1947 and 1952, when Pakistan finally earned Test status, the game became a vital expression of resilience and national aspiration.

The Pakistan Cricket Control Board (later the PCB) was formed in 1948, but it faced enormous hurdles. The country lacked developed infrastructure; Lahore Gymkhana and Karachi's Polo Ground were the only major venues of note, and most facilities had been left behind in India. Pakistan also had to recruit players rapidly, many of whom were displaced by Partition. Still, cricket carried symbolic weight. As a game shared with the former colonial rulers, it promised recognition in the Commonwealth. As a sport already popular among urban elites in Punjab, Karachi, and princely states like Bahawalpur, it had a cultural base to grow from.

In 1948, tragedy struck the new country when Muhammad Ali Jinnah, the founding father and Governor-General, passed away. Barely three years later, Prime Minister Liaqat Ali Khan was assassinated in Rawalpindi (1951). Politically, Pakistan was orphaned within its first decade, leaderless and vulnerable. Yet cricket provided continuity and hope. As historian Osman Samiuddin notes, "Pakistan cricket has always mirrored the nation: chaotic, fractured, yet remarkably resilient." The sport's trajectory from the late 1940s reflected precisely that spirit of defiance against odds.

Before Test status, Pakistan fielded strong teams against visiting sides. In 1948–49, the touring West Indies team, featuring George Headley and Everton Weekes, played Pakistan in Karachi. Though not a Test, the match was fiercely contested. Pakistan's bowling was spearheaded by the young Fazal Mahmood, whose deceptive seam movement was already making waves. Batting contributions from Nazar Muhammad (father of future opener Mudassar Nazar) and Imtiaz Ahmed, the elegant wicketkeeper-batsman, gave Pakistan credibility. Despite losing narrowly, Pakistan had shown that they could compete against the very best.

In 1949, the Commonwealth XI arrived for a series of unofficial games. These matches, though not formally recognized as Tests, were crucial. Players such as Nazar Muhammad and Imtiaz Ahmed held their ground, while Fazal Mahmood demonstrated the stamina and swing that would later humble England. These fixtures were followed by the Ceylonese (now Sri Lanka) tour of Pakistan in 1949–50. Pakistan won comfortably, asserting superiority over another aspiring cricketing nation. These early results mattered, as they sent a message to the MCC and the ICC: Pakistan was ready for recognition.

Abdul Hafeez Kardar emerged during this time as the pivotal figure in Pakistan cricket. Educated in the United Kingdom and having played for India before Partition, Kardar brought with him not just cricketing pedigree but also a cosmopolitan authority. Tall, charismatic, and fiercely nationalistic, Kardar believed that Pakistan deserved Test recognition, and he lobbied relentlessly. His connections in England, cultivated while at Oxford, allowed him to argue Pakistan's case in influential corridors of MCC. For a nation searching for international acknowledgment, Kardar's blend of diplomacy and leadership was invaluable. He was soon christened the "Father of Pakistan Cricket."

Kardar also shaped the early ethos of Pakistan cricket. He demanded discipline from players, instilled self-belief, and stressed that cricket was not just a pastime but a matter of national honor. His confrontational style—whether with administrators or opponents—reflected a determination that Pakistan should not be treated as a junior partner in world cricket. In later decades, this attitude became a hallmark of Pakistan teams: mercurial, defiant, and never cowed by bigger powers.

The resilience of Pakistan cricket was best symbolized by Nazar Muhammad, who became the first Pakistani to score a Test century (in 1952 against India) but whose career was tragically cut short by an injury. His contributions in the pre-Test era, however, had already made him a pioneer. Alongside him, Imtiaz Ahmed's free-flowing batting and wicketkeeping skills provided Pakistan with a dynamic cricketer admired even in England. Fazal Mahmood, meanwhile, was being groomed into Pakistan's strike bowler. His mastery of leg-cutters and control of length were already evident in matches against the Commonwealth XI, and it was clear he would be the spearhead of Pakistan's future Test attack.

Administratively, the newly formed PCB sought to organize domestic tournaments to nurture talent. The Quaid-e-Azam Trophy was inaugurated in 1953, named after Jinnah, but its roots lay in the early post-Partition years when provincial sides and railways teams carried the competitive spirit. These contests allowed players displaced by Partition to find new homes and careers in cricket, keeping alive a sense of continuity amid upheaval.

The push for Test status gained momentum by 1951. Kardar and PCB officials emphasized that Pakistan's performances against strong touring sides proved their readiness. The political climate also helped. Britain, keen to integrate Pakistan into the Commonwealth, saw cricket recognition as a symbolic gesture of inclusion. India, too, despite strained political relations after Partition and war in Kashmir, supported Pakistan's application. The rationale was partly political: bringing Pakistan into the cricketing fold would stabilize South Asian cricket and affirm continuity in the subcontinent's sporting culture.

In 1952, the ICC formally granted Pakistan Test status. For a nation that had been independent for only five years, it was a remarkable achievement. Pakistan's acceptance into the elite circle of Test nations reflected both its cricketing merit and Kardar's persuasive diplomacy. It was also a recognition of the resilience of players who had begun in difficult conditions—playing on matting wickets, with limited facilities, but with enormous national pride.

That same year, Pakistan embarked on its maiden Test tour to India. Symbolically, this was loaded with tension: the wounds of Partition were fresh, and the Kashmir conflict was unresolved. Yet cricket brought the two new nations face to face on a sporting field. Kardar led Pakistan with his usual intensity, while Fazal Mahmood and Nazar Muhammad carried the attack. Though India won the first series 2–1, Pakistan claimed a famous victory at Lucknow, announcing themselves with Fazal's match-winning spell. It was a fitting culmination of the struggles of 1947–52: Pakistan had arrived, no longer a cricketing orphan but a recognized Test nation.

These formative years thus set the tone for Pakistan cricket's identity. Born in turmoil, sustained by resilience, and shaped by figures like Kardar, Fazal, Imtiaz, and Nazar, the team embodied the same paradoxes as the nation itself—improvisational yet brilliant, fragile yet fearless. The deaths of Jinnah and Liaqat Ali Khan had shaken Pakistan, but on the cricket field, hope was alive. Recognition in 1952 was more than a sporting milestone; it was a statement that Pakistan, against all odds, was here to stay.

Readers' notes

Abdul Hafeez Kardar (1925–1996)

Oxford-educated, a former India Test cricketer who became Pakistan's first captain after independence. Known as the "Father of Pakistan Cricket," his leadership and diplomacy secured Test status in 1952 and shaped Pakistan's early cricketing ethos.

Fazal Mahmood (1927–2005)

Pakistan's first great fast-medium bowler, famed for his leg-cutters and stamina. His heroics at The Oval in 1954 made him a national legend, but his pre-Test performances in the late 1940s had already marked him as a spearhead.

Nazar Muhammad (1921–1996)

Stylish opener and father of Mudassar Nazar. He scored Pakistan's first Test century in 1952, but his promising career was tragically curtailed by injury. Before that, he was central in Pakistan's early representative matches.

Imtiaz Ahmed (1928–2016)

Dynamic wicketkeeper-batsman, among Pakistan's first attacking players. Played a vital role in early unofficial internationals against West Indies and the Commonwealth XI, and became one of the first to notch a Test double-century for Pakistan.

Pakistan Cricket Board (PCB)

Founded in 1948, the PCB took charge of organizing the young country's cricket structure. It inaugurated the Quaid-e-Azam Trophy in the early 1950s and spearheaded Pakistan's application for Test status, granted in 1952.

Liaqat Ali Khan (1895–1951)

Pakistan's first Prime Minister, assassinated in Rawalpindi. His death left the fledgling nation politically vulnerable, but the resilience that followed was reflected in cricket's rapid rise.

Muhammad Ali Jinnah (1876–1948)

Founder of Pakistan, revered as Quaid-e-Azam. His death in 1948 was a huge blow to the new nation, which had to navigate early crises without its guiding figure. Cricket became one of the unifying symbols of the country after his passing.

8.2 First Victories and Growing Identity (1952–1959)

When Pakistan took the field as a Test nation in 1952, it was the ultimate test of Abdul Hafeez Kardar's dream. Few expected a country so young, politically unsettled after the deaths of Jinnah in 1948 and Liaquat Ali Khan in 1951, to emerge quickly as a force in international sport. Yet within a decade, Pakistan not only won matches but also claimed historic series victories at home and abroad. Their progress was rapid, their identity unmistakable: a new Test nation with spirit, resilience, and a belief that cricket could reflect national pride.

The inaugural Test series against India in 1952–53 was the perfect theatre for a political and sporting statement. Pakistan, barely five years into existence, faced their giant neighbor in a five-Test series that carried more than runs and wickets—it carried the weight of partition. Kardar's side began nervously, losing the first Test in Delhi by an innings. Critics dismissed Pakistan as raw and unready. Yet the response was immediate and emphatic. In the second Test at Lucknow, Pakistan shocked India with a resounding victory by an innings and 43 runs.

145

Nazar Muhammad, the elegant right-hander, etched his name in history by scoring Pakistan's first ever Test century, carrying his bat for an unbeaten 124. Fazal Mahmood's mastery with the ball, supported by Mahmood Hussain, strangled the Indian batting. It was more than a win—it was a declaration. Within weeks of entering Test cricket, Pakistan had achieved what India had waited two decades for: a Test match victory. Though India went on to win the series 2–1, the message was sent to the cricketing world. Pakistan had arrived and arrived with fighting spirit.

Two years later came the tour that defined the decade: Pakistan in England, 1954. For a young team, the assignment looked daunting. England, with Len Hutton as captain and a formidable squad including Trevor Bailey and Peter May, had just regained the Ashes from Australia. Few believed Kardar's men could compete in English conditions. The first Test at Lord's ended in defeat, confirming expectations. But Kardar instilled resilience, urging his players to adapt to the seaming, swinging pitches. At The Oval, in the final Test, Fazal Mahmood produced one of the greatest spells of fast-medium bowling ever witnessed in England. Exploiting the damp pitch with relentless leg-cutters, Fazal returned figures of 6 for 53 and 6 for 46, bowling Pakistan to an 24-run victory. The match levelled the series 1–1, denying England a home series win against a side that had been playing Test cricket for less than two years. The Times of London called it "a miracle at The Oval." For Pakistanis back home, it was not just a cricket result but a moment of immense national pride—proof that their country could stand shoulder to shoulder with imperial powers. Fazal became a national hero, "our blue-eyed boy" as Kardar affectionately called him, and Oval '54 entered folklore as Pakistan's first great cricket triumph.

If the Oval victory showed Pakistan's ability to punch above its weight abroad, then home series results in the mid-1950s confirmed they were no one-hit wonder. India's tour of Pakistan in 1954–55 ended in a five-Test draw (0–0), with neither side able to force a win. Yet for Pakistan, merely holding their arch-rivals at home in their first bilateral series on home soil was seen as an achievement. The crowds in Karachi, Lahore, and Dacca (then East Pakistan) thronged stadiums, treating cricket as a new binding force for a divided young nation.

The years that followed brought more tangible success. In 1955–56, Pakistan hosted New Zealand and won the three-Test series 2–0, their first ever series triumph. The team had developed a balanced look: Fazal leading the attack, Imtiaz Ahmed providing dynamism with the bat and gloves, and Hanif Mohammad emerging as a reliable anchor. That momentum continued when Australia visited in 1956. Though the visitors only played a one-off Test, Pakistan shocked them by winning at Karachi. Fazal again was the destroyer, taking 13 wickets in the match, while Hanif provided the glue with the bat. Beating Australia, the most respected cricketing power of the postwar world, announced Pakistan's capacity to take on any opponent.

The real test of mettle came in 1957–58 when Pakistan toured the West Indies. Playing in the Caribbean was a daunting task for established sides, let alone a team barely six years into Test cricket. The West Indies, led by Gerry Alexander and featuring greats like Clyde Walcott, Frank Worrell, and Gary Sobers, were expected to dominate. They did win the series 3–1, but Pakistan's solitary victory at Bridgetown was hugely symbolic. It was their first Test win in the West Indies and showed that Kardar's insistence on self-belief was no hollow slogan. More importantly, the series produced one of the most extraordinary feats in cricket history. In the first Test at Bridgetown, chasing 600 to avoid defeat, Hanif Mohammad batted for 16 hours and scored 337—the longest innings in Test history. His defensive skill, mental strength, and sheer patience salvaged a draw that seemed impossible. Hanif became "The Little Master," and his innings became a symbol of Pakistani endurance against overwhelming odds. The 337 remains an immortal part of Test lore and established Pakistan's reputation as a side that could fight to the last.

The decade concluded on an even higher note when West Indies toured Pakistan in 1958–59. This time Pakistan not only competed but triumphed, winning the series 2–1. For a team less than a decade old in Test cricket, beating a full-strength West Indies side at home was remarkable. Hanif, Imtiaz, and Saeed Ahmed provided the runs, while Fazal remained the unerring match-winner with the ball. That victory was hailed by local and foreign observers as Pakistan's finest collective achievement of the 1950s.

By the close of the decade, Pakistan's record compared favourably with other new Test entrants. Where India had taken 20 years to win a Test, Pakistan had beaten England, Australia, West Indies, and New Zealand all within seven years of admission. They had won both at home and abroad, producing unforgettable performances like Fazal's Oval spell and Hanif's 337. More than just cricketing results, these achievements gave Pakistanis a sense of belonging on the world stage. In a decade marked by political upheaval and economic struggles, cricket became a unifying national passion.

The team's style also came to be defined: gritty batting centered on Hanif's obduracy, incisive medium-pace spearheaded by Fazal, and Kardar's uncompromising leadership. Their resilience reflected the broader resilience of a young state grappling with survival. As the 1950s ended, Pakistan cricket stood not as a fledgling experiment but as a fully recognized force, with an identity forged through sweat, discipline, and a fierce will to compete.

Readers' notes

Len Hutton (1916–1990)

England's legendary opening batsman, whose technique was a benchmark for post-war cricket. Pakistan's ability to dismiss him cheaply at The Oval in 1954 added immense prestige to their first series in England.

Denis Compton (1918–1997)

One of England's most stylish batsmen of the 1940s–50s, adored for his flair and attacking shots. Facing Fazal Mahmood during the 1954 Oval Test, Compton's struggles underlined Pakistan's rise as a genuine cricketing force.

Peter May (1929–1994)

England's captain in the 1950s, known for calm authority and elegant batting. His duels with Pakistan's seamers symbolized the respect England had to extend to their new Test opponents.

Godfrey Evans (1920–1999)

England's wicketkeeper and attacking lower-order batsman. His dismissals by Fazal Mahmood became a key highlight of the 1954 series, showing Pakistan could outclass even seasoned English pros.

Sir Everton Weekes (1925–2020)

Member of the West Indies' "Three Ws," renowned for his record run of consecutive Test centuries. His battles with Pakistan's bowling in 1957–58 and 1958–59 showcased the competitiveness of the new team against established giants.

Clyde Walcott (1926–2006)

Powerful West Indian batsman, another of the "Three Ws." His dismissals in Pakistan's early victories became symbolic of the side's growing confidence against world-class line-ups.

Sir Frank Worrell (1924–1967)

Later West Indies' first Black captain, Worrell was a cultured batsman whose grace made him beloved worldwide. Pakistan's ability to contest against him cemented their reputation as no pushovers in the 1950s.

8.3 Hanif and Fazal – Foundations of Legacy (1950s–early 1960s)

By the late 1950s, Pakistan cricket had already established two enduring icons whose influence extended far beyond their statistics: Hanif Mohammad and Fazal Mahmood. Hanif, affectionately known as the "Little Master," embodied discipline, patience, and technique. His epic 337 in 970 minutes at Bridgetown in 1958, the longest innings in Test history, was more than a record—it became a moral parable for a new nation. Generations of Pakistani batsmen, from Javed Miandad, Inzamam ul Haq to Younis Khan, would later draw inspiration from his ability to resist the fiercest attacks through sheer concentration. Hanif showed that Pakistan could produce batsmen who could thrive on the global stage, not merely survive.

Fazal Mahmood's contribution was equally transformative. His mastery of seam bowling, particularly under English conditions, had already stunned the cricketing world during the Oval Test of 1954. Fazal gave Pakistan a weapon that allowed them to challenge even the strongest sides. His aura as a match-winner defined the early character of the team: resilient, opportunistic, and unafraid. Later generations of fast bowlers—from Sarfraz Nawaz to Wasim Akram—would cite Fazal as the pioneer who made pace bowling the soul of Pakistan cricket. Alongside them, players such as Imtiaz Ahmed and Nazar Mohammad added depth, ensuring the 1950s were not just about two men but about laying down a cricketing ethos.

Yet Pakistan's progress was not without critique. The team's reliance on matting wickets at home—where the ball bounced and seamed unnaturally—drew attention from visiting teams. Richie Benaud, the astute Australian captain and later commentator, remarked that Pakistan would only become a truly great cricketing force if it shifted to turf pitches like the rest of the world. His words proved prescient. On turf, Pakistan would need to develop more rounded skills—spinners capable of longer spells, batsmen trained to handle swing, and fielders accustomed to faster outfields. This gradual transition, though slow, was part of the maturing of Pakistan cricket.

Meanwhile, the sporting landscape of Pakistan in this era was not dominated by cricket alone. From the mid-1950s onward, hockey emerged as the country's most celebrated sport. The 1960 Rome Olympics saw Pakistan win its first hockey gold, defeating traditional rivals India and ending their long domination of the sport. This victory electrified the nation, creating heroes like Naseer Bunda and laying the foundation for further triumphs. Pakistan went on to win another Olympic gold in 1968 in Mexico, and by clinching the inaugural Hockey World Cup in 1971, the nation had stamped its supremacy in the game. In the public imagination, hockey became the true stage for national pride, a martial display of discipline, skill, and stamina. Cricket, though important, remained in the shadow of hockey's golden era through the 1960s and 1970s.

Beyond hockey, Pakistan also began its rise in squash. Players like Hashim Khan had already made waves in the 1950s, capturing the British Open and inspiring a dynasty that would eventually dominate the sport for decades through Jansher and Jahangir Khan. Together with hockey and cricket, squash became part of Pakistan's identity as a sporting nation, showcasing that even a young country could compete at the highest levels globally.

Thus, the late 1950s and early 1960s were a paradoxical period. Cricket had its heroes in Hanif and Fazal, men who built a foundation of grit and professionalism, but the nation's popular imagination tilted towards hockey and squash, where world titles were being won. For Pakistan, this multiplicity of sporting achievements created a culture of resilience and ambition. Cricket might not yet have been the number one sport, but its foundations, built on the shoulders of Hanif and Fazal, ensured that its time would eventually come.

Readers' notes

Richie Benaud (1930–2015) – *Australian leg-spinning all-rounder and captain, later a legendary commentator. Benaud's advice to Pakistan in the 1950s to abandon matting wickets and adopt turf pitches was pivotal in shaping the nation's cricketing evolution.*

Naseer Bunda (1932–1993) – *Hero of Pakistan's 1960 Rome Olympics hockey final, scoring the decisive goal against India to secure Pakistan's first Olympic gold. Became a national sporting icon during hockey's golden era.*

Hashim Khan (c. 1914–2014) – *Pioneer of Pakistan squash. He won the British Open in 1951 and inspired a dynasty that dominated the sport for decades. His victories introduced Pakistan as a global force in squash.*

Rome 1960 Olympics – *The Games where Pakistan ended India's hockey dominance by claiming gold. A watershed moment for Pakistani sport, giving hockey precedence over cricket in popular imagination.*

Mexico City 1968 Olympics – *Pakistan secured its second hockey gold medal, reaffirming its supremacy in the sport during the 1960s.*

Hockey World Cup 1971 (Barcelona) – *The inaugural World Cup of field hockey, where Pakistan triumphed, stamping its dominance in world hockey and adding to its tally of Olympic successes.*

Matting Wickets – *Surfaces covered with coir or jute matting, commonly used in Pakistan's early Test years. They exaggerated seam movement and bounce, helping fast bowlers like Fazal Mahmood but often criticized for being unrepresentative of global conditions.*

8.4 The Lean Years of the 1960s

If the 1950s had signalled Pakistan's startling arrival on the world stage, the 1960s delivered a sobering reminder of how difficult it was to sustain success at the Test level. This decade remains etched as one of the leanest and most frustrating in Pakistan's cricketing history — a period marked by timid batting, defensive captaincy, poor crowd engagement, and above all, a mental block against the stronger cricketing nations of the Caucasian world, especially England and Australia.

The malaise began with the home series against Richie Benaud's Australians in 1959–60. After the highs of Fazal Mahmood's Oval heroics only a few years earlier, expectations were high, yet the Australians exposed Pakistan's vulnerabilities with ruthless efficiency, inflicting a 2–0 series defeat. The aura of Benaud's tactical acumen and the professional ruthlessness of Australian cricket left Pakistan's cricketers tentative, setting the tone for much of the decade. The defeats also demonstrated the gulf in class: while Pakistan had raw talent, their tactical nous and professionalism lagged far behind.

A drawn five-Test series against India in 1960–61 (all matches ending without a result) showed another weakness: Pakistan's tendency to play for safety rather than pressing for victory. Caution replaced aggression, and cricket became a joyless grind. Crowds, once excited by the Fazal-Hanif generation's exploits, grew restless with the endless stalemates. The press began to describe Pakistan's style as "timid cricket," where avoiding defeat seemed more important than chasing victory.

The England series of 1961–62 added insult to injury. Touring under Ted Dexter, England defeated Pakistan 1–0 in their backyard, exposing brittle batting and defensive captaincy. But it was the 1962 return tour to England that drove home the depths of Pakistan's struggles. Under dreary skies, on seaming wickets, Pakistan's batting repeatedly collapsed against Fred Trueman and Brian Statham. The result — a humiliating

4–0 defeat in the five-Test series — was the most comprehensive defeat Pakistan had suffered up to that point. It scarred an entire generation of players and entrenched the sense of inferiority against England that would linger until the 1970s.

The mid-1960s saw only marginal improvements. Pakistan managed to defeat New Zealand twice at home in 1964–65, their only Test wins of the entire decade. Against the Kiwis, pacer Asif Masood and batsman Saeed Ahmed played decisive roles, and Hanif Mohammad was still the bedrock of the batting order. Yet these victories were seen with scepticism, for New Zealand was then considered the weakest Test side. Against stronger opposition, Pakistan remained timid. That same year, Pakistan drew solitary Tests against Australia both home and away, but those stalemates were more a reflection of cautious tactics than genuine resilience.

Pakistan continued to falter abroad. The 1967 England tour ended in another winless disappointment — a 2–0 defeat where batting collapses and unimaginative captaincy again told the tale. Player's spoke of the intimidation factor: county-hardened English professionals bowled relentlessly, while Pakistan's amateurs seemed out of their depth.

The end of the decade was symbolic of the broader malaise. In 1969–70, New Zealand, long considered Pakistan's easiest prey, finally turned the tables. Touring Pakistan, the Kiwis won their first-ever Test on Pakistani soil and clinched the series 1–0. This result was a body blow: the very team against whom Pakistan had registered its few successes in the decade had now humiliated them in their backyard. For Pakistani cricket, this was the nadir of the 1960s.

Crowd enthusiasm also waned during this period. In contrast to the buzzing maidans of Bombay or Calcutta, many Pakistani Test matches were played before sparse or subdued audiences. The lack of flair and results turned cricket into a dry spectacle. Hockey, in contrast, gripped the imagination. Pakistan's Olympic gold in Rome in 1960 and its dominance in the following years shifted national attention away from cricket. For much of the decade, hockey was the true national sport, and cricket lagged as a frustrating, stop-start enterprise.

The 1960s in Pakistan were not only lean years on the cricket field but also turbulent ones politically and militarily. The decade witnessed skirmishes with India at the Rann of Kutch in 1965, followed by a full-scale war the same year. Stories of the Battle of Chawinda in Sialkot, where Pakistan's forces held off a far larger Indian advance, became part of national folklore, bolstering the young nation's sense of resilience. Yet these triumphs came at a cost—President Ayub Khan's health and popularity waned towards the decade's end, paving the way for the controversial leadership of General Agha Muhammad Yahya Khan, whose role in the eventual disintegration of Pakistan and the fall of Dhaka in 1971 is remembered critically. Despite such turmoil, sport in Pakistan endured, with cricket, hockey, and squash continuing to offer the people a stage for pride and identity even in difficult times.

Yet, even in this era of gloom, silver linings appeared. The 1960s quietly witnessed the debut of several players who would go on to form the backbone of Pakistan's golden generation in the 1970s. Majid Khan, with his elegant strokeplay, signalled the arrival of a batsman unafraid of fast bowling. Zaheer Abbas, who would later be hailed as the "Asian Bradman," began to make waves with his run-scoring potential. Asif Iqbal, a stylish all-rounder, emerged with resilience and a flair for counterattacking innings. These young cricketers represented a new mentality — one less cowed by the aura of England or Australia, and more willing to play positively. Their emergence hinted at better days to come.

In hindsight, the 1960s were Pakistan's most stagnant Test decade: only two wins in the entire ten years, both against New Zealand, and repeated losses against Australia, England, and even New Zealand at home. Yet, it also served as a necessary cleansing period. The timidity and fear of the 1960s created the hunger for change that would bear fruit in the following decade. The debuts of Majid, Zaheer, and Asif hinted that Pakistan's cricket would not forever remain cautious and defensive. From the ashes of a dull and disappointing decade would rise the bold, golden generation of the 1970s.

Readers' notes

Richie Benaud (1930–2015) – *Australian leg-spinning allrounder and captain who led Australia to a 2–0 series win over Pakistan in 1959–60. His sharp tactics and calm leadership made him one of the most influential captains of the era.*

Fred Trueman (1931–2006) – *England's fiery fast bowler, feared for his pace and aggression. He played a leading role in dismantling Pakistan's batting line-up during the 1962 series in England, which ended 4–0 in the hosts' favour.*

Brian Statham (1930–2000) – *English fast bowler, partner to Trueman, known for accuracy and relentless spells. He also inflicted repeated collapses on Pakistan's inexperienced batting in the 1962 tour.*

Ted Dexter (1935–2021) – *England's flamboyant batsman and captain who toured Pakistan in 1961–62 and masterminded England's 1–0 series victory on Pakistani soil.*

Colin Cowdrey (1932–2000) – *Stylish English batsman who became a tormentor of Pakistan in the 1960s, scoring prolifically during the 1962 home series.*

John Edrich (1937–2020) – *Another English batsman who cashed in on Pakistan's lack of penetrating bowling in the mid-1960s, cementing England's dominance at home.*

Bevan Congdon (1938–2018) – *New Zealand batsman and allrounder, part of the Kiwi side that shocked Pakistan by winning their first Test on Pakistani soil in 1969–70.*

Graham Dowling (1937–2021) – *New Zealand's captain during their historic 1969 victory in Pakistan, remembered as a turning point for Kiwi cricket.*

8.5 The 1970s – The Golden Generation

The 1970s were a watershed in Pakistan cricket, marking the arrival of a golden generation of talent that would go on to shape the team's destiny for decades. The decade began under the shadow of the national trauma of 1971, with the disintegration of East Pakistan and the fall of Dhaka, but the cricket field offered hope, identity, and a sense of collective pride. It was in this era that Pakistan unearthed some of its most charismatic players, whose flair and fighting spirit gradually built the team's reputation into one of the most feared sides in world cricket.

The turning point came at Edgbaston in 1971, when Zaheer Abbas, the "Asian Bradman," announced himself with a sublime 274 against England. It was a knock that immediately made him a household name, blending elegance with authority against a high-class English attack. The same match also saw the debut of a raw young medium pacer — Imran Khan, cousin of Majid Khan — who although did not impress immediately, would later redefine Pakistan cricket with his charisma and leadership.

Pakistan's first-ever Prudential World Cup campaign in 1975 ended narrowly, with Mushtaq Mohammad's team almost toppling the mighty West Indies in the group stage, only to be denied by Clive Lloyd's brilliance. Four years later, Pakistan again came agonizingly close in the 1979 semi-final at The Oval, where Asif Iqbal's spirited men fought valiantly before falling short against the same Caribbean juggernaut. These World Cup near-misses underscored Pakistan's potential but also their inability, at times, to seize the crucial moments on the global stage.

At home, however, Pakistan became virtually unbeatable. Stadiums filled with passionate crowds, and the aura of fortress-like dominance was established. The highlight came in 1978 when India returned to Pakistan after 17 long years, under Bishan Singh Bedi's captaincy. Mushtaq Mohammad marshaled his troops with discipline, and a resurgent Pakistan sealed a memorable 2–0 victory in the three-Test series. That triumph ignited national euphoria, symbolizing Pakistan's rise not just as a cricketing force but also as a country brimming with self-belief. The emergence of Javed Miandad, who had already made headlines with his fearless debut century in 1976, provided Pakistan with a precocious batsman who embodied grit and audacity in equal measure. Alongside Miandad, players like Majid Khan, Asif Iqbal, Sarfraz Nawaz, and Wasim Bari gave the side balance and depth.

Though Pakistan remained dominant at home, their away record in the 1970s was inconsistent. Yet, amidst setbacks in England and Australia, there were moments of brilliance that revealed their growing maturity. The most defining came at Sydney in 1976, when Imran Khan unleashed raw pace and hostility to claim 12 wickets in the match, scripting Pakistan's first-ever Test victory in Australia and leveling the series 1–1. It was a breakthrough performance that signaled the arrival of a new spearhead who would inspire generations. Just three years later, at Melbourne in 1979, Sarfraz Nawaz delivered one of Test cricket's most fabled spells, taking seven wickets for one run in a scarcely believable burst that dismantled Australia. This display not only stunned the cricketing world but also introduced the art of reverse swing, a craft that would become Pakistan's hallmark weapon for decades to come.

Despite such highs, Pakistan still struggled abroad against established Caucasian sides. Tours of England in 1974 and 1978, and of Australia in 1972–73 and 1976–77, exposed a lack of confidence in alien conditions. Yet these contests also hardened the team, teaching them resilience and tactical nous. At home, Pakistan's superiority was reasserted with a clinical 2–0 series win against New Zealand in 1976–77, further reinforcing their ability to dominate visiting sides.

The decade also unfolded against a backdrop of immense political turbulence. The execution of former Prime Minister Zulfiqar Ali Bhutto in 1979, the Iranian Revolution, the Soviet invasion of

Afghanistan, and General Zia-ul-Haq's military regime transformed the nation's political landscape. Sport, however, provided continuity and a unifying force. Pakistan's simultaneous triumph in the 1978 Hockey World Cup in Argentina reflected the country's broader sporting culture, where hockey and cricket together lifted national morale during difficult times.

Thus, the 1970s encapsulated Pakistan's transformation from a young, tentative cricketing nation into a team of flair and ambition, boasting players of extraordinary talent and resilience. The unbeaten home record throughout the decade created a fortress-like reputation, while iconic away performances by Imran Khan and Sarfraz Nawaz hinted at the birth of a truly world-class side. By the close of the decade, Pakistan cricket stood on firmer ground than ever before, its golden generation ready to script even greater triumphs in the years ahead.

Reader's notes

Mushtaq Mohammad (1943–) – *A versatile all-rounder who captained Pakistan in the late 1970s. Known for his gritty batting, clever leg-spin, and strong leadership, he guided Pakistan to notable successes, including the historic 2–0 win against India in 1978/79.*

Majid Khan (1946–2023) – *Stylish opening batsman and cousin of Imran Khan, remembered for his flowing drives and flair. Played county cricket for Glamorgan and became a symbol of elegance in Pakistan's top order during the 1970s.*

Zaheer Abbas (1947–) – *Nicknamed the "Asian Bradman," he was Pakistan's premier run-machine of the decade. His double century at Edgbaston in 1971 put him on the world stage, and he dominated both Test and ODI cricket with style.*

Sarfaraz Nawaz (1948–2024) – *Known as the pioneer of reverse swing, Sarfaraz produced one of the most remarkable spells in Test history at Melbourne in 1979, taking 7 wickets for 1 run against Australia. His contributions laid the foundation for Pakistan's fast-bowling legacy.*

Imran Khan (1952–) – *Made his Test debut in 1971. Although raw in his early years, he developed into a fearsome fast bowler and charismatic all-rounder. His 12-wicket haul at Sydney in 1976 was a landmark moment for Pakistan abroad.*

Javed Miandad (1957–) – *Debuted in 1976 as a teenage prodigy. His fearless batting, sharp cricketing brain, and match-winning temperament would define Pakistan's middle order for decades to come.*

Bishan Singh Bedi (1946–2023) – *Indian left-arm spinner and captain during the 1978/79 Indo-Pak series that resumed cricketing ties after 17 years. His clashes with Pakistan symbolized the revival of one of cricket's greatest rivalries.*

1975 Prudential World Cup – *The inaugural ODI World Cup in England, where Pakistan competed but fell short against the mighty West Indies in a memorable group stage clash.*

1979 Prudential World Cup Semi-final – *Pakistan nearly toppled the West Indies in another classic, falling just short of the final but proving themselves as a force in limited-overs cricket.*

Choudhry Zahoor Elahi Stadium (Gaddafi Stadium, Lahore) – *Pakistan's main cricketing venue by the late 1970s, where large crowds symbolized cricket's growing cultural hold, especially during the India-Pakistan revival series in 1978.*

8.6 Imran Khan's Rise – Test Conquests in England and India, ODI Glory at Sharjah, Nehru Cup 1989 and the 1992 World Cup

The 1980s marked Pakistan's transformation from an unpredictable side into one of the most formidable cricketing nations in the world. At the center of this renaissance was Imran Khan, a tall, charismatic all-rounder whose leadership, vision, and relentless will to win altered not only the trajectory of Pakistan cricket but also its identity. His impact on the game was such that many liken him to Franz Beckenbauer's influence on German football — a captain who combined talent, strategy, and inspiration, leading his team to an unprecedented peak.

The decade began with Pakistan maintaining its aura of invincibility at home. Except for a narrow defeat to the mighty West Indies in 1980, Pakistan remained unbeaten in home Test series throughout the 1980s. The fortress-like dominance was a hallmark of Imran's era. Under his stewardship, Pakistan demolished India 3–0 in the 1982/83 series on home soil, erasing the bitter memories of the 1979 defeat in India. Imran's personal haul of 40 wickets across the six Tests, alongside Miandad's towering 280 in Hyderabad, overwhelmed their archrivals. For Pakistanis, it was more than a cricketing triumph; it was a statement that they could dominate their neighbor in the game that mattered most to both nations.

Victories were not confined to the subcontinent. Imran made Pakistan a team to fear abroad. The defining moment came in 1987, when Pakistan toured India for a five-Test series. With the series tied 0–0 going into the final match at Bangalore, the tension was immense. On a spinning track, India were bowled out in a low-scoring contest, and Pakistan clinched the series 1–0 — their first-ever Test series win in India. It was considered the finest hour of Pakistan cricket to that date, cementing Imran's status as a national hero. That summer brought more joy when Pakistan, under Imran, defeated England 1–0 in a historic away series, courtesy of Wasim Akram's rise and a collective team effort. For a team that often carried an inferiority complex against England and Australia, this was symbolic of a new era of confidence.

Yet, Test cricket abroad remained a mixed bag. Pakistan narrowly lost away in Australia in 1981/82 and again in 1983/84, falling short despite flashes of brilliance. The 1990 series in Australia also ended in disappointment with a 1–0 defeat, though competitive performances, such as Sarfraz Nawaz's reverse-swing masterclass in Melbourne in 1979 and Imran's 12 wickets at Sydney in 1976, continued to inspire belief that Pakistan could challenge the strongest on their turf. Against the West Indies, then the most feared side in the world, Pakistan earned immense respect. Home and away draws in 1986, 1988, and 1990 against Clive Lloyd and later Vivian Richards' juggernaut were celebrated like victories. Few teams could boast parity with the Caribbean giants, but Pakistan, under Imran, matched them blow for blow. Briefly, Pakistan were even ranked as the number one Test side in the world, proof of the balance, depth, and steel that Imran had instilled.

One of the cornerstones of Imran's reign was his eye for talent. He personally scouted and nurtured players like Wasim Akram, Waqar Younis, Aaqib Javed, Mushtaq Ahmed, and later Inzamam-ul-Haq, giving Pakistan a conveyor belt of world-class cricketers. His philosophy was fearless: he wanted his bowlers to intimidate, his batsmen to dominate, and his team to fight until the last ball. In many ways, he engineered the cultural shift from Pakistan being talented but inconsistent to becoming a ruthless cricketing machine.

If Test cricket showed Pakistan's rising pedigree, limited-overs cricket captured the imagination of the masses. The iconic moment came at Sharjah in April 1986, when Javed Miandad hit a last-ball six off Chetan Sharma to seal victory against India in the Austral-Asia Cup final. That six became folklore, changing Pakistan's psychological approach to ODIs. It was the beginning of a new belief that Pakistan could chase any target, fight to the last ball, and emerge victorious. The win also intensified the India–Pakistan rivalry, tilting momentum in Pakistan's favor during the late 1980s. The impact of Miandad's last-ball six at Sharjah in 1986 ran far deeper than just one match. It inflicted a psychological wound on India that lingered for years. From that point until the famous Bangalore quarter-final in the 1996 World Cup, Pakistan enjoyed a stranglehold over India in limited-overs cricket. Time and again, India found themselves in winning positions only to falter at the last moment, while Pakistan, driven by a new-found belief, snatched improbable victories. For nearly a decade, the balance of power in ODIs decisively tilted in Pakistan's favor, giving the team and its supporters an edge that defined the rivalry during this era.

The momentum carried into other tournaments. In 1989, Pakistan stunned the cricketing world by winning the Nehru Cup at Eden Gardens, defeating a star-studded West Indies side led by Viv Richards. The victory on Indian soil in front of more than 100,000 spectators was especially sweet, symbolizing Pakistan's growing stature in the limited-overs format. The Nehru Cup triumph was followed by further dominance in Sharjah, where Wasim Akram's hat-trick in the 1990

Australasia Cup final became another legendary moment. Pakistan had mastered the art of tournament play, combining aggression with resilience. Wins in the Rothmans Cup (1989) and the Sharjah Cup (1991) consolidated their reputation as the kings of ODI cricket outside the World Cup.

Yet, not all was smooth. The 1987 Reliance World Cup, co-hosted by India and Pakistan, was both a triumph and a heartbreak. The tournament was organized impeccably, drawing crowds comparable to Italy's World Cup in football three years later. For the first time, cricket felt like a festival across South Asia. Pakistan, playing at home, were tipped as favorites. But in the semifinal at Lahore, Australia stunned them in front of a packed Gaddafi Stadium. It was a bitter defeat, yet the passion and enthusiasm around the tournament cemented cricket's role as Pakistan's national sport.

The redemption arc came in 1992. By then, Imran was in the twilight of his career, but he rallied his team with the "cornered tigers" philosophy. Wearing color kits and playing under floodlights, Pakistan embraced the modern World Cup in Australia and New Zealand. The campaign began disastrously, with defeats against India, West Indies, and South Africa. But Imran's belief galvanized the squad. Pakistan won crucial games against Australia and Sri Lanka, then edged New Zealand in a dramatic semifinal, thanks to Inzamam-ul-Haq's explosive 60 off 37 balls. In the final at the Melbourne Cricket Ground, Pakistan defeated England by 22 runs. Imran, in his final international innings, top-scored with a captain's knock, before lifting the Benson & Hedges Cup from Colin Cowdrey. For Pakistan, it was the culmination of 40 years of struggle, a victory that inspired millions and permanently etched Imran's name in history.

This golden period in cricket coincided with Pakistan's sporting supremacy in other disciplines. In hockey, Pakistan won the 1982 World Cup in Bombay and the 1984 Olympic gold in Los Angeles, further reinforcing their global dominance. They also reached the final of the

1990 Hockey World Cup in Lahore, underlining a sustained legacy. In squash, Jahangir Khan and Jansher Khan ruled the courts, making Pakistan synonymous with the sport. Such simultaneous excellence across cricket, hockey, and squash gave Pakistan an aura of being a sporting giant, something never replicated in later decades.

The broader national landscape also shaped cricket's trajectory. The Soviet invasion of Afghanistan in 1979 brought millions of Afghan refugees into Pakistan, altering demographics and fueling geopolitical turbulence. Domestically, General Zia-ul-Haq's authoritarian regime loomed large, yet cricket thrived as a unifying outlet. Matches against India, especially after Zia's "cricket diplomacy" visit to Jaipur in 1987 during the Test series, became more than sport — they were extensions of national identity and politics.

Imran Khan's leadership style deserves special attention. Unlike many before him, he combined aristocratic charm, Oxford education, and a global outlook with deep national pride. He demanded discipline, fitness, and professionalism, qualities often missing in South Asian cricket. He also stood tall in controversies, whether it was disputes with administrators, selection debates, or clashes with the press. His charisma made him more than just a captain; he became the face of Pakistan cricket, a statesman on the field who commanded global respect.

By the time Imran retired after the 1992 World Cup, Pakistan had scaled cricket's highest peak. The journey from a new Test nation in 1952 to world champions in 1992 was complete. For Pakistanis born in the 1970s and 1980s, Imran's team defined their childhood, their pride, and their national dreams. It was not just about winning a trophy; it was about proving to the world that Pakistan could rise against all odds, combine flair with fight, and rule the biggest stage.

This golden age of Pakistan cricket unfolded alongside a turbulent but defining political transformation in the country. Remarkably, just a week before Javed Miandad struck his famous last-ball six in Sharjah in April 1986, Benazir Bhutto — daughter of the executed Prime Minister Zulfiqar Ali Bhutto — returned from exile to Lahore, where she was greeted by an electrifying crowd of over a million supporters. The immense reception symbolized the beginning of the gradual decline of General Zia-ul-Haq's powerful military regime. His sudden death in the Bahawalpur air crash of 1988 ended a decade of martial rule, and later that year Pakistan held its first free elections since the 1970s. Benazir Bhutto's Pakistan People's Party triumphed, though her government was short-lived, toppled by 1990, when the conservative Islami Jamhoori Ittehad (IJI), led by industrialist Nawaz Sharif, rose to power. It was under Nawaz Sharif's tenure that Pakistan lifted the 1992 World Cup, with Imran Khan's "cornered tigers" immortalized at Melbourne. When the victorious team was invited to the Prime Minister's residence, Nawaz light-heartedly suggested that Imran should join his government — a prophetic quip, for few could have imagined then that cricket's greatest captain and the rising Punjabi politician would one day become the fiercest of rivals on Pakistan's political battlefield.

Reader's notes

Imran Khan (Pakistan) – *Charismatic all-rounder and inspirational captain who redefined Pakistan cricket in the 1980s and early 1990s, culminating in the 1992 World Cup triumph.*

Javed Miandad (Pakistan) – *Pakistan's most dependable middle-order batsman of the era, remembered for his last-ball six off Chetan Sharma in the 1986 Australasia Cup final.*

Chetan Sharma (India) – *Indian fast bowler who became part of cricketing folklore after conceding Miandad's iconic last-ball six at Sharjah in 1986.*

Wasim Akram (Pakistan) – *Left-arm fast bowler whose devastating pace, swing, and reverse swing made him one of the greatest bowlers in cricket history. Instrumental in Pakistan's 1992 World Cup win.*

Waqar Younis (Pakistan) – *Known as the "Toe-Crusher," Waqar revolutionized fast bowling with his lethal yorkers and reverse swing in the late 1980s and early 1990s.*

Inzamam-ul-Haq (Pakistan) – *Explosive middle-order batsman who announced himself with a match-winning innings against New Zealand in the 1992 World Cup semi-final.*

Aaqib Javed (Pakistan) – *Young fast bowler in the early 1990s, remembered for his aggression and hat-trick against India in Sharjah October 1991.*

Mushtaq Ahmed (Pakistan) – *Leg-spinner whose variations gave Pakistan a fresh attacking edge in the early 1990s and who played a key role in the 1992 World Cup.*

Viv Richards (West Indies) – *Fearsome batsman of the West Indies and global superstar of the 1970s and 1980s, symbolizing dominance in both Tests and ODIs.*

Malcolm Marshall (West Indies) – *One of the most feared fast bowlers in cricket history, renowned for his pace, swing, and aggression during the 1980s.*

Allan Border (Australia) – *Inspirational Australian captain of the 1980s, under whom Australia revived its cricketing fortunes, including victory in the 1987 World Cup in Pakistan.*

Martin Crowe (New Zealand) – *Stylish Kiwi batsman and leader whose tactical genius almost carried New Zealand to the 1992 World Cup final before falling to Pakistan.*

Colin Cowdrey (England) – *Former England captain who presented Imran Khan with the 1992 World Cup trophy at the Melbourne Cricket Ground.*

Jahangir Khan (Pakistan) – *Legendary squash player who dominated the sport through the 1980s, setting records and bringing global sporting prestige to Pakistan.*

Jansher Khan (Pakistan) – *Successor to Jahangir Khan in squash, extending Pakistan's dominance in the sport well into the 1990s.*

Hassan Sardar (Pakistan) – *Iconic field hockey player who starred in Pakistan's 1982 World Cup and 1984 Olympic gold medal triumphs.*

General Muhammad Zia-ul-Haq – *Pakistan's military ruler (1977–1988), under whom cricket and Sharjah flourished; died in the 1988 Bahawalpur plane crash.*

Zulfiqar Ali Bhutto – *Founder of the Pakistan People's Party (PPP), executed in 1979 under Zia.*

Benazir Bhutto – *Daughter of Zulfiqar Ali Bhutto, returned in 1986, became Prime Minister in 1988; symbolized Pakistan's democratic revival.*

166

Nawaz Sharif – *Punjabi industrialist politician, rose under Zia's patronage, leader of the Islamic Democratic Alliance (IJI); became PM in 1990.*

PPP (Pakistan People's Party) – *Center-left political party, founded by Zulfiqar Ali Bhutto, led by Benazir in this period.*

IJI (Islami Jamhoori Ittehad) – *Conservative political alliance led by Nawaz Sharif against the PPP.*

8.7 Instability and Missed Opportunities (1993–2008)

The curtain fell on an era of extraordinary brilliance when Imran Khan, having led Pakistan to their most iconic cricketing triumph in the 1992 World Cup, retired from international cricket. That victory at the MCG did not just symbolize success on the field but was seen as the culmination of a golden age in Pakistan's sporting history. With Imran's departure, the leadership baton was passed to Javed Miandad, one of the most prolific and aggressive batsmen in Pakistan's cricketing legacy. It was Miandad's stewardship that marked the beginning of a new era— a period defined by individual brilliance, impressive but scattered victories, and eventually, the start of a long, painful decline.

Pakistan carried forward the momentum of the World Cup win into the Test arena with an emphatic 2-1 Test series victory in England in 1992. The series was dominated by the reverse swing mastery of Wasim Akram and Waqar Younis, whose devastating spells left the English batting order in tatters. This was the era where Pakistan's pace attack was unmatched, and the team looked a genuine global force in Test cricket. The following winter, Pakistan toured New Zealand and secured another series win, beating a Martin Crowe-led side 1-0. These back-to-back away victories hinted that Pakistan was not just a sporadically successful team but a side capable of sustained excellence.

However, the cracks began to show in the One Day International (ODI) format. In the limited-overs leg of the 1992 England tour,

Pakistan slumped to a 4-1 defeat. The loss exposed a worrying inconsistency in the middle order, coupled with tactical naivety and poor fielding—elements that would continue to haunt Pakistan in the years to come. The team also struggled in the tri-series in Australia later that year and produced mixed results in Sharjah and South Africa through 1993. Despite the ODI hiccups, Pakistan remained imperious in the Test arena at home. From 1992 to 1994, no touring side could breach the fortress. Zimbabwe were dispatched 2-0 in the 1993/94 series, and New Zealand fell 2-1 in a hard-fought contest. The crowning moment of this period came in 1994, when Pakistan beat Australia 1-0 in a three Test series at home. This win was significant not just for the result, but for what it represented: the culmination of nearly 25 years of Test dominance at home. Since 1969, barring a solitary defeat to the West Indies in 1980, no side had conquered Pakistan in their own backyard. The series win over Australia marked the end of an era.

In parallel, Pakistan's sporting prowess extended beyond cricket. The men's hockey team triumphed at the 1994 Hockey World Cup in Sydney, defeating the Netherlands in a dramatic final. This victory marked Pakistan's fourth Hockey World Cup title — still a world record — and, when combined with the 1992 Cricket World Cup win, represented the zenith of national sporting pride. Between 1968 and 1994, Pakistan claimed four Hockey World Cups, one Cricket World Cup, multiple Hockey Olympic gold medals, and dominated the world of squash through the unparalleled exploits of Jahangir and Jansher Khan. After a long hiatus, Arshad Nadeem's gold medal victory in javelin at the 2024 Olympics, defeating his Indian counterpart, ended a 32-year Olympic medal drought.

However, 1994 would also prove to be the final peak before a slow and steady descent began to erode the foundations of Pakistan's dominance. While the victory in Sharjah's Australasia Cup in 1994— where Pakistan once again beat India in a high-pressure final—offered one last limited-overs trophy, it would remain their final major ODI title for 23 years. The decline began in 1995 with a home Test series loss to Sri Lanka, their first at home in 15 years. The aura of invincibility had been punctured. The defeat was compounded by poor showings in the Asia Cup and further failures in Sharjah.

The 1996 World Cup quarterfinal against India in Bangalore was a seismic moment. Despite scoring with rapid good start in the first 10 overs, Pakistan failed to chase 288. The loss was not just a cricketing defeat; it carried deep emotional and psychological resonance for a cricket-obsessed nation. While Pakistan did avenge some pride by defeating England 2-0 in a 1996 away Test series, the tide had begun to turn. The subsequent years saw a string of unsettling losses at home: South Africa in 1997, Zimbabwe in 1998, Australia later that year, and England in 2000. Visiting teams, once intimidated by playing in Pakistan, now arrived with belief—and increasingly, success.

In 1997, under Hansie Cronje's leadership, South Africa toured Pakistan for the first time in a Test series. The Proteas, packed with stars like Lance Klusener, Shaun Pollock, Allan Donald, Pat Symcox, and Gary Kirsten, played with grit and confidence. The first two Tests were closely fought, but the decisive third Test in Faisalabad was unforgettable: Symcox's unexpected counterattacking innings and incisive bowling ensured Pakistan failed to chase a modest 146, losing by 53 runs. South Africa sealed their first-ever away Test series in Pakistan. The series was notable not only for its cricket but also for the state visit of Queen Elizabeth II, who attended one of the Tests to meet both teams. The pain deepened when South Africa went on to win a tri-nation ODI series in Pakistan the same month, beating Sri Lanka in the final while Pakistan failed to qualify. A year later, Mark Taylor's Australians arrived and carved their own place in history. Taylor's epic 334 not out in Peshawar, declared overnight in deference to Don Bradman's iconic score, became a symbol of dominance. Australia clinched their first Test series win in Pakistan in nearly four decades and followed it with a 3-0 sweep in the ODIs. Even Zimbabwe shocked Pakistan in 1998, winning 1-0 in a two-match series, exposing vulnerabilities once unimaginable. The nadir of this sequence came in 2000 when Nasser Hussain's England achieved the unthinkable, beating Pakistan in Karachi during the fading light of Maghrib to win their first Test series in the country in nearly forty years. It was a series of shocks that revealed fragility in Pakistan's cricketing foundations.

Amid this turbulent stretch, one tour stood out as both politically symbolic and cricketing historic. In early 1999, Pakistan traveled to India for a much-anticipated Test series against the backdrop of Prime Minister Atal Bihari Vajpayee's landmark visit to Lahore, where he addressed crowds at Minar-e-Pakistan in a gesture of reconciliation. On the field, the cricket was nothing short of gripping. At Chennai, Pakistan secured a nerve-wracking 12-run victory in front of a packed stadium, a result that evoked memories of their famous 16-run win at Bangalore in 1987. The drama reached another crescendo at Eden Gardens in Kolkata during the Asian Test Championship. In front of one of the largest cricket crowds in history, Shoaib Akhtar's electrifying pace silenced the home supporters as Pakistan defeated India emphatically. That triumph carried them to Asian Test Championship title, one of the few major Test honors the team achieved after their away series wins in England in 1992 and 1996. These moments offered fleeting reminders of Pakistan's resilience and flair, even as inconsistency and decline increasingly defined the broader arc of their cricketing journey.

The inconsistency in major ICC events mirrored the broader disarray of Pakistan cricket in that era. Campaigns in the 1998, 2000, 2004, and 2006 ICC Champions Trophy all ended in disappointing exits, reflecting a side that could not find stability in big tournaments. The 1999 main World Cup, however, initially seemed to promise redemption. Pakistan stormed through the group stages and the semi-final with a dominant bowling attack led by Wasim Akram, Shoaib Akhtar, and Saqlain Mushtaq, complemented by Saeed Anwar's elegance at the top of the order. The nation's hopes soared as they reached the final at Lord's, only for those dreams to be brutally dashed. Against Australia, Pakistan collapsed in what remains the most one-sided World Cup final in history, dismissed for just 132 runs and overwhelmed by a clinical opponent. The defeat was not merely a loss; it was the manner of surrender—uncompetitive and anticlimactic—that shook national morale and scarred fans who had expected their team to rise to the occasion.

Worsening matters were the swirling allegations of impropriety and corruption that began to dominate headlines. While not all claims were legally proven, the shadow of match-fixing loomed large over some of the senior-most players although no concrete evidence was ever presented. Hearings, inquiries, and speculation eroded trust between the public and the team, damaging the credibility of Pakistan cricket at home and abroad. For a sport that had been a source of unity and pride, the scandals created a sense of betrayal, deepening the disillusionment that was already spreading after the on-field inconsistencies.

In 2002, Pakistan hit one of its lowest points in Test cricket. Playing Australia in Sharjah, Pakistan were bowled out for under 100 in both innings of the same Test—an ignominious record that epitomized the team's mental fragility and technical deficiencies. Meanwhile, the team's standing at home continued to erode. In 2004, India toured Pakistan and won the Test series, marking a historic moment not just for cricketing rivalry but for India's ascension and Pakistan's diminishing stronghold at home.

Pakistan's performances in the 2003 and 2007 main World Cups were equally deflating. Both tournaments ended with early exits, and the team never came close to challenging for the title. These years were marked by a lack of consistency, confused selection policies, and tactical incoherence. Despite possessing talented individuals, Pakistan struggled to forge a cohesive unit. There were bright spots—such as a drawn away series in India in 2005 and a home Test series win against

India in 2006—but these moments were outliers in an otherwise downward spiral.

A statistical overview of Pakistan's Test series between 1992 and 2008 reveals the tale clearly. From 1969 to 1994, the team enjoyed dominant home form. But from 1995 onward, Pakistan began to lose Test series regularly—both at home and abroad. Between 1995 and 2008, they suffered whitewashes in Australia (1999, 2004) and defeats at home to teams like Zimbabwe, England, Australia, South Africa, and India. Even when not losing outright, Pakistan struggled to assert dominance in drawn series, a sharp contrast to the previous decades.

The shift in focus towards limited-overs formats, especially T20 cricket, became increasingly apparent. While the cricketing world embraced the rapid rise of T20 leagues and commercialization, Pakistan seemed to drift without direction. The team failed to play a five-Test series after 1992, reflecting both scheduling limitations and a dwindling appetite for the traditional format. Younger players gravitated towards the glitz of T20 cricket, often at the expense of red-ball discipline. The domestic cricket structure, once a reliable pipeline for elite talent, became outdated and under-resourced. As a result, bench strength weakened, and the team became over-reliant on a handful of stars like Shoaib Akhtar, Abdul Razzaq, and Azhar Mahmood, all of whom were nearing the twilight of their careers by the mid-2000s.

External factors also played a pivotal role. The 9/11 attacks and their geopolitical aftermath changed the global security landscape. In 2002, the New Zealand team aborted its Pakistan tour after a bombing incident near their hotel. This was a major setback. Over time, several top-tier teams became hesitant to visit Pakistan, and the cricketing calendar increasingly pushed the team into neutral venues like the UAE. This isolation stripped Pakistan of its home advantage and deprived fans of witnessing their team in person.

Meanwhile, Pakistan's other sporting icons fell into decline. The hockey team, once a global powerhouse, failed to win a single World Cup or Olympic medal post-1994. Squash, which had produced legends like Jahangir and Jansher Khan, faded without succession. The wider sporting system in the country was crumbling—underfunded, mismanaged, and unable to cope with modern demands. In this larger context, cricket still held public attention, but with increasing frustration and disappointment.

By the end of 2008, Pakistan cricket was a shadow of its former self. A team that once ruled the world stage with flair, aggression, and unpredictability had lost its way. The golden years from 1968 to 1994, marked by World Cups, Olympic medals, and home dominance, had given way to an era of uncertainty. The long wait for another major ODI title—finally ending with the 2017 Champions Trophy—only underscored how long the drought had lasted.

Reader's Notes

Saeed Anwar *emerged as Pakistan's premier opening batsman of the 1990s, blending elegance with consistency and becoming the face of Pakistan's top-order stability until the early 2000s.*

The 1994 Australasia Cup *victory in Sharjah marked Pakistan's last major ODI title for 23 years, a symbolic high before the prolonged drought that followed.*

Inzamam-ul-Haq *rose from Imran's protégé to captaincy, known for his calm presence at the crease and longevity across eras of turbulence.*

Shoaib Akhtar, *the "Rawalpindi Express", added extreme pace and theatre to Pakistan's bowling arsenal, but his career was marred by injuries and inconsistency.*

Pakistan remained unbeaten at home in Test series *from 1980 to 199, extending a dominant streak that had lasted since 1969 with only one interruption.*

The 1995 home Test series loss to Sri Lanka *broke a 15-year unbeaten record at home and is widely seen as the symbolic beginning of Pakistan's long decline.*

Security concerns post-9/11, *including New Zealand's mid-tour withdrawal in 2002, led to Pakistan's increasing isolation from international cricket and forced a shift to neutral venues.*

No 5-match Test series has been played by Pakistan since 1992, indicating a shift in priorities toward shorter formats and diminishing stature in Test scheduling.

*From 1994 to 2008, Pakistan's once-dominant Olympic and world-stage performance in sports like **hockey and squash** also collapsed, paralleling the cricketing downturn.*

8.8: Younis Khan, Misbah, and the Highs of 2009–2017

The end of 2008 had already cast a shadow over Pakistan cricket, but the events of early 2009 brought a seismic rupture. The attack on the Sri Lankan team in Lahore in March that year marked the last international Test match played on Pakistani soil for over a decade. The game's heartbeat in Pakistan moved to sterile, lifeless stadiums of the UAE. The loss of home conditions, familiar pitches, passionate crowds, and national morale was more than symbolic—it altered the very fabric of the team's cricketing evolution.

It was in these trying circumstances that Younis Khan, a rugged, proud Pathan from Mardan, stepped up to lead the national side. A man of few words but immense grit, Younis brought discipline, unity, and character to a dressing room battered by security crises, administrative disarray, and public disillusionment. His crowning achievement came swiftly. In the ICC World T20 2009, held in England, Pakistan rallied under his captaincy to clinch the title, burying the ghosts of their heart-wrenching defeat in the final of the 2007 edition against India. It was poetic redemption. From being a nation without a home to becoming world champions, Pakistan had found a rare moment of collective exhale. Younis retired from the shortest format at the summit, leaving behind a legacy of resilience and leadership forged in exile.

The longer format, however, demanded rebuilding. In came Misbah-ul-Haq, a mature presence in the lineup and, over time, the most stabilizing figure Pakistan cricket had seen in decades. Misbah inherited a team in turmoil—tainted by the 2010 spot-fixing scandal involving captain Salman Butt and fast bowlers Mohammad Amir and

Mohammad Asif. The scandal rocked the sport and compounded Pakistan's image crisis. Yet, Misbah's understated authority, sharp cricketing mind, and almost zen-like demeanor offered Pakistan a rare commodity: calm.

From 2010 onwards, with the UAE serving as their home venue, Misbah orchestrated an era of tactical pragmatism. Under his watchful leadership, Pakistan turned the UAE into a fortress. The highlight came in 2012 when they whitewashed England 3-0 in a Test series. England, then ranked number one in the world under Sir Andrew Strauss, were humbled on dry, turning tracks where spin duo Saeed Ajmal and Abdur Rehman ran riot. Misbah's ability to maximize the strengths of his squad was on full display. With Ajmal bamboozling world-class batsmen and the middle order anchored by Younis, Azhar Ali, and Asad Shafiq, Pakistan found the kind of stability rarely seen in previous decades.

The path wasn't without setbacks. Away performances remained inconsistent. Tours to Australia and South Africa exposed Pakistan's continued struggles with pace, bounce, and discipline. Australia completed 3-0 whitewashes in both 2010 and 2016/17, underlining the gap in standards. Yet, every setback seemed to add resolve. In Sri Lanka, Pakistan scripted a brilliant 2-1 Test series win in 2015, with Younis Khan producing a masterclass in the fourth innings in Pallekele. These moments stood out as beacons during the years of wandering.

One of the most symbolic moments of this chapter came in 2016. After a closely fought 2-2 Test series draw in England—featuring a famous century and celebratory push-ups by Misbah at Lord's—Pakistan ascended to the number one spot in the ICC Test rankings for the first time in the 21st century. The team received the prestigious Test mace, marking a full-circle moment. The feat had only been achieved once before, in 1988 under Imran Khan. That Misbah's team achieved this while playing all their 'home' cricket in foreign lands made it even more admirable.

Parallel to the Test highs, Pakistan continued to show fighting spirit in ICC limited-overs tournaments, despite lacking the structural depth of the more resourced cricketing nations. In the 2011 World Cup, held in the subcontinent, a weakened Pakistan—led by Shahid Afridi—surprisingly topped their group, defeating Sri Lanka and Australia. With the dark cloud of the 2010 spot-fixing bans hanging overhead, few expected a deep run. Yet, Afridi's team made it to the semi-final in Mohali, only to lose a tense contest to India. The match was marred by dropped catches—most notably of Sachin Tendulkar—and a controversial DRS decision reversal that kept Tendulkar at the crease. Pakistan were left to rue their missed opportunities, but the team had restored some pride.

In 2015, another spirited but limited Pakistan side again made it to the quarter-finals in Australia. With an ageing squad, and Misbah and Afridi both playing their last World Cup, the team pushed eventual champions Australia in the knockout game. At one stage, Australia were reeling, but dropped catches and missed chances once again proved costly. The team exited the tournament with their heads held high, but with the writing on the wall: it was time for transition.

The most astonishing moment in Pakistan's ODI history post-1992 came in 2017, when under the unassuming leadership of Sarfaraz Ahmed, they won the ICC Champions Trophy. Entering the tournament as the lowest-ranked team, and having lost heavily to India in the group stage, Pakistan pulled off an extraordinary turnaround. They defeated South Africa, Sri Lanka, and tournament favourites England to set up a final rematch with India. What followed at The Oval was one of Pakistan's most clinical performances in ODI history. Fakhar Zaman's fearless century, Mohammad Amir's early blitz dismantling India's top order, and a 180-run victory margin stunned the world. In many ways, this triumph exorcised the trauma of the 2011 semi-final and 2007 T20 final defeats to India. It also ended a 23-year drought of major ODI titles since the 1994 Australasia Cup in Sharjah.

By 2017, Younis Khan and Misbah-ul-Haq had announced their retirement. Their final Test series in the West Indies ended in fitting fashion—Yasir Shah's dramatic last-over dismissal of Shannon Gabriel secured Pakistan's first ever Test series win in the Caribbean. The sight of Misbah and Younis walking off together, victorious and dignified, brought closure to a chapter defined by professionalism, patience, and pride amidst chaos. They had held the team together through one of its most fractured decades and left behind a legacy not measured in just wins, but in character.

The exile years from 2009 to 2017 were not just about logistics and venues. They were about identity. Playing in front of empty stands in Abu Dhabi and Dubai, Pakistan had to reinvent its cricketing soul. The players had to draw energy from within, as the roars of Lahore or Karachi were replaced by the eerie quiet of neutral grounds. Yet, despite the absence of crowds, and in the presence of shadows from the past, Pakistan found ways to stay relevant. Misbah and Younis, Afridi and Sarfaraz, Ajmal and Amir, Azhar and Asad—they carried forward a tradition that could easily have withered.

Pakistan once again displayed the spirit of a resilient nation. During the long and painful exile phase, when no international cricket was played on home soil, the team not only survived but soared in unexpected ways. Against all odds, Pakistan won 2 major ICC trophies—a feat they hadn't achieved from 1993 to 2008—even as they played without the comfort of home conditions. The triumphs in the 2009 T20 World Cup and 2017 Champions Trophy, a historic Test series win in the West Indies, ODI series win in India and South Africa and a climb to the number one Test ranking under Misbah-ul-Haq reflect an era of grit and substance. These accomplishments, secured by a group of players often considered less naturally gifted than the golden generation of the 1993–2008 period, arguably eclipse their predecessors' record. It was a phase of quiet excellence, carved out not with flamboyance, but with discipline, heart, and remarkable self-belief.

177

Pakistan may have lost the right to host, but they refused to lose the will to fight.

8.9 – Decline and Contemporary Challenges (2018–Present)

After the dramatic high of the 2017 ICC Champions Trophy triumph, many believed that Pakistani cricket had found its next golden generation. That afternoon at The Oval, when Pakistan thrashed India in one of the most one-sided finals in ICC history, seemed to herald a new dawn. But instead, it turned out to be the final gust of a brief resurgence, before the winds of decline began to blow once more—this time fiercer and more destabilizing than ever.

Pakistan's post-2017 cricketing narrative has been shaped not only by what happened on the field but also by an increasingly fractured and volatile political landscape off it. Within weeks of the Champions Trophy victory, the sitting government led by Nawaz Sharif was disqualified from office following the Panama Papers verdict. It was a moment of political earthquake in the country, one that had a domino effect across all institutions—including sport. By 2022, Imran Khan, the very man who once lifted Pakistan's most iconic cricket trophy, was also removed from power, and the nation's already unstable governance plunged further into chaos. Within the Pakistan Cricket Board, the leadership carousel turned relentlessly. Chairman after chairman, selector after selector, coach after coach, and captain after captain—everyone came and went, but stability never came to stay. In the span of eight years, the team had more than half a dozen coaches and at least five captains across formats. Each came with promises of change, of rebuilding, of new strategies—but all left behind more questions than answers.

Meanwhile, on the field, the afterglow of 2017 faded rapidly. From a team that had once turned UAE into a fortress during the Misbah era, Pakistan began to suffer Test defeats even in their adopted home. The 2017/18 Test series whitewash by Sri Lanka was a loud alarm bell. New Zealand edged out Pakistan 2-1 in 2018/19, followed by a 3-0 hammering at the hands of South Africa. When Test cricket returned to Pakistan in 2019, there was momentary optimism. The return of Sri

179

Lanka and Bangladesh brought some joy as Pakistan secured wins. But Australia's 2022 tour exposed glaring flaws. Pat Cummins' men outplayed Pakistan across three Tests, winning the series 1-0 with absolute control.

Then came the historic 2022/23 home series against England. A Bazball-charged English team swept Pakistan 3-0 in one of the most dominant visiting performances ever seen on Pakistani soil. It was not just the scoreline that hurt, but the sheer gulf in tactical planning, fielding intensity, and execution. The same trend repeated against New Zealand, where Pakistan failed to win a single match in a two-Test home series. Even in the 2024/25 season, Pakistan could only manage a 1-1 draw with West Indies—a team they once routinely outclassed.

The truth had become undeniable. In the red-ball format, Pakistan had fallen dangerously behind modern standards. The pitches remained dull, selection strategies incoherent, and player development stagnant. There was no clear batting backbone nor a settled spin attack in home conditions. Yasir Shah's decline post-2018 created a vacuum, and while players like Nauman Ali, Sajid and Abrar Ahmed showed glimpses of brilliance, none consistently delivered match-winning performances.

Emerging talents dried up as the domestic structure remained fragmented and lacked proper incentives. The Pakistan Super League (PSL) launched in 2016 became successful commercially and in terms of unearthing T20 talent, but it failed to serve as a feeder for longer format cricket. While England, India, and Australia refined their systems, integrated sports science, and invested in data analytics, Pakistan's approach remained reactive and archaic.

The white-ball formats told a mixed story. In the 2019 World Cup, Pakistan began poorly but showed fight towards the end. Yet, they missed out on the semifinals due to net run rate—a technicality that stung deeply. But the 2023 World Cup was far more disappointing. Poor planning, tactical confusion, and underwhelming performances led to an early group-stage exit. It was a harsh reminder that the system was producing individual talent but not cohesive units capable of enduring pressure.

There were, however, flashes of the old Pakistan brilliance. In the 2021 T20 World Cup, the team played with swagger and beat India for the first time in a World Cup, a massive psychological breakthrough. They reached the semi-finals but stumbled against Australia in a tense contest. In 2022, Pakistan made it all the way to the final in Melbourne, but once again failed at the last hurdle—losing to England in a closely fought battle. The Asia Cup 2022 final loss to Sri Lanka was especially painful. After reducing their opponents to 58 for 5, Pakistan's bowlers inexplicably let the game slip, highlighting issues of temperament and mental strength under pressure.

The core group of Babar Azam, Mohammad Rizwan, Shaheen Afridi, Fakhar Zaman, and Shadab Khan were seen as generational talents. And in many ways, they were. But in critical moments—semifinals, finals, deciding Test matches—the team repeatedly faltered. Whether it was Babar's reluctance to innovate tactically or the middle order's inability to absorb pressure, something always went missing.

By 2025, Pakistan cricket entered yet another phase of transition. Babar Azam stepped down, and Salman Ali Agha along with Mohammad Rizwan took over leadership roles in the Test and white-ball formats. The upcoming WTC cycle in 2025-27, the 2026 T20 World Cup in India & Sri Lanka, and the 2027 main ODI World Cup in South Africa now loom large on the horizon. These tournaments will not just define the careers of the current crop but may also decide whether Pakistan continues its slide or reclaims a competitive place in world cricket.

It would, however, be unfair to say Pakistan lacks talent. The issue lies deeper—in how that talent is nurtured, mentored, and tested under pressure. Modern cricket demands strategic planning, high-performance environments, and adaptive thinking—areas where Pakistan continues to lag behind. Fitness standards remain questionable, fielding is inconsistent, and mental conditioning largely absent.

Compounding Pakistan's cricketing challenges is the broader geopolitical climate. Since the 2008 Mumbai attacks, Indo-Pak relations have remained strained, with diplomatic engagement limited and bilateral cricket suspended. India's refusal to travel to Pakistan for the recently concluded 2025 ICC Champions Trophy—insisting on neutral venues—along with the handshake controversy during the Asia Cup and the trophy handover from PCB Chairman Mohsin Naqvi, have further underscored the deepening isolation. The brief military escalation—India's Operation Sindhoor and Pakistan's reciprocal Operation Bunyan al-Marsus—has added a layer of political complexity that continues to cloud sporting cooperation. Within this context, the increasing influence of the BCCI over global cricket governance—particularly in ICC scheduling, policy decisions, and revenue models—has significantly tilted the institutional balance.

Pakistan's cricketing voice on the international stage has been notably diminished. No longer part of the so-called "Big Three," and now structurally overtaken by South Africa, Pakistan faces the urgent need to catch up across multiple domains—administration, coaching, player development, and cricket diplomacy. To restore its stature and recalibrate its standing within the global cricketing architecture, Pakistan will need more than just institutional reform; it must start winning major international trophies sooner rather than later. Success on the field remains one of the most effective ways to reclaim relevance off it.

Yet, history shows that Pakistan thrives when its back is against the wall. The team's DNA is still wired for the improbable. Whether it's Sarfaraz's men shocking India in 2017, or Misbah's side rising to No. 1 in 2016 without a single home Test, or Shaheen's magical opening spell in the T20 World Cup 2021—moments of magic continue to shine through. What is needed now is not just more moments, but sustained structure and stability. Only then can Pakistan hope to emulate the steel of its 1970s, 1980s, and early 1990s generations. As of 2025, Pakistan cricket stands at a fragile crossroads. The next two years will tell whether this phase was a nadir before a rebirth—or the continuation of a long, agonizing decline.

Special Capsule -The Pakistan Super League: Resilience Through Franchise Cricket

In 2016, amid national security challenges and an absence of international cricket at home, Pakistan took a bold leap into the modern cricket economy with the launch of the Pakistan Super League (PSL). Modeled on franchise leagues like the IPL and Big Bash, the PSL began as a five-team tournament held entirely in the UAE—primarily in Dubai and Sharjah. It was born not in celebration but in necessity. With Pakistan deprived of international fixtures following the 2009 attack on the Sri Lankan team in Lahore, the PSL became both a symbol of defiance and a vehicle for revival.

The PSL not only kept Pakistan relevant in global cricket discussions but also offered fans, players, and administrators a professional platform to showcase their capabilities. Despite its offshore beginnings, it quickly earned credibility through its competitive matches, strong production values, and its embrace of young local talent. Over the years, the league expanded to six teams—Karachi Kings, Lahore Qalandars, Islamabad United, Peshawar Zalmi, Quetta Gladiators, and Multan Sultans—each cultivating loyal fan bases and city rivalries.

What made the PSL particularly significant was its timing and perseverance. The league endured logistical hurdles, political opposition, and even a global pandemic. During COVID-19, while leagues around the world were paused or scaled back, the PSL innovated with bio-secure bubbles and rescheduled formats. Gradually, as security improved, matches began returning to Pakistan—first in Lahore and Karachi, and later in Multan and Rawalpindi—culminating in full home-based tournaments. This shift marked not just a logistical triumph but a psychological victory for a country starved of live cricket.

The PSL has been instrumental in developing Pakistan's player pipeline. Fakhar Zaman, Haris Rauf, Shadab Khan and Saim Ayub are standout examples—emerging from relative obscurity through PSL exposure. Lahore Qalandars' player development program has become a blueprint for talent discovery in economically underdeveloped regions. The league has thus complemented domestic cricket, often proving more efficient in fast-tracking raw talent to the national setup.

However, not all aspects of the PSL are beyond critique. A recurring concern has been the reliance on aging or internationally sidelined players—particularly from Western nations—who may no longer add elite competitive value. While marquee names help attract attention, an overemphasis on nostalgia risks undermining the PSL's credibility as a platform for high-performance cricket. More strategic recruitment and investment in emerging international talent may address this imbalance and raise the league's standard.

Economically, the PSL has become a vital revenue stream for the Pakistan Cricket Board (PCB), helping fund infrastructure, player contracts, and grassroots programs. It has also drawn sponsorship from global brands, tech platforms, and local conglomerates, showing that Pakistan cricket has commercial appeal when packaged correctly. The league's success has even sparked calls for a Champions League-style competition featuring franchise teams across Asia—a signal of the PSL's growing stature.

The PSL is more than just a cricket tournament. It is Pakistan's answer to sporting isolation, a mechanism for soft power, and a tool for national cohesion. In uncertain times, the league has delivered certainty—both in terms of entertainment and in developing the next generation of Pakistani cricketing stars.

Special Capsule - India–Pakistan Finals and Trophy-Deciders

Few rivalries in world sport carry the same intensity as India versus Pakistan, and nowhere has this been more visible than in tournament finals. From Melbourne to Mirpur, these clashes have repeatedly transcended sport, becoming symbols of pride, politics, and power. Yet the balance of history tells a surprising story: Pakistan has consistently held the upper hand in finals. India's triumph at the 1985 World Championship of Cricket in Melbourne marked the first great milestone, a dominant victory that seemed to herald a long period of supremacy. But a year later, Javed Miandad's last-ball six in the 1986 Austral-Asia Cup Final turned the narrative. That moment did not merely win Pakistan the match; it etched a psychological scar that lingered for years. The Sharjah years of the late 1980s and early 1990s cemented Pakistan's reputation as a finals team. They beat India decisively in the 1989 Rothmans Champions Trophy, the 1991 Wills Trophy, and the 1994 Pepsi Austral-Asia Cup, each time asserting dominance in front of packed Gulf crowds where the expatriate South Asian community turned Sharjah into a cauldron.

India did strike back memorably in the 1998 Independence Cup in Dhaka, chasing 316 in the decider, one of their most famous ODI victories. But 1999 proved brutal: Pakistan thrashed India in both the Pepsi Cup Final in Bengaluru and the Coca-Cola Cup Final in Sharjah, winning by massive margins.

The new millennium brought shifts in momentum. Under MS Dhoni's leadership, India clinched a dramatic victory in the 2007 World T20 Final in Johannesburg — a symbolic win that marked the beginning of India's prominence in the T20 format. Pakistan, however, reasserted their strength in key regional and multilateral clashes, securing the 2008 Kitply Cup Final and, most memorably, the 2017 ICC Champions Trophy Final at The Oval, where they defeated India by 180 runs. More recently, India claimed the 2025 Asia Cup title with a win over Pakistan, narrowing the head-to-head tally in tournament finals.

While India has maintained an excellent record against Pakistan in ICC World Cup matches, Pakistan has traditionally held the upper hand in final and Test encounters, leading 12–9. This asymmetry — where each side has excelled in different pressure environments — remains one of the defining dynamics of their storied rivalry.

Reader's Notes

Salman Ali Agha – *Newly appointed captain in 2025, Salman is seen as a technically solid batter and mature cricketing mind. He now faces the challenge of leading Pakistan through a turbulent transitional phase.*

Mohammad Rizwan – *A passionate and dependable wicketkeeper-batter known for his discipline and consistency across formats. Rizwan has been handed white-ball leadership responsibilities and remains a core pillar of the team.*

Babar Azam – *Regarded as one of Pakistan's most gifted batters in recent memory. Though he stepped down as captain, his elegant batting and leadership between 2019–2024 defined a generation striving for relevance.*

Shaheen Shah Afridi – *Pakistan's pace spearhead post-2019, Shaheen delivered some iconic spells, particularly in T20 cricket. Injuries and inconsistency have sometimes hampered his rhythm, but he remains crucial to Pakistan's plans.*

Shadab Khan – *An energetic all-rounder with leadership experience, Shadab was expected to be the long-term T20 captain. His flair and versatility in the middle overs remain vital, especially in white-ball formats.*

Naseem Shah – *A teenage sensation who burst onto the scene with a five-wicket haul and a Test hat-trick. Seen as the next fast-bowling great if managed carefully through injuries and form fluctuations.*

Abrar Ahmed – *A mystery spinner with a unique action, Abrar has emerged as a promising Test asset, particularly on turning tracks. He impressed with sharp turn and control in home Tests post-2022.*

Agha Salman – *Apart from captaincy, Salman has brought middle-order stability in Tests, often stepping up when the top order fails. His ability to bat long and offer off-spin makes him a vital team balance figure.*

Saud Shakeel – *A patient and compact batter, Saud made a name for himself in Test matches with a calm temperament and ability to occupy the crease for long innings.*

Operation Sindhoor & ICC Fallout – *The recent Indo-Pak military flare-up (2024–2025) had sporting consequences too. India's refusal to play ICC Champions Trophy matches in Pakistan shifted fixtures to UAE, reigniting debates over neutrality, diplomacy, and BCCI's influence on global cricket structures.*

The Pakistan Super League (PSL) *is a professional Twenty20 cricket league founded in 2015, featuring city-based franchises competing annually.*

It was established to revive high-quality cricket in Pakistan during a period of international isolation and has since become a key platform for talent development and fan engagement.

Chapter 9 – Sri Lanka's Journey: From Outsiders to World Champions

9.1 Early Years and Test Status (1981–1984)

Sri Lanka's journey to becoming a Test-playing nation was not a tale of overnight elevation but a long, defiant walk through years of marginalization, global skepticism, and an early thirst for recognition. Their presence in the inaugural Prudential World Cup in 1975, while largely symbolic, announced their intent to the cricketing establishment. Competing as a non-Test nation, Sri Lanka faced full-member giants with limited experience and scant resources. The results were predictably one-sided in both the 1975 and 1979 editions—Sri Lanka lost most of their matches convincingly—but there were glimmers of possibility. The watershed moment came in the 1979 World Cup when Sri Lanka stunned a full-strength Indian team at Old Trafford. That upset was more than just a win—it was a geopolitical statement. It legitimized their potential and stirred murmurs in the corridors of the International Cricket Council that perhaps the "outsiders" from the island deserved a seat at the main table.

Among the key catalysts that supported their cause was the growing international sentiment around expanding the Test fraternity beyond the colonial core. Sri Lanka's cricket board was assertive, lobbying strongly for full membership, and the political goodwill from nations like India and Pakistan, both of whom were pushing for regional solidarity in cricket, further strengthened their case. It also helped that during this period, players like Roy Dias, Duleep Mendis, and Bandula Warnapura were gaining reputations as technically sound and fiercely competitive cricketers in the limited international opportunities they were afforded.

In 1981, the long wait ended—Sri Lanka was granted full Test status, becoming the eighth nation to join the elite club. Their inaugural Test came against England in Colombo in February 1982. It was a grand occasion, not just in cricketing terms but also culturally and nationally, attended by dignitaries and watched with pride across the island. Though Sri Lanka lost the match by seven wickets, they impressed observers with their discipline and resilience. Ian Botham, the talismanic English all-rounder, who had visited Sri Lanka on prior tours, remarked positively about their potential and temperament, offering a kind of validation that resonated in the media back in England.

The early Test years were predictably difficult, as Sri Lanka faced more experienced and physically dominant teams. They lost series to Pakistan and New Zealand in quick succession, both away and at home. However, the team began showing grit. They secured a respectable draw in India and again during their visit to England in 1984. These results, though modest in numbers, signaled that Sri Lanka was not just here to participate—they were learning, absorbing, and evolving quickly. The cricket world began taking note that the islanders, who once played as cheerful underdogs, were slowly transforming into a nation that would someday challenge the world order.

9.2 – Arjuna Ranatunga's Leadership and the 1996 Wills World Cup

Sri Lanka's transformation from a team of underdogs to world champions was far from linear. The mid-1980s brought a mixture of occasional milestones and long spells of frustration. However, even in these early years, a spirit of defiance began to stir within Sri Lankan cricket—a will to assert identity, not just as participants in the global game but as serious contenders. This quiet revolution found its voice in the steady emergence of domestic stalwarts and an eventual leader who would rewrite Sri Lanka's cricketing destiny—Arjuna Ranatunga.

The first breakthrough came in 1985 when Sri Lanka registered their first-ever Test series victory, and that too against mighty India. The 1–0 triumph in a three-match home series was a bold declaration that the islanders were no longer merely filling the fixture list. Roy Dias, Arjuna Ranatunga, and Duleep Mendis formed the spine of a team learning to punch above its weight. Yet, this moment of triumph was fleeting. Over the next eight years, Sri Lanka would struggle for consistency in the Test arena. Series after series, both at home and abroad, exposed their lack of depth, experience, and at times, mental resilience. Not until 1992/93 would they again win a Test series.

In the limited-overs format, however, signs of promise flickered earlier. The 1986 Asia Cup was a defining moment. Sri Lanka, still not considered serious contenders in ODIs, pulled off a stunning triumph over tournament favorites Pakistan in the final. It was a statement win—proof that the islanders had both the tactical acumen and raw aggression to rattle top teams. The win brought Sri Lanka their first major silverware in international cricket and added a layer of belief to their growing confidence.

The Reliance World Cup in 1987 offered another glimpse into their evolving character. While they didn't advance deep into the tournament, Sri Lanka competed with intent, pushing stronger sides and improving their net run rate and match discipline. These were formative years in which they were often outgunned but rarely out-spirited. It was becoming increasingly evident that Sri Lanka was not merely trying to survive at the top—they were preparing to thrive.

Still, their Test form remained brittle. A notorious example came during the 1992 home Test series against Australia, where Sri Lanka suffered one of the most heartbreaking chokes in their history. Having dominated large portions of the match and well poised to win the series, the team crumbled at crucial moments. Tactical lapses and nerves exposed the side's struggle with sealing victories against elite opposition, a recurring issue during this era.

Yet even amid these frustrations, Sri Lanka began carving out a reputation in ODIs as a team capable of the spectacular. The 1992 World Cup saw one of the most memorable chases of the time. Against Zimbabwe, they chased down a then-record target of 312, showcasing a previously unseen explosiveness in their batting approach. This was followed by a victory over South Africa—one of the tournament's strongest teams. Though they didn't reach the semifinals, Sri Lanka had demonstrated flashes of the fearless cricket that would later become their signature.

The years leading up to 1996 were a period of quiet foundation-building. Wins in tri-nation tournaments, particularly the 1995 Sharjah Cup, were symbolic. They weren't just competing anymore—they were beginning to win consistently. But the seismic shift came during their historic 1995 tour of Pakistan. There, Sri Lanka not only stunned the hosts by winning the Test series 2–1—Pakistan's first home series loss in 15 years—but did so with authority. It was a triumph that validated years of struggle and rebuilding. It was the series where Arjuna Ranatunga's leadership truly matured, where players like Sanath Jayasuriya and Romesh Kaluwitharana were unleashed with a new sense of freedom, and where the groundwork was laid for something unprecedented.

Ranatunga was no flamboyant figure. He was stocky, slow between wickets, and disinterested in the aesthetics of cricket. But he was a thinker—a master of cricketing psychology, a strategic manipulator of game situations, and a man who understood that leadership in Sri Lanka meant more than just field placements. He shielded his team from criticism, confronted bullying from more powerful cricketing boards, and re-engineered the team's mindset from inferiority to insurgency.

The 1996 Wills World Cup was the culmination of this ideological and tactical overhaul. Sri Lanka came into the tournament as dark horses. Their preparation had been unconventional transforming their batting style to embrace all-out aggression at the top. Jayasuriya and Kaluwitharana were assigned a singular role: go berserk in the first 15 overs. And they did. Their revolutionary approach tore apart oppositions, setting a new blueprint for ODI batting.

In their group stage match against Zimbabwe, Sri Lanka piled on 397 runs—then the highest team total in ODI history. The cricketing world was stunned by the relentlessness of their batting. The victory against India in the group stage was another psychological landmark; they chased a steep target with unnerving ease, again headlined by Jayasuriya's blitzkrieg.

However, not all teams agreed to play in Sri Lanka. Australia and the West Indies refused to travel to Colombo, citing security concerns. Their matches were forfeited, giving Sri Lanka free points. Critics scoffed at their route to the knockout stages, but Sri Lanka silenced them with cricketing authority.

The quarterfinal against England was nothing short of a blitz. Jayasuriya smashed the English attack with impunity, turning the match into a lopsided affair. But it was the semi-final at Eden Gardens, Calcutta, that would etch Sri Lanka's name in cricketing folklore.

Facing a red-hot Indian side that had just eliminated Pakistan, Sri Lanka were put in to bat by Azharuddin on a pitch expected to deteriorate. Srinath removed both Jayasuriya and Kaluwitharana in the first over, and soon Gurusinha was also gone. At 35/3, in front of 100,000 partisan fans, India seemed to have booked their place in the final. But Aravinda de Silva had other plans. He counterattacked with a majestic 66, a mix of classical and modern stroke play. His assault was not just about runs—it was about psychological disruption. With support from

Roshan Mahanama, Tillakaratne and Ranatunga, Sri Lanka clawed their way to 251—a total that looked defendable on a slow, crumbling pitch.

India began confidently, with Sachin Ramesh Tendulkar holding the innings together. But when he was run out for 65, panic set in. What followed was a dramatic collapse. From 98/1, India slumped to 120/8. As the Eden Gardens crowd turned hostile and began setting the stadium on fire, Clive Lloyd—the match referee—awarded the game to Sri Lanka by default. It was a dark, chaotic end to a high-voltage semi-final, but it marked the beginning of a new world order.

In the final against Mark Taylor's Australia, played in Lahore, Sri Lanka completed their fairy tale. Australia batted first and posted 241. It was a challenging total because again Sri lanka lost early wickets, but the pressure was handled very well by Ranatunga and man of the match Aravinda De Silva. Once again on big occasion, Aravinda de Silva rose to the occasion. After taking 3 wickets with the ball, he produced one of the greatest innings in a World Cup final—an unbeaten century that guided Sri Lanka to a comprehensive 7-wicket win.

The symbolism was powerful. Australia, who had refused to play in Sri Lanka, were beaten in a World Cup final held in the subcontinent. The image of Benazir Bhutto handing the trophy to Arjuna Ranatunga captured the regional and political resonance of the victory. For the first time, a co-host nation had won the World Cup, and Sri Lanka had also become the first team to win a final while chasing. It was a historic performance that shattered colonial hierarchies in cricket and redefined the art of one-day batting.

Sri Lanka's triumph was not just a sporting achievement; it was a socio-cultural moment of seismic importance. It validated a decade of sacrifice, of being overlooked, of bearing condescension from the so-called 'Big Three.' A team once viewed as soft underdogs had dismantled the very structures that doubted them. The legacy of Ranatunga, De Silva, Jayasuriya, Muralitharan, and others was now eternal. The small island nation had climbed to the summit, not by copying the powerful, but by inventing a style of their own.

Reader's Notes

Arjuna Ranatunga – *Sri Lanka's first great captain and the architect of their 1996 World Cup triumph. Known for his shrewdness, defiance, and strategic mind, Ranatunga commanded immense respect and helped shape a fearless Sri Lankan side that believed it belonged on the world stage.*

Sanath Jayasuriya & Romesh Kaluwitharana – *This explosive opening pair changed the landscape of ODI cricket. Jayasuriya's brutal hitting and Kaluwitharana's unorthodox aggression made full use of the fielding restrictions in the first 15 overs, laying the foundation for Sri Lanka's revolutionary batting approach.*

Aravinda de Silva – *The most elegant and technically refined Sri Lankan batter of his era. His match-winning century and three wickets in the 1996 World Cup final are part of cricket folklore. De Silva played a pivotal role in Sri Lanka's rise through the 1990s.*

Mark Taylor – *The Australian captain during the 1996 World Cup final. Taylor's side were favourites, but were comprehensively outplayed by Sri Lanka in the final.*

Asanka Gurusinha – *A stoic and dependable No. 3 batter who often held the innings together. Known for his gritty style, Gurusinha was instrumental in stabilizing collapses and provided the glue between explosive openers and finishers in the 1996 squad.*

Roshan Mahanama – *A stylish top-order batsman and later one of cricket's most respected match referees. Mahanama played several key innings in the 1996 World Cup and was admired for his professionalism, fielding prowess, and calm temperament.*

Hashan Tillakaratne – *A gritty left-hander known for his fighting spirit in the middle order. Tillakaratne was part of the transitional phase in the late '80s and early '90s and added depth to the 1996 team with valuable contributions in pressure situations.*

Chaminda Vaas – *Emerging in the mid-90s, Vaas brought left-arm seam quality to a spin-heavy attack. Known for his control, swing, and accuracy, he was crucial in both ODIs and Tests and would later go on to become Sri Lanka's greatest pace bowler.*

Muttiah Muralitharan (early years) – *Just beginning to make his mark during this era, Murali's mysterious off-spin added teeth to Sri Lanka's bowling attack. By 1996, he was already playing key roles in dismantling opposition batting lineups and would later become a world record-holder.*

1996 Eden Gardens Semi-Final vs India – *A turning point in South Asian cricket drama. After a blistering Indian start, Sri Lanka mounted a stunning comeback. Sachin Tendulkar's run-out triggered a collapse that led to crowd violence, forcing match abandonment and default victory for Sri Lanka.*

1986 Asia Cup Win – *Sri Lanka's first major international trophy, defeating Pakistan in the final. This was the start of their ascendancy in limited-overs cricket and marked a psychological breakthrough against the stronger subcontinental sides.*

1995 Test Series Win in Pakistan – *A massive moment in Sri Lanka's Test history—beating Pakistan 2-1 in their own backyard, breaking Pakistan's 15-year unbeaten home record. It gave the team a platform of belief just months before the 1996 World Cup.*

1985 Test Series Win vs India – *Sri Lanka's first Test series victory, and it came against a strong Indian side at home. The series was a pivotal step in establishing themselves as a credible force in the longer format.*

9.3 From Underdogs to Global Contenders (1996-2007)

The 1996 World Cup triumph marked the dawn of a new cricketing era for Sri Lanka. No longer seen as outsiders or minnows, they had emphatically announced themselves as a powerhouse in the making. But the years that followed were perhaps even more important—they would reveal whether Sri Lanka could sustain that brilliance or fade into one-tournament wonders. What transpired from 1996 to 2007 was a compelling transformation: a decade of growth, regional dominance, away struggles, and a steady transition into global contenders.

Following the euphoric World Cup win, Sri Lanka embarked on a mission to build consistency across all formats. The challenge was immense: transitioning from inspired one-off performances to becoming a team that could win regularly—home and away, in Tests and ODIs.

Their first defining moment in Test cricket came in 1998, when they defeated England at The Oval in a one-off Test—Sri Lanka's first-ever away Test series win on English soil. That match is now legendary, largely due to Muttiah Muralitharan's magical 16-wicket haul. Murali, already a known force, had now graduated to wizard status. That performance validated Sri Lanka's arrival not just as limited-overs specialists but as serious red-ball contenders.

At home, Murali made Sri Lanka nearly unbeatable. Between 1996 and 2007, they won a string of Test series in Colombo, Kandy, and Galle, conquering the likes of Australia (1999), India (2001), South Africa (2004 and 2006), West Indies (2001/02), Zimbabwe, and Bangladesh. Defeating Australia in the 1999 home Test series was a landmark achievement for Sri Lanka. Coming just months after Steve Waugh's side had lifted the World Cup, the series win underscored Sri Lanka's growing maturity in the longest format. Murali's spinning web, backed by the disciplined pace of Chaminda Vaas and emerging talents like Dilhara Fernando, Herath and Nuwan Zoysa, gave Sri Lanka the variety and potency needed to consistently challenge visiting teams.

One of the most iconic Test batting feats came in 1997 against India, when Sri Lanka posted a still-unbroken world record of 952/6 declared. Sanath Jayasuriya's marathon 340 was a hallmark of endurance and flair, while Roshan Mahanama's 225 demonstrated grit. That innings didn't just crush India—it redefined what the cricketing world thought Sri Lanka could achieve in the longest format.

Overseas, they still struggled in traditionally hostile territories. They lost in Australia (1996, 2004), South Africa (1997, 2001, 2003), and had mixed results in New Zealand. These away performances exposed deficiencies in adapting to seam, bounce, and pace. But there were also flashes of brilliance—especially in the subcontinent and in England.

Notably, Sri Lanka won another famous Test series in Pakistan in 1999–2000.

The Asian Test Championship, won in 2001–02, was another feather in their cap. It was a format designed to promote Test cricket in the region, and Sri Lanka's win against traditional rivals underscored their growing confidence and tactical maturity.

While Sri Lanka's home record between 1996 and 2007 was largely formidable, there were a few notable blips that reminded the cricketing world of the game's inherent unpredictability. In 2000/01, Nasser Hussain's England side stunned the hosts by clinching a hard-fought 2–1 Test series win—marking one of the few occasions an overseas team conquered Sri Lanka's spin-heavy conditions during that era. Similarly, in 2003/04, Australia, under Ricky Ponting, displayed clinical precision in sweeping the Test series 3–0, showing that even the Galle and Kandy fortresses could be breached. These rare defeats did little to tarnish Sri Lanka's overall dominance at home but served as valuable lessons and benchmarks in their evolving journey as a cricketing powerhouse.

In ODI cricket, Sri Lanka evolved into one of the most exciting and unpredictable sides in the world. Their ODI structure, spearheaded by Arjuna Ranatunga and later transitioned to Marvan Atapattu, was enriched by the infusion of youth. Players like Mahela Jayawardene, Kumar Sangakkara, Tillakaratne Dilshan, Atapattu, Russel Arnold, and Upul Chandana began emerging, blending with the experience of Jayasuriya, Muralitharan, and Vaas to create a potent mix.

Their limited-overs success was immediate and consistent. In 1997, they won a historic tri-series in India involving India, Pakistan and New Zealand, defeating Pakistan in the final. That same year, they captured the Asia Cup beating India, further asserting their dominance in the region. In 1998, they reached the final of the Independence Cup, narrowly losing to South Africa in Lahore, but their performances were lauded for consistency and aggression.

Despite a disappointing campaign in the 1998 ICC Champions Trophy and a forgettable 1999 World Cup group-stage exit, Sri Lanka continued to regroup and rebuild. They bounced back by winning the 2002 ICC Champions Trophy. The final was washed out twice, resulting in a shared trophy with India, but Sri Lanka's path to the final was marked by disciplined bowling and clinical finishes. The Champions Trophy win was their first global trophy since 1996—and a strong message to the cricketing world that Sri Lanka was no fluke.

They won the Asia Cup again in 2004, defeating India and Pakistan in dominant fashion. Their ODI record against top teams, particularly in the subcontinent, became increasingly impressive. In 2004 and 2006, they defeated South Africa in bilateral ODI and Test series at home, showing their increasing comfort against one of the game's most feared pace attacks.

The 2003 World Cup campaign in South Africa saw them reach the semi-finals, defeating teams like South Africa and West Indies along the way. Jayasuriya led from the front, Vaas was sublime with the new ball, and Sangakkara and Jayawardene played key supporting roles. Though they were eventually eliminated by a dominant Australia in the semis, the campaign had plenty of positives.

The 2004 and 2006 ICC Champions Trophy campaigns were less successful, marred by inconsistency and fragile middle-order collapses. Yet Sri Lanka kept churning out strong bilateral series performances— winning in Pakistan, Bangladesh, and India. The bowling attack evolved with the inclusion of Lasith Malinga, whose slinging action and deadly yorkers brought a new edge to their arsenal.

Kumar Sangakkara and Mahela Jayawardene came to define this era. Elegant, intelligent, and fiercely competitive, they were the twin engines of Sri Lankan cricket. Jayawardene's ability to anchor innings and Sangakkara's flair and grit behind the stumps made them one of the most iconic duos in modern cricket. Together, they would go on to

198

carry Sri Lanka through its next great phase, but their roots were firmly planted in this foundational decade.

Other notable players who emerged during this phase included Thilan Samaraweera, a technically sound Test batsman; Malinga Bandara, a leg-spin option; Jehan Mubarak, who showed early promise; and Farveez Maharoof, a seam-bowling all-rounder who gave balance to the ODI side. Though not all reached the heights expected, they reflected a widening talent pool.

Sri Lanka had also begun improving in terms of fielding and athleticism—areas long considered weaknesses. Under foreign coaches like Dav Whatmore and Tom Moody, there was a new focus on fitness, match awareness, and data-driven preparation.

The decade wasn't without challenges. Administrative instability, an underperforming domestic structure, and political interference continued to affect selection and long-term planning. The team remained vulnerable in SENA conditions, losing Test series in Australia (2004), South Africa (multiple), and New Zealand (2004/05). Their batting lineup occasionally crumbled in conditions with lateral movement or steep bounce. But crucially, they never lost their fighting spirit.

By 2007, Sri Lanka stood on the cusp of another golden generation. Having laid solid foundations through the late 1990s and early 2000s, they had built a well-rounded, experienced, and talented squad capable of challenging any team in the world.

The journey from post-1996 volatility to mid-2000s stability was neither smooth nor linear. There were dips and detours. But the overarching story was one of remarkable transformation—from world-beaters to global contenders with staying power. As Sangakkara and Jayawardene prepared to take over the reins, Sri Lanka was no longer defined by a single World Cup win. They were now a mature cricketing nation, respected for their skill, feared for their passion, and admired for their resilience.

Readers' Notes

Muttiah Muralitharan – *The cornerstone of Sri Lanka's bowling attack, Murali's unmatched spin wizardry transformed home Tests into one-sided affairs and defined the era.*

Sanath Jayasuriya – *A trailblazing opener whose aggressive batting redefined ODI powerplays; also played a vital role as a handy left-arm spinner.*

Mahela Jayawardene – *Stylish and intelligent, he emerged as a dependable batsman and future captain, helping cement Sri Lanka's batting order.*

Kumar Sangakkara – *Technically refined and fiercely competitive, he brought class behind the stumps and with the bat, evolving into a generational figure.*

Tillakaratne Dilshan – *A dynamic stroke-maker who added depth with his all-round ability and later innovation (like the "Dilscoop").*

Thilan Samaraweera – *Provided solidity in the Test middle order, especially valuable on challenging wickets.*

Lasith Malinga – *Entered international cricket in the early 2000s, soon recognized for his slinging action and deadly yorkers, especially in ODIs.*

Rangana Herath – *Quietly emerged in the shadow of Muralitharan; a crafty left-arm spinner who later became Sri Lanka's lead spinner post-Murali era.*

Russel Arnold – *A versatile left-hander who played a supporting role in the middle order, contributing in key moments across formats.*

Upul Chandana – *Leg-spinning all-rounder known for his athletic fielding and useful lower-order hitting.*

Dilhara Fernando & Nuwan Zoysa – *Key seam options in this period, bringing pace and height to complement Vaas's control.*

Farveez Maharoof – *Emerging all-rounder toward the end of the period, known for his seam-up bowling and lower-order contributions.*

Marvan Atapattu – Stylish and composed top-order batsman who later captained the national team; known for his textbook technique, patience, and key centuries in both home and away series. He played a pivotal role in stabilizing the batting lineup in the early 2000s.

2002 ICC Champions Trophy – Shared Glory

Under Sanath Jayasuriya's captaincy, *Sri Lanka defeated Pakistan, New Zealand, and Australia before rain forced a shared final with India. This was their first ICC trophy since 1996.*

Ricky Ponting – Australia's captain in the 2003/04 series, where his team whitewashed Sri Lanka 3–0 in a rare home defeat for the islanders.

Nasser Hussain – England captain who masterminded a surprise Test series win in Sri Lanka in 2000/01, exploiting reverse swing and smart tactics.

9.4 Golden Generation, Narrow Misses: Sri Lanka's Era of ICC Finals and T20 World Cup Redemption (2007–2014)

The period between 2007 and 2014 marks a golden yet bittersweet era in Sri Lankan cricket—a time defined by brilliance, heartbreak, and eventual redemption. Rarely in the history of the game has a team consistently reached the summit so often, only to fall agonizingly short. Yet, this period also witnessed the maturation of a golden generation—Mahela Jayawardene, Kumar Sangakkara, Lasith Malinga, Tillakaratne Dilshan, and Rangana Herath—players who helped elevate Sri Lanka from proud challengers to permanent fixtures among the world's cricketing elite.

This golden run began with the 2007 ICC Cricket World Cup in the Caribbean. Sri Lanka entered the tournament with a balanced and battle-hardened squad, built around experience and youth. Jayasuriya was still a force at the top, and the Sangakkara-Jayawardene partnership was maturing into one of the finest in the world. Malinga was developing into a world-class death bowler, and Muralitharan remained at the peak of his powers. Sri Lanka defeated South Africa, England,

and New Zealand to storm into the final against the mighty Australians led by Ricky Ponting.

The final at Bridgetown, Barbados, started under heavy clouds, both literally and metaphorically. Chasing Australia's daunting 281 in a rain-reduced 38-over final, Sri Lanka got off to a steady start, but when Sanath Jayasuriya and Kumar Sangakkara were at the crease, the chase still looked plausible. However, quick wickets in the middle overs saw the effort unravel. Despite Jayawardene's calm presence, the collapse proved decisive. Australia clinched the title, and Sri Lanka had to settle for runners-up—again.

The 2009 ICC T20 World Cup in England brought renewed hope and an impressive unbeaten run into the final. Sri Lanka had overcome the trauma of the Lahore terrorist attack earlier that year, when the team bus was ambushed during a Test tour of Pakistan. The tragedy bonded the side and added emotional gravity to their T20 campaign. Malinga, Dilshan, and Sangakkara starred throughout, particularly Dilshan, whose innovative batting won him the Player of the Series award. Yet, in the final against Pakistan at Lord's, Sri Lanka faltered. Early wickets derailed their innings, and their modest total of 138 was never going to be enough. Pakistan chased it down with relative ease, giving Sri Lanka their second ICC final defeat in just two years.

If 2007 and 2009 were painful, the 2011 ODI World Cup final was excruciating. Co-hosted by Sri Lanka, India, and Bangladesh, the tournament felt like a homecoming for the Lankans. Sri Lanka played high-quality cricket throughout, with Dilshan and Tharanga providing explosive starts and the ever-dependable Sangakkara and Jayawardene controlling the middle. Malinga's ability to strike early gave the bowling unit menace. The final, held at Wankhede Stadium in Mumbai, saw Jayawardene produce a magnificent century—elegant, composed, and purposeful—to guide Sri Lanka to a competitive 274. India, however, responded with composure. Although Malinga removed Sehwag and Tendulkar early, Gautam Gambhir and MS Dhoni turned the tide.

Dhoni's famous six to seal the win relegated Sri Lanka to bridesmaids once again. This was their third ICC final loss in five years.

The 2012 ICC T20 World Cup at home should have been the redemption arc. Sri Lanka looked confident and composed throughout, feeding off home support and playing tactically astute cricket. The bowling attack, led by Malinga, Herath, and Ajantha Mendis, was varied and dangerous. In the final at R. Premadasa Stadium in Colombo, they faced a West Indies side captained by Darren Sammy. Chasing just 138, the script seemed written for a Sri Lankan win. But the pressure of the final proved too much—batsmen collapsed, and Sunil Narine spun a web around them. Losing by 36 runs on home soil was devastating. The tears of Sangakkara and the stunned silence of the Colombo crowd reflected the heartbreak.

Despite these setbacks, Sri Lanka kept pushing. The resilience of the team, and the refusal to allow disappointment to define them, were perhaps the greatest hallmarks of this era.

Finally, in 2014, the stars aligned. The ICC T20 World Cup in Bangladesh became the stage for Sri Lanka's long-awaited redemption. Captained by Lasith Malinga after Dinesh Chandimal stepped down during the tournament, the team played with measured aggression. The bowlers were miserly and incisive throughout the tournament. In the final at Mirpur, Sri Lanka faced India, a formidable team led by MS Dhoni. Sri Lanka's bowlers were superb, limiting India to just 130 in 20 overs. Herath's control and Malinga's yorkers stifled the Indian middle order. In response, Kumar Sangakkara played a match-winning innings of 52* in his final T20 international, ensuring Sri Lanka won by six wickets. The scenes of celebration were cathartic—after losing four ICC finals, Sri Lanka finally had their moment. For Mahela and Sanga, both nearing retirements, it was a fairy-tale finish.

Parallel to their ICC campaigns, Sri Lanka remained a potent force in the Asia Cup. They lifted the trophy in 2008 under Jayawardene and again in 2014 under Angelo Mathews. These victories, against competitive regional rivals like India, Pakistan, and Bangladesh, underlined Sri Lanka's continued relevance in the ODI format.

The Test arena saw mixed results. At home, Sri Lanka continued to be a challenging side. They won Test series against India (2008), New Zealand (2009), and Pakistan (2009 and 2014), and drew with England in 2011 and 2012. However, they also suffered defeats at home to Australia and South Africa during that phase. Away from home, the struggles persisted. Heavy defeats in Australia (2007, 2012/13) and South Africa (2011/12) exposed their vulnerabilities in pace-friendly conditions. Nonetheless, the team registered a historic Test series win in England in 2014—a landmark achievement, marking their second Test series triumph on English soil since 1998. That win, built around gritty batting and disciplined bowling, was one of the high points of the era.

A monumental chapter closed when Muttiah Muralitharan retired in 2010, finishing with an unmatched 800 Test wickets. His final delivery in Test cricket yielded a wicket—a poetic ending to a career that had redefined spin bowling. Murali's records are staggering, and his influence incalculable. No bowler, before or since, has dictated games so completely through sheer spin wizardry.

Meanwhile, Rangana Herath seamlessly filled the void left by Murali. Understated but supremely effective, Herath emerged as Sri Lanka's spin lynchpin, especially in the latter half of this period. His left-arm orthodox spin proved decisive in victories against Pakistan, India, and New Zealand. Herath's rise was symbolic of Sri Lanka's ability to renew itself even as legends departed.

Leadership during this period was stable and thoughtful. Jayawardene, Sangakkara, and later Angelo Mathews captained with a blend of tactical acumen and calm. Coaches like Trevor Bayliss and Graham Ford brought international professionalism, helping the team adapt to evolving demands of the modern game.

Beyond statistics and silverware, what defined this era was its consistency. Between 2007 and 2014, Sri Lanka reached five ICC finals—more than any other side from Asia in that span.

This level of consistency was unprecedented for a team from the subcontinent. Not even Pakistan, with its glorious past, or very strong Indian side, with its vast resources, could match this feat during the same timeframe. The disappointment of the near misses only enhances the value of their eventual triumph.

Several players etched their names into cricket history during this time. Dilshan's innovation at the top, especially with the "Dilscoop," redefined T20 batting. Sangakkara and Jayawardene not only amassed runs but elevated the standard of Sri Lankan cricket through their leadership, discipline, and vision. Malinga's unique slinging action made him a feared bowler globally, particularly in T20s. Mathews emerged as a dependable all-rounder, anchoring both innings and leadership in the post-Sanga-Mahela era.

Nuwan Kulasekara, Thisara Perera, Chamara Kapugedera, and Jehan Mubarak provided depth and flexibility. The team fielded better, ran harder, and embraced innovation in formats where adaptability was key.

Still, challenges remained. The domestic structure struggled to produce replacements at the rate required. Political interference in team selections and board governance remained issues. But the team's resilience, forged through repeated heartbreak, helped mask these structural concerns for the time being.

By 2014, as the careers of Sangakkara and Jayawardene approached their twilight, the golden generation could look back with immense pride. They had not just won matches—they had redefined Sri Lankan cricket's global identity. From humble beginnings to a feared multi-format powerhouse, Sri Lanka's rise was inspirational.

The journey from the heartbreak of 2007 to the redemption of 2014 is one of the most compelling arcs in modern cricket history from Asia. For seven years, Sri Lanka hovered near greatness, only to fall just short—until the final burst brought glory. This era left a legacy of belief, a blueprint for consistent performance, and a generation of players who became heroes not for just winning but for daring to chase greatness.

Reader's Notes

Sri Lanka reached five ICC finals between 2007 and 2014, *including two ODI World Cup finals (2007, 2011) and three T20 World Cup finals (2009, 2012, 2014), an unmatched feat in that era.*

2007 ODI World Cup Final: *Sri Lanka lost to Australia. The chase looked promising with Jayasuriya and Sangakkara, but a middle-order collapse derailed the effort.*

2009 ICC T20 World Cup Final: *Played at Lord's, Sri Lanka's early batting collapse led to a below-par total, which Pakistan chased comfortably. Tillakaratne Dilshan had been Sri Lanka's star performer leading to the final.*

Lahore Attack, 2009: *The Sri Lankan team was targeted in a terror attack in Pakistan, an event that shook the cricket world. Despite the trauma, the team displayed immense courage and went on to play the 2009 T20 final just months later.*

2011 ODI World Cup Final: *Despite dismissing Sehwag and Tendulkar early, Sri Lanka couldn't contain MS Dhoni, who led India to a memorable win. Jayawardene's classy century went in vain.*

2012 T20 World Cup Final (at home): *Sri Lanka failed to chase down a modest target of 138 against West Indies. Sunil Narine's bowling and Marlon Samuels' big hits were decisive.*

2014 ICC T20 World Cup Triumph: *Sri Lanka finally broke the final jinx, defeating India in Dhaka. Sangakkara played a calm match-winning knock in his farewell T20I, sealing an emotional victory.*

Muttiah Muralitharan retired in 2010 *with* **800 Test wickets**, *the highest in Test history—a milestone considered nearly unbreakable.*

Sri Lanka won Asia Cups in 2008 and 2014, showcasing their continued regional dominance in ODIs and T20s.

Emerging and Key Players (2007–2014): Lahiru Thirimanne, Dilshan, Thisara Perera, Angelo Mathews (as an all-rounder and future captain), Rangana Herath (Murali's successor), and Nuwan Kulasekara were central to the team's success during this period.

9.5 – A Slow Unravelling: Decline, Transition, and the Elusive Resilience (2015–Present)

The story of Sri Lankan cricket since 2015 has been a sobering contrast to the heady heights of the previous two decades. Once celebrated for their flair, tactical innovation, and competitive consistency, Sri Lanka entered a turbulent period that saw them regress from tournament finalists to early exits, from home dominators to hosts who frequently lost their stronghold, and from producers of generational legends to a team still searching for stability. While there have been sparks of brilliance, the broader narrative has been one of decline—on the field, in administrative decision-making, and in public enthusiasm.

The moment many point to as the beginning of this downward spiral came in 2015, when Pakistan toured Sri Lanka and defeated the hosts 2-1 in a Test series. This defeat wasn't merely a loss in numbers—it symbolized the end of an era. Coming off the retirements of stalwarts like Kumar Sangakkara and Mahela Jayawardene, Sri Lanka had suddenly become a team with a leadership vacuum and an untested core. The psychological impact of losing at home to a subcontinental rival underlined the vulnerability that would plague the team in the coming years.

The losses didn't stop there. That same year, India also came and beat Sri Lanka 2-1 in a closely fought Test series. The transition was in full swing, and while there was hope in some emerging talents, the weight of replacing players with over 10,000 runs and double-century pedigrees was a task beyond the new generation's readiness. Sri Lanka's reputation as a near-invincible team at home—especially in the spin-friendly dustbowls of Galle and Colombo—began to erode, with foreign teams exploiting cracks that were once impenetrable.

Ironically, just a year after the 2015 nadir, Sri Lanka produced one of their most stunning performances of the modern era—whitewashing the then number one ranked Test team, Australia, 3-0 in the 2016 series. This was a high point that seemed to signal a potential turnaround. Rangana Herath, the wily left-arm spinner who had emerged from Murali's shadow, ran riot on turning tracks. The likes of Dinesh Chandimal and Kusal Mendis chipped in with crucial runs. Australia, boasting players like Steve Smith and David Warner, looked clueless against Sri Lanka's renewed aggression and spin assault. This victory was not only emphatic but also historic—it marked Sri Lanka's first-ever series whitewash against Australia.

Again in 2018, they displayed another astonishing feat: defeating South Africa 2-0 at home, with commanding displays that revived their fortress reputation, albeit briefly. But even more impressive was what followed. In 2019, Sri Lanka became the first-ever Asian team to win a Test series in South Africa, defeating the Proteas 2-0 away from home. Led by Dimuth Karunaratne and propelled by sensational performances from Kusal Perera, including a once-in-a-generation fourth-innings 153* in Durban, this victory stood as a beacon of hope—a sign that the team was still capable of producing magic.

However, these highs have been few and far between. The broader pattern since 2015 has been defined by inconsistency, collapses, and missed opportunities. Sri Lanka have regularly lost Test series at home, something unthinkable in the era of Muralitharan and Jayawardene. England defeated them in 2018 and again in 2021. India, Pakistan, and even Bangladesh have come away with results. Their overseas performances have remained poor, with series defeats in Australia (2018/19, 2024/25), South Africa (2020/21, 2024/25), and New Zealand (multiple occasions). Despite occasional drawn series and standalone Test victories, Sri Lanka have failed to string together consistent performances.

In the limited-overs formats, their decline has been even more glaring and alarming. After reaching five ICC finals between 2007 and 2014, Sri Lanka have not appeared in a single ICC tournament final since. Their World Cup campaigns in 2019 and 2023 were particularly forgettable. The 2019 edition saw them finish outside the top five, winning only three matches. Sri Lanka failed to finish in the top 8 of the 2023 World Cup standings and thus did not qualify for the 2025 ICC Champions Trophy in UAE/Pakistan. It marked the first time in history that Sri Lanka missed out on participation in a global 50-over ICC event purely due to performance. Humiliating 50 all out against India in the Asia Cup final 2023 was also one of the lowest points in Sri Lanka's cricket history. Touted as an exciting, youthful side before the tournament, the capitulation brought back memories of the team's deep-rooted structural issues.

Their T20 World Cup performances have fared no better. In the 2016, 2021, 2022 and 2024 editions, Sri Lanka failed to reach the semi-finals. The decline was sharp compared to the golden stretch where they reached three T20 finals and won in 2014. The once-feared bowling attack, particularly in the death overs, lost its sting. Malinga's retirement left a void that has yet to be filled convincingly.

Amidst all this, Sri Lanka's Asia Cup win in 2022 remains a glowing outlier. Under Dasun Shanaka's captaincy, the team stunned favorites India and Pakistan to lift the title in the UAE. The likes of Bhanuka Rajapaksa, Wanindu Hasaranga, and Pathum Nissanka played fearless cricket, drawing comparisons to Sri Lanka's bold 1996 side. The victory showed that talent still existed—what was lacking was direction, development, and consistent nurturing.

This period also saw Sri Lanka's entry into the T20 franchise world with the Lanka Premier League (LPL), launched in 2020. Modeled after the

IPL and other global leagues, LPL was designed to bring structure, revenue, and international exposure to local players. Though still finding its footing, the league has provided a platform for emerging stars like Matheesha Pathirana and Dunith Wellalage to share dressing rooms with global icons. However, its long-term impact remains uncertain, especially in a cricketing ecosystem marred by inconsistent governance.

One of the root causes of this decline has been administrative instability. Constant changes in selectors, frequent captaincy switches, and a revolving door of head coaches have made it impossible to build momentum. Political interference and short-term thinking have undermined team cohesion and player confidence. Financial issues and poor domestic infrastructure have also contributed to the stunted growth of potential stars.

Another glaring issue has been the failure to replace the old guard. With the retirement of Sangakkara, Jayawardene, Malinga, and Dilshan, Sri Lanka were left with a leadership vacuum. While players like Dinesh Chandimal, Angelo Mathews, and Karunaratne have had their moments, none have consistently provided the performances or aura that defined their predecessors. Young talents such as Avishka Fernando, Charith Asalanka, and Hasaranga have shown promise but lacked long-term consistency.

Despite these challenges, it's important to note that Sri Lanka still produces quality cricketers. Their school cricket system remains among the most passionate and widespread in the world. The problem isn't the pipeline—it's the transition. Talents are identified but not developed. Players shine briefly before fading due to poor fitness standards, technical deficiencies, or mental burnout.

In Tests, even as performances have dipped, individual milestones have brought pride. Rangana Herath's final years were a masterclass in spin bowling, and he retired with over 400 Test wickets. Dimuth

Karunaratne has been one of the few stable batting figures, anchoring innings amid collapses. Young spinners like Prabath Jayasuriya and Maheesh Theekshana suggest there's spin talent waiting in the wings.

Off the field, cricket's cultural position in Sri Lanka is also under strain. With poor results and lack of heroes to idolize, public interest has waned. The days of packed Galle Fort stadiums and schoolchildren painting their faces with Sri Lankan flags are less common now. Media scrutiny has intensified, often pointing fingers at the board rather than players. Calls for reform have grown louder, but change has been slow and superficial.

One of the defining symptoms of Sri Lanka's decline in this era has been their inability to close out crucial matches, even from winning positions. A particularly painful example came during the 2017 ICC Champions Trophy, in a virtual quarterfinal against Pakistan. Sri Lanka had their regional rivals on the ropes, with just one wicket standing between them and a spot in the semi-finals. However, a series of dropped catches—most notably reprieves given to Sarfaraz Ahmed—proved costly. Sarfaraz capitalized on those chances, steering Pakistan to a dramatic victory. Their ICC rankings have plummeted across formats, and in some years, they've had to play qualifying rounds just to enter major tournaments. For a team that once set trends, they now chase shadows.

Yet, not all hope is lost. The 2022 Asia Cup win, the LPL's growing traction, and performances like the Test win in South Africa show that with the right strategy, Sri Lanka can revive. But it will require introspection, investment in grassroots cricket, and above all, patience. Sri Lanka need to stop searching for the next Sangakkara and start building players who can define their own era.

This is a time of reckoning for Sri Lankan cricket. The golden generation is gone. The legacy they left behind demands more than nostalgia—it demands accountability, planning, and a vision for the future. The nation that once captured the world's imagination with flair and fight now stands at a crossroads. Whether they descend further or rise again depends not just on talent but on the will to rebuild.

As of 2025, Sri Lanka remains a cricketing nation with proud traditions, immense potential, and a passionate fan base. What it lacks is direction. The next chapter will not write itself—it must be earned, one gritty innings, one inspired spell, and one bold decision at a time. A strong Sri Lankan team is not just vital for the nation's pride but essential for the health of world cricket, ensuring balance, diversity, and richer competition on the global stage.

Special Capsule Lanka Premier League: Sri Lanka's Domestic Lifeline in the T20 Era

The Lanka Premier League (LPL), launched in 2020, represents Sri Lanka's strategic entry into the world of franchise-based T20 cricket. Modeled on the success of global leagues like the IPL and PSL, the LPL was conceived not just as a sporting event, but as a platform for economic recovery, talent development, and global visibility for Sri Lankan cricket—particularly during a period marked by financial instability and post-2015 team decline.

The timing of its launch—during the height of the COVID-19 pandemic—was as audacious as it was risky. With limited international cricket and commercial activity, Sri Lanka Cricket (SLC) partnered with private investors and international stakeholders to create a product that could revive domestic interest, attract foreign players, and engage fans globally via digital platforms. The league's initial seasons were held in bio-secure bubbles in Hambantota, under tight health protocols, yet they managed to draw millions of online viewers and generate strong social media traction.

The LPL features city-based franchises such as Colombo Strikers, Galle Titans, and Jaffna Kings, which bring regional flavor to the national game. Importantly, the league has been a launchpad for Sri Lanka's emerging talents. Players like Charith Asalanka, Pathum Nissanka, Matheesha Pathirana, and Maheesh Theekshana gained recognition through strong LPL performances—subsequently earning national call-ups and even IPL contracts. The league has also given seasoned domestic performers a new stage to showcase their skills and extend their careers.

However, the LPL also faces several challenges. Frequent changes in franchise ownership, delayed payments to players, and governance concerns have raised questions about its long-term financial stability. Furthermore, the league has occasionally leaned heavily on foreign players who are either past their prime or excluded from top-tier international selection—raising concerns similar to those surrounding the PSL and other second-tier leagues.

Despite these flaws, the LPL remains Sri Lanka's most commercially viable cricket product outside the national team. It provides SLC with much-needed broadcasting revenue, creates off-season engagement, and—perhaps most crucially—helps retain young Sri Lankan cricketers within the domestic system rather than losing them to global franchise circuits too early.

Moving forward, the LPL's credibility will depend on consistent scheduling, transparent governance, and strategic alignment with the national team's talent pipeline. If managed effectively, it can play a crucial role in reversing the post-2015 decline of Sri Lankan cricket and contribute to rebuilding the golden aura last seen in the Sangakkara-Jayawardene era.

In a cricketing ecosystem where T20 leagues have become central to financial survival and narrative relevance, the Lanka Premier League is not a luxury—it is a necessity. For a proud cricketing nation trying to rediscover its footing, the LPL offers not just entertainment, but a roadmap back to global competitiveness.

Reader's Notes

Kusal Mendis – *A stylish right-hander who burst onto the scene in 2016 with a memorable century against Australia; hailed early as a successor to Sangakkara but has struggled with consistency.*

Dinesh Chandimal – *Former Test captain known for his gritty middle-order batting; part of the transitional core, providing experience amid frequent team changes.*

Dimuth Karunaratne – *Became Sri Lanka's most dependable Test opener in the post-Sanga era and captained the side during a turbulent phase with steady hands.*

Angelo Mathews – *One of the few consistent performers during the decline; former captain whose all-round ability often carried the side in crucial matches.*

Niroshan Dickwella – *An aggressive wicketkeeper-batsman known for flair and unpredictability; symbolic of Sri Lanka's raw but inconsistent talent pool.*

Dhananjaya de Silva – *A technically sound batsman and handy off-spinner who became a reliable figure in both red and white ball formats.*

Pathum Nissanka – *A promising modern-day opener who has shown glimpses of solidity and temperament, especially in Test cricket.*

Lasith Malinga (T20 captain) – *Played a pivotal leadership role in the 2014 T20 World Cup triumph and remained a T20 specialist until retirement, mentoring the next generation.*

Wanindu Hasaranga – *A new-age all-rounder and leg-spinner with match-winning T20 abilities; his performances have been one of the few bright spots in recent years.*

Lanka Premier League (LPL) – *Launched in 2020, Sri Lanka's T20 franchise competition aimed to emulate the IPL model; while still growing, it has helped unearth emerging talent and keep the domestic game relevant.*

Part V – Emerging Nations and Global Expansion

Chapter 10 – Against the Tide: Bangladesh Cricket's Journey Through Turmoil and Triumph (1971–2025)

The story of Bangladesh cricket is one of slow-burning resilience, heartbreak, and small glories carved through long struggles. Emerging from the ashes of a brutal war in 1971 that led to its independence from Pakistan, Bangladesh pursued cricket with a conviction that defied structural, economic, and political limitations. The nation's sporting story is intrinsically tied to its national identity, and its cricketing rise has symbolized both ambition and aspiration on the world stage.

Cricket in Bangladesh, introduced during British colonial rule, began taking national significance after the country's independence. Early efforts at developing a coherent domestic structure met several challenges — limited infrastructure, low investment, and frequent political instability. Nonetheless, cricket spread widely through schools, universities, and local clubs, often in the absence of well-maintained grounds or formal training.

In 1977, the ICC recognized Bangladesh as an Associate Member, giving them access to international tournaments such as the ICC Trophy. Their performances in these early competitions were spirited but inconsistent. However, the cricketing world took notice in 1997 when Bangladesh won the ICC Trophy in Malaysia, thereby qualifying for the 1999 Cricket World Cup — their first appearance at a global ICC event.

It was in that 1999 World Cup that Bangladesh delivered a defining moment in their cricket history: a stunning victory over Pakistan. The win, driven by disciplined bowling and inspired fielding, shook the cricketing world and galvanized national pride back home. It was also a significant political moment; defeating a regional giant like Pakistan had implications beyond sport, serving as a soft-power triumph for a still-developing nation. The World Cup victory laid the foundation for Bangladesh's elevation to Test status the following year.

In June 2000, Bangladesh was granted full Test status by the ICC, becoming the tenth nation to enter the format. The decision was met with optimism and skepticism alike — while their passion and potential were acknowledged, their competitiveness in the longest format was in doubt. Unfortunately, many of those concerns would be realized in the coming years.

Bangladesh's entry into Test cricket came against the mighty India in November 2000 in Dhaka. The occasion was historic and emotionally charged, with Bangladesh putting on a fighting performance in their debut innings. However, India comfortably won by 9 wickets, and it set the tone for what became a prolonged period of struggle for the fledgling Test side.

Between 2000 and 2005, Bangladesh played a staggering 35 Test matches without winning a single one. Most of them ended in heavy defeats, often by an innings. In fact, their maiden Test victory only came in January 2005 against a depleted Zimbabwe side, and their first Test series win arrived during the same tour.

The early 2000s were marked by severe defeats to almost every Test-playing nation. Bangladesh was whitewashed by Australia, South Africa, England, Pakistan, and Sri Lanka repeatedly. In 2003, they came agonizingly close to defeating Pakistan in Multan, only to be denied by an Inzamam-ul-Haq masterclass. His unbeaten 138, aided by tailenders and dropped catches, rescued Pakistan to a one-wicket victory. That single match — so near yet so far — haunted Bangladesh for years. It symbolized their frustrating inability to close out games even when in commanding positions.

Throughout the 2000s, Bangladesh lacked experience, depth, and a bowling attack capable of sustaining pressure across five days. While players like Habibul Bashar, Mohammad Ashraful, and Mashrafe Mortaza offered moments of brilliance, the overall structure was too weak to challenge top-tier teams.

It wasn't until the mid-2010s that Bangladesh began to seriously turn heads in the Test arena. With a more professional domestic structure in place, greater investments from the BCB (Bangladesh Cricket Board), and a maturing generation of players, the Tigers began to hold their own — particularly in home conditions.

The first significant signs of improvement came in 2016 and 2017. Bangladesh achieved their first Test victory over England at home in 2016, and in 2017, they drew a two-Test series 1-1 against Australia — including a historic victory in Dhaka. Their long-standing hoodoo against Pakistan was finally broken in 2015 in the limited-overs format, and although Pakistan won the lone Test of that series, it reflected a shifting power dynamic.

In the same period, Bangladesh won a Test in Sri Lanka (2017), drew with India at home, and began showing resilience against top teams. Mehidy Hasan Miraz's emergence as a world-class spinner, alongside the pace duo of Taskin Ahmed and Mustafizur Rahman, gave the attack some teeth, particularly on subcontinental pitches.

The series win against West Indies in 2009 and 2018 (home and away), a drawn series with New Zealand in 2023, and their 2024 Test series victory over Pakistan marked notable highs in what had historically been a difficult Test journey. However, Bangladesh's away record still leaves much to be desired. The team has often been non-competitive on bouncier or seaming tracks in South Africa, New Zealand, and Australia — a reflection of both technical limitations and a lack of exposure to such conditions.

No discussion of Bangladesh cricket is complete without Shakib Al Hasan — arguably the country's greatest ever cricketer. A world-class all-rounder, Shakib has carried the side across all formats for nearly two decades. His consistency, temperament, and ability to deliver under pressure elevated Bangladesh's competitiveness and global standing.

Tamim Iqbal, with his audacious strokeplay; Mushfiqur Rahim, the steady middle-order anchor; and Mahmudullah, the quiet match-winner, have all formed the core of the team during its most successful phases. Mustafizur Rahman's arrival in 2015 brought a rare x-factor to Bangladesh's bowling attack, while bowlers like Taijul Islam and Shoriful Islam have developed into dependable options.

Soumya Sarkar and Litton Das, though inconsistent, have shown flashes of brilliance, underlining that the talent pipeline exists — but consistency and discipline remain developmental gaps.

In the shorter formats, Bangladesh have shown more promise but are still plagued by inconsistency. Their ODI journey began with a bang — a stunning win over Pakistan in the 1999 World Cup that catapulted them toward Test status. In 2007, they stunned India in the World Cup, knocking them out and advancing to the Super 8 stage. The 2015 World Cup quarterfinal appearance and victories over South Africa, England, and Pakistan in bilateral series built the case for Bangladesh being a strong ODI unit.

Yet, despite all that, Bangladesh have never reached an ICC event final in either ODIs or T20Is. Their only semifinal appearance remains the 2017 ICC Champions Trophy, where they were dismantled by India. The 2012 Asia Cup final against Pakistan — which Bangladesh lost by just 2 runs — remains a painful near-miss in their quest for silverware.

With a passionate fanbase and home advantage, expectations have often outweighed delivery.

In T20Is, Bangladesh's record is modest. Their performances in global T20 tournaments have been underwhelming, with frequent first-round exits. The shorter format has exposed their lack of big-hitters and death bowlers — critical components in modern-day T20 cricket.

The launch of the Bangladesh Premier League (BPL) in 2012 was aimed at injecting professionalism, money, and exposure into the national setup. Although the league has faced challenges — including corruption allegations and administrative missteps — it has served as a platform for young talent and foreign-player interaction.

Players like Mustafizur Rahman and Mehidy Hasan made their mark through the BPL pipeline, and the league has brought cricketing visibility to smaller cities. However, the league still lags behind the IPL, PSL, or even the CPL in terms of organization and global reach. A more structured and transparent BPL could help Bangladesh build greater depth, especially in white-ball cricket.

Cricket in Bangladesh does not exist in a vacuum. The sport is often enmeshed in the nation's political discourse, with the BCB being a politically influenced body. Leadership changes, allegations of favoritism in selections, and inconsistent management have all stymied growth at times.

The team also carries the burden of immense public expectation. Even minor defeats spark outrage, and victories are often seen as national triumphs. This pressure has, at times, helped players thrive under scrutiny, but it has also led to burnout and controversies.

After nearly 25 years as a Test nation, Bangladesh finds itself at a crossroads. The progress is undeniable — from being the perennial whipping boys of world cricket to becoming giant-killers at home. They have talent, a solid domestic structure, and a fan base that lives and breathes cricket.

But the gaps are equally glaring: a poor away record, inconsistent limited-overs campaigns, and a dearth of clutch performances in ICC tournaments. That Bangladesh, despite being a Full Member for two and a half decades, has yet to play in a World Cup final or consistently challenge in global tournaments reflects both a journey of improvement and a persistent underachievement.

Yet, there is reason for hope. The pipeline of players is stronger than ever, the domestic structure has improved, and recent performances show they are no longer pushovers. With better leadership, investment in coaching and analytics, and continued faith in youth, Bangladesh can aspire to not just participate in global events but also contend.

Cricket demands all-round excellence — technical, tactical, mental. Bangladesh has shown it can beat top-tier teams on its day. The next step is to become the team that does it every day.

Special Capsule: The Bangladesh Premier League: Ambition, Adversity, and a Work in Progress

The Bangladesh Premier League (BPL), inaugurated in 2012, was Bangladesh's bold attempt to insert itself into the lucrative world of franchise T20 cricket. Launched with the dual aim of nurturing domestic talent and boosting revenue for the Bangladesh Cricket Board (BCB), the BPL drew immediate attention with its vibrant crowds, passionate fan base, and aggressive marketing. Franchises like the Dhaka Dynamites, Comilla Victorians, and Chattogram Challengers introduced a regional flavor to cricket in a country where the sport is almost a second religion.

Despite early promise, the BPL has experienced a rocky journey. Match-fixing scandals in its early years, payment delays, and inconsistent franchise management have marred its credibility. These issues led to periodic suspensions and structural overhauls, including a controversial edition in 2019 where the BCB took over direct control of the league, sidelining private franchises. Yet, each iteration has demonstrated the league's resilience and underlying popularity.

On the field, the BPL has served as a key development platform. Players like Mustafizur Rahman, Mehidy Hasan Miraz, and Najmul Hossain Shanto have used the BPL to sharpen their skills and gain exposure to international players and high-pressure scenarios. Foreign stars such as Chris Gayle and AB de Villiers have brought global attention, although concerns linger around reliance on retired or fringe overseas players.

While not as polished as the IPL or as structured as the PSL, the BPL remains a vital part of Bangladesh's cricketing ecosystem. With better governance, consistent scheduling, and long-term franchise stability, it has the potential to evolve into a premier T20 destination and a cornerstone of Bangladesh's sporting economy.

Reader's Notes

Shakib Al Hasan – *Widely regarded as Bangladesh's greatest all-rounder, Shakib has been ICC's top-ranked all-rounder across formats multiple times and has carried the team through numerous key moments in both Tests and ODIs.*

1999 World Cup Upset – *Bangladesh's stunning win over Pakistan in the 1999 World Cup was a defining political and sporting statement that paved the way for their Test status.*

2003 Inzamam Test Escape – *Inzamam-ul-Haq's legendary one-wicket rescue in Multan denied Bangladesh a historic win; the match remains a haunting near-miss and symbol of early heartbreak.*

Mashrafe Mortaza – *The "Narail Express" became not just a pace spearhead but a symbol of national hope and captaincy leadership during the team's transitional years.*

Victory in the Caribbean (2009) – *Bangladesh's first overseas Test series win came against a weakened West Indies side, marking a rare away triumph.*

BPL (Bangladesh Premier League) – *Launched in 2012, the league has helped develop domestic talent and brought global attention to Bangladesh's T20 circuit.*

2012 Asia Cup Final Heartbreak – *Bangladesh nearly clinched their first major title, losing to Pakistan in a last-over thriller that captured hearts despite defeat.*

2015 Home Surge – *Bangladesh dominated Pakistan, India, and South Africa in ODIs at home, signaling a mini-golden phase of limited-overs form.*

Test Consistency Issues – *Despite isolated wins (like vs. England in 2016 and Australia in 2017), Bangladesh's Test form remains erratic, particularly overseas.*

ICC Knockout Record – *Bangladesh has only reached one ICC event semi-final (Champions Trophy 2017) and is yet to appear in a final, underscoring a long road ahead at the elite level.*

Chapter 11 – Afghanistan: From Conflict to Cricketing Ascent (2001–Present)

Afghanistan's cricket journey is one of the most remarkable in modern sporting history. A nation that spent decades entrenched in conflict, economic hardship, political instability, and international isolation, somehow carved out a unique identity through the game of cricket—a game that found unexpected roots in refugee camps and blossomed on the global stage within two decades. From dusty pitches in Peshawar refugee camps to playing in ICC World Cups, Afghanistan's rise is a testament to the power of sport to unite, inspire, and transcend.

The seeds of cricket were sown during the 1980s and 1990s, when millions of Afghans fled to Pakistan as a result of the Soviet invasion and subsequent civil war. It was in Pakistan's cricket-crazed culture, particularly in cities like Peshawar, that young Afghan refugees picked up the game. Many future stars such as Mohammad Nabi and Asghar Stanikzai began their cricketing education in these makeshift refugee camp setups. Cricket, thus, emerged not just as a pastime but as a cultural bridge, a sense of stability in chaos.

In 2001, the Afghanistan Cricket Board was officially formed. The timing coincided with the fall of the Taliban regime, which had previously banned most sports. This allowed the Afghan people, now reeling from decades of instability, to embrace the sport openly and nationally. The early years were challenging. Afghanistan, as an affiliate member, had to begin its journey in Division Five of the ICC World Cricket League in 2008. What followed was a stunning run of success: back-to-back promotions, culminating in Afghanistan achieving One

Day International (ODI) status in 2009. Just a year later, they were playing in their first ICC World T20.

The dream of Test cricket, however, would take longer. Afghanistan had to prove themselves not just in the shorter formats but as an administration, a cricketing system, and a sustainable national project. After years of consistent performances and global admiration for their rapid rise, Afghanistan was awarded Full Member status by the ICC in 2017, alongside Ireland, making them the 12th Test-playing nation.

Their inaugural Test came in 2018 against India at Bengaluru. It ended in a one-sided defeat, with Afghanistan bowled out twice in two days, but the significance of that moment was lost on no one. Here was a country that, not long ago, had no official stadiums, no domestic structure, and no home matches—now playing against the biggest cricketing nation in a full-fledged Test match.

Afghanistan would go on to win their second-ever Test match against Ireland in 2018/19, and followed it with an historic overseas Test win against Bangladesh in 2019. That victory, led by the likes of Rashid Khan and Ibrahim Zadran, was a defining moment. However, Afghanistan's Test record since has remained underwhelming, with losses to India, Sri Lanka, Bangladesh, and Ireland in subsequent fixtures. Their challenges in the Test arena are deeply structural lack of consistent fixtures, an underdeveloped domestic first-class system, and the inability to play at home.

Unlike other Full Members, Afghanistan has no home Test ground. Due to ongoing security issues and political turbulence, they have played their Test matches in India or the UAE. This has hindered their ability to build a fortress-like dominance seen with other Test nations. Test cricket thrives on conditions, crowds, and familiarity—Afghanistan has had none of that in red-ball cricket.

Where Afghanistan truly began to shape their international reputation was in the shorter formats. After a tough initiation into elite competition, they registered their first-ever ICC World Cup victory in 2015, defeating Scotland in a tense, unforgettable single-wicket thriller in Dunedin. Chasing 211, it was Samiullah Shinwari's gritty 96 and Shapoor Zadran's dramatic last-wicket stand that sealed the win — a moment that brought tears to Afghan fans worldwide and drew praise from across the cricketing world. Even Imran Khan, Pakistan's World Cup-winning captain and then political leader, publicly congratulated Afghanistan, calling it a monumental achievement for a war-torn nation finding pride through sport. That win remains etched as one of the most symbolic milestones in their cricketing ascent.

Despite that spark, the 2019 World Cup was a harsh reminder of their limitations—they lost all nine group stage matches. But it was the 2023 World Cup in India that marked a true breakthrough. Afghanistan shocked the defending champions England in Delhi, then clinically dismantled Pakistan in Chennai with a display of complete dominance in both batting and bowling. The defining moment, however, came against Australia at the Wankhede Stadium in Mumbai. Having reduced the five-time world champions to 91 for 7 in a chase of 292, Afghanistan seemed destined for their biggest win ever. But in one of the most astonishing innings in ODI history, Glenn Maxwell's unbeaten 201 turned the match on its head. Afghanistan's hopes of a semi-final were shattered—but their reputation was solidified. This was no longer a plucky underdog side looking to survive; it was a team fully capable of toppling giants and redefining the competitive balance of white-ball cricket.

In the 2024 ICC T20 World Cup in the West Indies, Afghanistan finally broke through to the semi-finals. Their group stage performance was highlighted by a stunning win over defending champions Australia. Led by Rashid Khan and an explosive Rahmanullah Gurbaz, Afghanistan charged into the final four, only to succumb meekly to South Africa in the semi-final—a match that exposed their lack of temperament under pressure. Still, the achievement was historic and confirmed their credentials as a T20 powerhouse.

Afghanistan's victories have not been limited to ICC tournaments. They beat Pakistan in a T20 series, defeated Sri Lanka, and shocked England in the 2025 ICC Champions Trophy. Afghanistan is still to qualify for the final of any ICC or Asia Cup event. The team has yet to develop the consistency needed to win over long tournaments, and their over-reliance on individual brilliance—especially Rashid Khan and Mohammad Nabi—remains a structural weakness.

Rashid Khan, of course, is the poster boy of Afghan cricket. Widely regarded as one of the best white-ball bowlers in the world, Rashid has played in nearly every global T20 league, bringing both visibility and financial stability to Afghan cricket. Mohammad Nabi, the elder statesman, has been crucial as a mentor, finisher, and off-spinner. Players like former captain Asghar Afghan (formerly Stanikzai), Najibullah Zadran, and Rahmanullah Gurbaz have also played key roles in establishing Afghanistan's presence in global cricket.

But for all their talent, the future hinges on two key factors: governance and infrastructure. The Afghanistan Cricket Board has seen multiple leadership changes, and the country's political instability—especially after the return of the Taliban in 2021—has thrown the future of sports, including cricket, into uncertainty. While the Taliban government has allowed cricket to continue, concerns remain over women's participation, press freedom, and international isolation—all of which could harm Afghan cricket's long-term prospects.

Another major roadblock is the absence of a proper home structure. With no first-class league that functions regularly, Afghan players lack the multi-day match practice that is vital for Test success. Their domestic cricket largely focuses on limited-overs and T20 formats. Without foundational investments in longer format cricket, Afghanistan may continue to stagnate in Tests despite individual talent.

Still, there is plenty of reason for optimism. The Shpageeza Cricket League, Afghanistan's T20 tournament, has grown steadily in popularity and now features several international players. The league is broadcast to multiple countries, and despite obvious challenges, it has become a vital talent pipeline. Young players like Fazalhaq Farooqi, Azmatullah Omarzai, Noor, Mujeeb and Ibrahim Zadran represent the next generation, and have already shown glimpses of brilliance.

With time, support from the ICC, stable governance, and consistent international fixtures, Afghanistan can grow into a consistent all-format side. Their recent performances show they are no longer content with moral victories. They want—and are capable of—winning on the world stage.

What makes Afghanistan unique is that it is not just a cricket story—it is a human story. The tale of a nation that rose from the ashes of war and displacement to challenge cricket's superpowers is both humbling and inspiring. Cricket has given the Afghan people hope, unity, and identity.

If Afghanistan can translate its T20 confidence into ODI and Test consistency, and if they can finally play in front of packed home crowds in Kabul or Kandahar, there is no reason why they cannot become one of cricket's elite nations.

Their cricketing journey is still in its early chapters. The script is unwritten, but the ink is filled with promise.

Reader's Notes

Rashid Khan – *their talisman, a global T20 superstar and fearless leader.*

Mohammad Nabi – *veteran all-rounder and spiritual leader of the side.*

Asghar Afghan – *the captain who shaped the team's culture during its formative years.*

Fazalhaq Farooqi – *a sharp left-arm pacer emerging as a game-changer in white-ball cricket.*

Rahmanullah Gurbaz – *an explosive top-order batter with the potential to dominate across formats.*

Ibrahim Zadran – *a technically sound, temperamentally solid top-order anchor.*

Mujeeb Ur Rahman *and* **Noor Ahmad** – *mystery spinners keeping Afghanistan's spin legacy alive on the global stage.*

Part VI – Cricket in the Age of Innovation and the Future

Chapter 12 – Artificial Intelligence and the Future of Decision-Making

12.1 Umpiring, DRS, and Predictive AI Models

In the evolving landscape of cricket, technology has become deeply embedded in the fabric of the game's decision-making. One of the most transformative shifts has occurred in the domain of umpiring, where artificial intelligence (AI) and advanced data systems now assist and, in some cases, challenge the authority of human officials. Cricket has always prided itself on fairness, and the margin for error in elite-level matches has never been narrower. With millions of viewers and high-stakes outcomes riding on split-second decisions, the call for more precision is understandable—and increasingly led by AI.

The introduction of the Decision Review System (DRS) marked a watershed moment. Technologies like Hawk-Eye for ball tracking, UltraEdge for sound detection, and real-time replay systems have become mainstream. These tools don't replace umpires but offer an added layer of objectivity. However, their success has sparked a provocative question: if machines can assist so effectively, could they eventually take over umpiring responsibilities altogether?

Research into this possibility is ongoing. One notable effort is the framework proposed by Iyer and BalaVignesh (2021), which used computer vision, trajectory modelling, and AI-based inference systems to simulate third-umpire decisions. Their model demonstrated over 90% accuracy on various dismissal types—run-outs, stumpings, and LBWs—suggesting that AI can, in principle, make faster and more consistent calls than humans in many scenarios. Real-time video feeds can be processed with predictive overlays, allowing on-screen indicators to present probabilities of dismissals within moments of an incident.

Despite this, the proposition of full AI umpiring must be examined critically. Cricket is not played in sterile, controlled environments. The game is subject to dust, rain, crowd noise, worn pitches, and even power failures. AI systems, especially those trained in controlled datasets, may falter when faced with the unpredictable theatre of live sport. Partial visibility, sudden obstructions, or reflective surfaces can confuse machine vision. Additionally, AI systems often struggle with contextual judgment—when to allow spirit-of-the-game considerations, or how to interpret borderline situations where common sense may trump binary logic.

Moreover, cricket's history is filled with iconic moments that underscore the deeply human, and often controversial, nature of umpiring. In 1987, the infamous altercation between Pakistan umpire Shakoor Rana and England's Mike Gatting in Faisalabad—where the latter pointed his finger at the umpire and accused him of bias—sparked an international incident. The fallout wasn't just about a no-ball call; it was about authority, colonial baggage, and respect. Similarly, in 1995, Australian umpire Darrell Hair called Sri Lanka's Muttiah Muralitharan for "chucking," sparking a decade-long debate on cultural perception, racial undertones, and biomechanical legitimacy. Even in the modern era, the 2018 "Sandpaper Gate" scandal in South Africa raised uncomfortable questions about human oversight, accountability, and moral policing—questions AI cannot yet answer.

These events remind us that human umpiring brings with it not just error, but a mirror to the game's ethical and emotional fabric. The drama of a close call, the dissent of a batter, the calm or fire of an umpire under pressure—all are integral to the lived experience of cricket. AI, for all its brilliance, lacks this moral compass, the ability to weigh subtle nuances, to feel pressure, or to stand as a cultural symbol. Would AI have managed the Gatting-Rana crisis with diplomacy?

Would it have recognized the implicit racial dynamics of calling Muralitharan, or the need for human discretion in volatile match atmospheres?

Still, AI is not the enemy—it is a tool. Many argue for a hybrid future, where umpires and AI systems collaborate. Already, automated front-foot no-ball detection has been used with great success. Other low-stakes, high-frequency tasks—like edge detection, stumping frame analysis, or boundary reviews—could be fully automated. This would allow human umpires to focus on managing players, game tempo, and intangible elements of match control.

Critics of full automation also raise concerns about AI bias and transparency. AI systems trained predominantly on data from one region or format may underperform elsewhere. Moreover, opaque algorithms could alienate fans if decisions appear arbitrary. Explainable AI (XAI) models—where logic pathways are made clear to broadcasters and audiences—will be crucial in gaining trust.

The future may also include real-time AR-assisted umpiring, where officials wear glasses that overlay predictive information, or predictive analytics for crowd-informed decision-making. Still, at its core, cricket is a human game. It thrives on tension, unpredictability, and judgment under pressure. AI can elevate fairness, but it must not strip away the soul of the sport.

Umpiring is not just about making the right decision—it's about making it in the right way. For all its promise, AI must remain a servant, not the master. Cricket's challenge in the coming decades will be to blend human judgment and machine accuracy without losing the charm that has made the game endure. Only then can the umpire of the future be truly complete—part machine, part maestro, and fully accountable.

12.2 – AI in Player Selection, Strategy, and Performance Analytics

In modern cricket, decision-making is no longer solely dictated by the instincts of captains or the experience of coaches. As of 2025, Artificial Intelligence (AI) and machine learning models have become integral tools for shaping not only team strategy but also player selection, match planning, and even game-day adjustments. The confluence of data science and cricket has transformed the sport from a traditional, feel-driven contest into one increasingly governed by predictive modelling and real-time analytics.

Over the past decade, national teams and franchise leagues have embraced AI not just as a tool for analysis, but as a strategic partner. These systems can process vast amounts of player data—ball-by-ball match events, biomechanical motion capture, training load, pitch conditions, opposition analysis, and even player psychology. The goal is to anticipate outcomes, reduce uncertainty, and guide teams toward data-backed decisions in moments that would otherwise rely solely on instinct.

One of the most impactful applications of AI has been in player selection and workload management. Fast bowlers have benefited from AI models that track fatigue, injury risk, and peak performance windows. Leading teams like Australia, India, and England have adopted rotation policies informed by AI tools that process GPS-based training data, match fatigue metrics, and historical injury patterns. These models help boards protect their pacers for key tournaments while ensuring squad depth is tested across formats. In a crowded global calendar, such load-balancing has become a strategic necessity.

On the tactical side, AI now provides pre-match simulations and in-game suggestions based on opponent matchups. Coaches and analysts use predictive models to simulate thousands of virtual matches—what happens if a batter faces a certain type of bowler, or if a spinner is introduced in a specific over? These insights can shape batting orders, field placements, and bowling changes. In T20 leagues like the IPL and Big Bash, franchises invest in AI-powered decision engines such as IBM Watson, SAS Viya, and custom-built cricket-specific algorithms to optimize playing XIs and simulate pressure situations.

This real-time potential is not merely theoretical. As far back as 1999, disgraced former South African captain Hansie Cronje was spotted using an earpiece to communicate with coach Bob Woolmer during a World Cup match—drawing widespread attention for bypassing traditional decision-making boundaries. While that incident had darker connotations in retrospect, it also hinted at a future where real-time strategic guidance could be provided to captains via wearable tech, such as AI-integrated earpieces or heads-up displays. If allowed by future ICC regulations, AI-driven tactical nudges could assist teams—especially associate nations—in navigating complex match scenarios, helping them bridge the gap in tactical acumen.

Already, coaches and captains review win-probability graphs, risk matrices, and "matchup blueprints" mid-match. In coming years, this could evolve into live decision assistance, where the captain receives tactical cues from a supercomputer fed by ball-tracking, weather, and opposition tendencies. Such systems could prove transformative for newer cricketing nations lacking strategic depth, offering them real-time insight to punch above their weight in key moments.

At the individual level, AI-enhanced systems now dissect performance with surgical precision. For example, computer vision tools like Hawk-Eye and KinetiX capture every nuance of a bowler's release point or a batter's head position during strokeplay. Combined with biomechanical inputs, these tools allow support staff to correct inefficiencies, identify scoring zones, or design training plans. Elite players now use AI to self-correct technique based on simulations that predict performance under different pitch, venue, or opposition conditions.

12.3 Risks of Over-Reliance on Algorithms in a Human Game

The revolution is not confined to the elite. Grassroots and domestic systems are catching up. Apps like CricViz and SmartCrick now allow local academies and smaller boards to access rudimentary AI insights on player strengths, opposition weaknesses, and even match tactics. This democratization of data means the next Rashid Khan or Shubman Gill could be discovered and refined far earlier in their careers, with tailored development pathways supported by AI.

However, challenges persist. A key concern is the ethical use and accessibility of these systems. Boards with deeper financial resources can afford proprietary analytics suites and data scientists, potentially creating a technological divide. Another concern is algorithmic bias— models trained on elite-level data may undervalue performances in associate leagues or on atypical pitches. There's also a philosophical debate on whether AI might deskill intuitive leadership. Should captains always follow what the model says? Or should they override it based on feel and experience?

And then there's the human element. Cricket is not a video game—it is played in uncertain weather, under emotional strain, and in front of passionate crowds. AI cannot simulate adrenaline or interpret body language in the way a veteran captain might. Pitch reading remains one of the most nuanced and misunderstood aspects of cricket strategy. Over the years, even the most experienced captains have been guilty of misreading conditions—electing to bat or bowl first with costly consequences. The surface's behavior, moisture content, grass coverage, and rate of deterioration are notoriously hard to assess with the naked eye. In this regard, AI-powered pitch analysis tools offer a compelling future. By combining historical ground data, live environmental sensors, and surface imagery processed by computer vision, these tools can provide captains and coaches with real-time assessments of how a pitch might play across sessions or days. These systems can simulate ball bounce, spin, and carry potential based on surface microstructure. Instead of relying on instinct alone, captains will soon have the option to receive data-backed recommendations—a hybrid of science and gut feel. For associate nations or less experienced captains, such tools could be the difference between a match lost at the toss and one won with informed clarity.

Thus, while AI will continue to shape cricketing strategy, its role must remain that of an assistant, not a commander. The beauty of the game lies in its unpredictability—AI can narrow the odds, but it cannot eliminate risk or emotion. Great captains still make bold, human decisions. Great players still defy the data.

Moving forward, the most successful teams will be those that blend AI precision with human intuition. Cricket, in its essence, will remain a human drama—but in the data age, it will be staged with the lights of powerful machines guiding the way. As the boundary between man and machine continues to blur, one thing is certain: in cricket's future, the captain and the computer will walk side by side.

Readers' Notes

DRS (Decision Review System) – *A combination of Hawk-Eye, UltraEdge/Snickometer, and ball-tracking technology used to assist umpires with close calls. It has transformed decision-making in cricket, though controversies remain.*

UltraEdge vs Snickometer – *Two audio-based tools to detect bat-ball contact. While Snicko uses traditional audio waveforms, UltraEdge synchronizes with video, offering improved clarity but still vulnerable to misinterpretation.*

Glenn McGrath's 2005 Edgbaston LBW – *Often cited as one of the first major DRS-like cases (pre-DRS) where technology might have overturned a pivotal on-field decision, had it existed.*

Mike Gatting–Shakoor Rana controversy (1987) – *A famous umpire-player confrontation that illustrated the human tension in cricket officiating. Technology like AI could eliminate such emotional outbursts, but at the cost of cricket's human edge.*

DRS Controversy – Kohli vs South Africa (2022–23) – *Virat Kohli questioned the accuracy of DRS when South African batter Dean Elgar was reprieved. His animated criticism at the stump mic reignited the trust-versus-tech debate.*

AI-Powered Player Tracking – *Used in modern leagues like the IPL, where player fatigue, sprint count, and positioning are tracked in real-time to inform tactical decisions and substitutions.*

Hansie Cronje's Ear-Piece Scandal (1999) – *During the World Cup, Cronje was allegedly spotted using an earpiece to receive coaching instructions mid-game — now viewed as a precursor to legal, AI-driven tactical guidance.*

Australia, India, and England's Rotation Policy (2020s) – *These nations now use AI to track workload and rotate fast bowlers, preserving them for marquee matches — especially in packed international calendars.*

Real-Time AI Captaincy Assistants – *Conceptual tools that, if allowed by ICC in future, could provide captains live suggestions on field placements, bowling changes, or DLS forecasts via ear implants or AR glasses.*

Azhar Ali's 2022 Gaddafi Stadium Dismissal – *A 5-minute third umpire delay and inconclusive UltraEdge call highlighted how technology still leaves room for uncertainty, with the decision significantly affecting the series outcome.*

12.4 Ethics and AI Bias in Cricket Technology

As technology increasingly defines the modern cricketing landscape, the ethical dimensions of its application demand greater scrutiny. While tools like the Decision Review System (DRS), Hawk-Eye, Snickometer, and UltraEdge have improved the accuracy of decisions, they are not infallible. More critically, they are not neutral. Behind every algorithm, camera angle, and sensor lies a human design, which can introduce biases—whether unintentional or systemic.

One of the most famous recent controversies involving DRS came during the 2021–22 Test series between South Africa and India, when South African batter Dean Elgar survived a close LBW appeal after ball-tracking showed the delivery narrowly going over the stumps. To many observers, including seasoned commentators, the decision seemed suspect. The Indian players, visibly frustrated, questioned the accuracy of the system. Virat Kohli walked up to the stump mic and openly accused the host broadcaster of manipulating the ball-tracking. The moment went viral, igniting debate over how much control broadcasters have in framing or influencing technological output. It raised broader questions around transparency, standardization, and the potential for subconscious bias even within supposedly objective systems like Hawk-Eye.

Another historic example remains etched in cricket folklore: Sachin Tendulkar's LBW reversal against Saeed Ajmal in the 2011 World Cup semi-final in Mohali. With millions watching, Hawk-Eye projected the ball missing leg stump by a marginal degree. Pakistani players were visibly stunned. Years later, Ajmal himself would question the decision in interviews. Could a slight change in angle or speed calibration have altered the outcome? This wasn't merely a technical query—it had emotional and nationalistic overtones, demonstrating the moral weight technology now bears in cricket.

There are further examples that expose the limits of AI and tech tools in grey areas. The "conclusive evidence" standard remains vague in many scenarios. For instance, Snickometer or UltraEdge may pick up a spike, but without synchronized visuals, it is hard to determine whether it was bat hitting pad or ball brushing edge. A telling example came during the 2022 third Test between Pakistan and Australia at the Gaddafi Stadium, where Azhar Ali was controversially given out after an extended third umpire review that took over five minutes. Despite inconclusive replays and a debatable UltraEdge spike, the decision was upheld — much to the shock of fans and commentators. The dismissal proved critical, as Pakistan collapsed soon after, ultimately losing the Test and the series. The episode underlined how even the best tech can leave umpires in a quandary, relying more on educated guesses than certainties — and how such decisions can shape the course of entire series. Similarly, low catches remain contentious, as cameras cannot always determine whether fingers were cleanly underneath the ball. The soft signal — where the on-field umpire makes an initial call — used to play a role in such decisions, but its removal has increased the onus on technology, even when visual ambiguity persists.

As cricket is rapidly moving fast, it is imperative in the modern age to fully scrutinize cricket equipment and supply chain companies using advanced tools such as quantum mechanics–driven AI. Furthermore, the proliferation of mini-breaks during matches needs closer evaluation — what exactly is being changed or exchanged in these pauses, and whether their frequency is healthy for the rhythm and fairness of the sport.

One often overlooked ethical concern is data disparity between nations. Richer boards like India, England, and Australia can afford multiple high-speed cameras, thermal imaging, and enhanced ball-tracking, while poorer nations may only deploy the bare minimum. This raises a serious question of equity: if a key LBW appeal or catch review in an ICC tournament is denied due to inferior tech infrastructure in certain matches or venues, has the game really been fair?

Moreover, AI algorithms themselves can carry hidden biases. For example, a predictive model built largely on data from subcontinent pitches may misjudge bounce or swing in English conditions. A batter from an associate nation, with limited data points, may be poorly profiled by selection AIs. Without deliberate checks, these biases can creep into tactical decisions and even career opportunities.

Given these complexities, the need for transparency and regulatory oversight is urgent. Every AI model used in international cricket—be it in officiating or player analysis—should be audited by an independent body. Host nations must be held to uniform technological standards. There should be compliance protocols, ensuring that ball-tracking, Snicko, and other tools are calibrated identically for every match in a series or tournament.

There's also room to embed human oversight into technological decisions—not to override tech, but to contextualize it. For example, third umpires could be given a "margin of uncertainty" guideline, allowing for nuanced interpretation rather than blind reliance on frames and spikes. AI, after all, should assist, not dominate.

As cricket moves deeper into the digital age, its ethical backbone must evolve in parallel. Technology may reduce human error, but it must not come at the cost of fairness, transparency, and trust. The spirit of the game depends not only on the tools we use—but how responsibly we wield them.

12.5 Innovative Captains in the Age of Intelligence: Past Lessons, Future Blueprints

While artificial intelligence continues to reshape cricket's technological and analytical backbone, the essence of cricketing success still rests — and may always rest — in the intuition, nerve, and imagination of human leadership. The role of the captain, once romanticized as a gentleman tactician or inspirational general, is now entering a new era — one that must blend data fluency with strategic innovation, emotional intelligence with real-time problem-solving, and tradition with transformation.

Historically, cricket has often progressed through the minds of its most innovative captains. Don Bradman, widely revered for his batting, was also ahead of his time as a strategist. During the 1948 Ashes tour in England, he once reversed the batting order on a damp Leeds pitch, sending in tailenders first to protect the main lineup — an early example of match awareness trumping orthodoxy. Innovative Mark Taylor's decision to promote Shane Warne up the order in the 1996 World Cup quarter-final against New Zealand was bold, catching opponents off-guard and altering the match's tempo. These are not just anecdotes; they are historical data points for how courage and creativity can trump logic.

Imran Khan's leadership in the late 1980s and early 1990s transformed Pakistan's cricketing landscape. He didn't just lead from the front — he reengineered the team's DNA by blending youthful fast bowlers with seasoned all-rounders and mystery spinners, creating an unpredictable yet potent force. Arjuna Ranatunga's decision to unleash Sanath Jayasuriya and Romesh Kaluwitharana as pinch-hitting openers in the 1996 World Cup rewrote ODI conventions, proving that innovation often emerges from the periphery.

Martin Crowe's tactical genius was exemplified in his choice to open the bowling with spinner Dipak Patel in the 1992 World Cup — a maneuver that disrupted batting rhythms and maximized field restrictions. Graham Gooch, though less flamboyant, was a master of mental resilience and strategic self-reliance, leading England through a difficult era with clarity and steel. Sourav Ganguly, as earlier discussed, instilled belief and aggression into Indian cricket, changing its psychological framework.

Hansie Cronje — a name permanently shadowed by scandal — cannot be overlooked for his instrumental role in South Africa's rapid post-apartheid cricketing resurgence. His tactical acumen and adaptability helped shape a team that was both formidable and innovative. Mark Taylor's 1995 series victory over the West Indies in the Caribbean ended a 15-year unbeaten streak, not merely through skill, but through brave declarations, flexible fielding strategies, and self-assurance.

Even Mike Brearley, known for modest personal statistics, remains a towering figure in captaincy literature. His understanding of psychology, team dynamics, and man-management — as well as his timely tactical calls — are still studied in leadership seminars today. Brearley demonstrated that captains need not be the best players on the field, but they must be the best readers of it.

Among the modern architects of tactical innovation, Michael Vaughan's captaincy during the 2005 Ashes stands as a defining chapter. Vaughan combined aggressive bowling rotations with psychological clarity — maintaining composure and an unflinching approach even in the most volatile moments. One such moment came when Steve Harmison's first-ball bouncer struck Ricky Ponting on the cheek, drawing blood. While many expected a gesture of concern, Vaughan instructed his team to hold formation, signaling a new, steely English intent. This cold, calculated discipline was emblematic of a side that had absorbed years of failure and was finally ready to respond with strategy rather than sentiment. Under Vaughan's leadership, England ended a 16-year Ashes drought — not just through individual brilliance, but through a collective recalibration of belief, tempo, and tactical precision.

Among modern leaders, Australia's Pat Cummins offers a compelling case study in composed, data-aware, and situationally responsive captaincy. In the 2023 ICC World Cup final, held in front of over 100,000 spectators at Ahmedabad's colossal stadium, Cummins executed a tactical masterclass. Against a red-hot Indian side and a nation-sized crowd, he calmly read the pitch and game conditions, tailoring a strategy that relied not just on raw pace or power but on calculated pressure. His subtle bowling changes, disciplined field placements, and clinical containment of India's top order led to one of the most memorable upsets in modern ODI history.

Cummins' leadership acumen also shone in Australia's World Test Championship victory, where his trust in Travis Head — both as a counterattacking middle-order batsman and as a game-turner — paid massive dividends. His mental strength was perhaps best exemplified during the 2023 Ashes at Edgbaston, where he helped chase down a tense fourth innings target with the bat, exorcising the ghosts of the 2005 heartbreak on the same ground. In doing so, he redefined the archetype of a modern fast-bowler captain: one capable of carrying physical burden and mental clarity in equal measure.

As cricket leadership continues to evolve alongside AI and advanced analytics, captains like Michael Clarke exemplify a new paradigm — one that fused innovation with instinct. His tenure demonstrated that the future belongs to those who can combine tactical logic with emotional intelligence, adapt to shifting game contexts, and lead not just by numbers, but by nuance.

Looking ahead, the captains of the AI age will be hybrid thinkers: data literate yet instinct-driven, analytically sharp but emotionally attuned. They may hold degrees in sports science, behavioral economics, or systems engineering, but their real edge will lie in how they synthesize inputs from data models, player intuition, and match context in real time. Future captains might use AR visors to visualize field placements, rely on predictive fatigue models to rotate bowlers, or override algorithmic suggestions based on —gut feell — a trait technology has yet to replicate. What distinguishes innovative captains is not just their willingness to experiment, but their ability to do so under pressure. In an age where decisions may increasingly be supported by AI, the captains who thrive will be those who can question AI — not blindly follow it. The ability to balance empirical logic with instinctive insight will become the most valued trait in cricket leadership.

In essence, the future belongs not just to those who embrace technology — but to those who know when to depart from it.

12.6 Ben Stokes and the Bazball Paradigm: Innovation or Disruption?

In the increasingly data-driven and commercially intense ecosystem of modern cricket, the emergence of Bazball under Ben Stokes and Brendon McCullum has been one of the most disruptive and compelling innovations in Test cricket strategy. Characterized by high-risk batting, bold declarations, attacking field placements, and an unapologetic quest for results, Bazball is both a cricketing philosophy and a marketing narrative — one that has succeeded in re-engaging spectators, reviving Test atmospheres, and challenging long-standing norms.

Under Stokes' captaincy, England's red-ball team began to operate with a clarity of purpose: to make Test cricket not just viable, but vibrant. Matches were played at an accelerated tempo, with scoring rates exceeding five or six runs an over, and results engineered through calculated disruption. Their historic Rawalpindi Test win in 2022 — on a flat pitch where England scored 506 runs on Day 1 — signalled that the rules of Test engagement were being rewritten.

Yet, the approach is not without its vulnerabilities. The one-run loss to New Zealand in 2023, after enforcing a bold follow-on, and the aggressive declaration at Edgbaston during the Ashes — which arguably cost England the series — illustrate how fine the margins can be between innovation and overreach. Moreover, despite its success in home conditions, Bazball has not yet delivered an Ashes series victory, nor has it triumphed in India, where spin-friendly conditions and strategic depth demand more nuance than narrative. These shortcomings raise important questions about the adaptability and longevity of such an all-in philosophy.

Still, what Bazball has undeniably achieved is the re-animation of Test cricket's public image. Crowds have returned. Conversations have shifted. Players, once shackled by fear of failure, appear to play with license and clarity. And for broadcasters and boards, the "Bazball effect" has provided new storytelling arcs in a format often seen as less commercially attractive than T20.

Looking forward, Bazball offers fascinating possibilities within hybrid cricket models. Imagine a three-day format, combining the depth of Test cricket with the urgency of ODIs — 55 overs per side across two innings, played in white kits, under pink-ball floodlights, in front of packed crowds. Such a format, fuelled by Bazball's tempo and theatre, could redefine how long-form cricket is consumed and understood. It represents not merely entertainment, but strategic recalibration for a future audience raised on speed and spectacle.

Innovation is not a luxury; it is a civilizational imperative. As the world transitions from traditional banks to fintech, from physical gold to digital assets, and from analogue systems to algorithmic ecosystems, cricket too must evolve within the same planetary trajectory. Sport cannot remain insulated from broader societal shifts. To outpace opponents — both tactically and culturally — continuous innovation is not just desirable; it is essential. History offers sobering lessons: once-dominant sides like the West Indies and Pakistan, long celebrated for their flair and instinctive brilliance, now struggle to keep pace in an era defined by systems, data, and strategy. Without adaptation, even legacies built on genius risk being reduced to nostalgia.

Bazball may or may not become a global standard. But its cultural significance is already assured — as both a provocation and a proposal.

It is a reminder that cricket, even at its most traditional, remains a space for reinvention.

Chapter 13 – Formats, Franchising, and the Future of Cricket

13.1 Test Cricket's Survival and ODI Decline

Cricket, since its formal inception in 1877, was built around the Test match—two innings per side, spread across days, layered with complexity, strategy, and patience. From that foundational format emerged the One Day International (ODI) in 1971, which condensed cricket into a single day, suiting both broadcasters and modern audiences. The inaugural Prudential World Cup in 1975 showcased the spectacle of this new format, while Kerry Packer's World Series Cricket in the late 1970s revolutionized player payments, TV presentation, and global appeal. Fast forward to 2005, the T20 format was born, and the 2007 ICC World T20 cemented its legitimacy. The IPL, launched in 2008, took the shortest form of the game to commercial stratospheres.

Thus, each cricketing century has brought with it a new format: the 19th century gave birth to Test cricket; the 20th refined ODIs; and the 21st is unmistakably owned by T20s. As we approach the dawn of the 22nd century, a question looms large—can Test cricket survive in its traditional form, and where does that leave the ODI format?

The truth is sobering. The survival of Test cricket over the last quarter-century has been dependent on three economic and viewership powerhouses: India, Australia, and England. Series such as The Ashes or the Border-Gavaskar Trophy continue to produce iconic moments and attract decent viewership. However, outside this axis, the Test arena has visibly thinned. Once-formidable Test nations like West Indies, Pakistan, and Sri Lanka have struggled to sustain competitiveness due to structural, economic, or political challenges.

The World Test Championship (WTC), introduced by the ICC to provide greater context and stakes to bilateral Test matches, has shown promise. The three finals so far have generated solid global attention. Yet, the problem remains structural—WTC still primarily thrives when the big three are involved. If competitive equilibrium isn't broadened, public interest will eventually wane.

A declining diversity of competitive teams makes Test cricket appear more exclusive and archaic. And exclusivity in a sport that seeks global expansion is a contradiction. It becomes difficult to argue for Test matches in nations where revenue, crowd interest, and development funding are all heavily weighted towards shorter formats. The format needs more than nostalgia to survive—it needs a structural evolution that balances heritage with practicality.

On the other hand, ODI cricket faces an identity crisis. Neither as steeped in tradition as Tests nor as thrilling and time efficient as T20s, the format is increasingly struggling for relevance. While the 50-over World Cup remains prestigious and commercially viable—as evidenced by vibrant editions in 2011, 2015, 2019, and 2023—bilateral ODI series have started to resemble filler content, often played out in half-empty stadiums and consumed passively by viewers already saturated with franchise leagues and T20 content.

A deeper problem compounds this issue: the domination of a few elite nations. Since Sri Lanka's stunning win in 1996, nearly three decades have passed without a team outside the 'Big Three' (India, Australia, and England) lifting the ODI World Cup trophy. These very nations also serve as the custodians of Test cricket, with financial clout, broadcast leverage, and large domestic followings. While South Africa (WTC 2025 winners) and New Zealand (WTC 2021 winners) have made inroads in red-ball cricket, they operate in nations where cricket is not the primary sport, often overshadowed by rugby. Their limited domestic pull raises questions about sustainability and grassroots growth. That is not to say the 'Big Three' are solely responsible for the

249

decline of longer formats in other traditional cricketing nations. The regression of Pakistan, West Indies, and Sri Lanka in both Test and ODI cricket stems largely from internal mismanagement, inconsistent domestic structures, and a lack of long-term vision by their respective boards. Yet, if the goal is to elevate the standard of global competition, then isolating these teams through minimal or symbolic engagement won't help. Instead of limiting encounters to token two-match Test series, boards and the ICC should consider expanding them to minimum three or even four-match series—allowing for narrative arcs, player development, and more meaningful contests. Yes, there are commercial realities and broadcaster demands, but a broader scheduling philosophy driven by competitive growth rather than short-term metrics is essential if cricket is to sustain relevance in its longest formats.

This overconcentration of success and influence is dangerous for global cricket. If tournaments continue to be monopolized by a few nations, and if longer formats remain viable only within these borders, the game risks turning into a semi-global niche—exclusive rather than inclusive. The promise of globalisation, which ODI cricket once represented in the late 1990s and early 2000s, is now at risk of receding.

For cricket to thrive—across all formats—it cannot remain confined to three or four nations. The health of ODIs and Tests is intimately tied to the diversity of strong, competitive national teams and broader geographic engagement. Without this, the formats may survive in structure but wither in spirit.

Attempts to revive ODIs with reduced overs—such as 40-over versions or split innings—have not found favor. Cricket audiences are more polarized now: they either demand a timeless, strategic epic (Test cricket), or an evening of drama-packed entertainment (T20). ODI, which used to be the perfect middle ground, now risks being neither here nor there.

This erosion is not just theoretical. The ICC Champions Trophy, once the second-most important ODI event, has struggled for meaning. Scheduled again for 2029, its very purpose is questioned in an already congested calendar. Unless drastically reimagined, its days may be numbered.

A viable path forward for ODI cricket could be to retain the 50-over World Cup as the sole marquee event, eliminating bilateral ODI series entirely. This would streamline the congested international calendar, reduce player fatigue, and sustain public anticipation around the format. Much like how the Olympics preserves enthusiasm for niche sports through infrequent, high-stakes competition, a four-year ODI World Cup cycle could maintain relevance without overexposure.

However, such a strategy requires thoughtful inclusivity. It was a troubling spectacle to witness West Indies—winners of the first two World Cups in 1975 and 1979—fail to qualify for the 2023 edition in India. Similarly, Sri Lanka's absence from the 2025 ICC Champions Trophy signals a worrying trend. Unlike football, which enjoys a global base of 175+ competitive nations and can justify a 48-team World Cup, cricket remains a niche sport. Excluding iconic Test-playing nations in favor of inconsistent Associate teams does more harm than good. Competitive legitimacy, brand value, and fan interest suffer when legacy teams are absent.

Rather than simply expanding for the sake of inclusion, the ICC must confront the deeper structural issues behind the decline of once-promising cricketing nations. Zimbabwe's descent and Kenya's erosion—despite their historic high points, such as Kenya's win over West Indies in 1996 and their semi-final run in 2003—highlight how certain regions have been neglected in the developmental roadmap. At the same time, an overemphasis on allocating events and resources to the Big Three has reinforced a lopsided ecosystem where other nations are reduced to peripheral participants.

South Africa's absence from the 1975,1979, 1983 and 1987 World Cups was rooted in apartheid and geopolitical isolation—an entirely different context. But today's exclusions are the result of administrative apathy, commercial centralization, and an uneven playing field. Unless international cricket sustains a strong cohort of at least 12 highly competitive, financially stable, and structurally sound national teams, both ODIs and Test cricket risk losing their global footprint. Rebuilding strength in traditional cricketing heartlands is not just nostalgic—it is strategic necessity.

Test cricket, meanwhile, must embrace reforms while protecting its core. Limited-over hybrid formats—like 3-day, double-innings matches with capped overs—might provide one route, though such discussion belongs more fully in the next chapter. What Test cricket cannot afford is stagnation. Day-night Tests, points-based systems, and greater funding for smaller boards must be explored aggressively.

The ultimate success of both formats will depend on competition, audience, and broadcast adaptability. Technology can help with reach and interactivity, but the soul of these formats lies in a plurality of nations participating with pride and proficiency. A cricketing world where only three or four countries can afford to care about Test or ODI cricket is a world where both formats risk slow extinction.

In an era defined by speed, cricket must remember that time alone doesn't define quality. For Test cricket to survive, and ODIs to remain relevant, reform isn't optional—it's existential.

13.2 Hybrid Cricket: 3-Day, Double-Innings, 55-Over Formats

As cricket continues to evolve in response to the demands of a rapidly changing world, there is growing recognition that traditional formats may not remain sustainable in their current form. One possible direction the sport could take in the late 21st or early 22nd century is the introduction of hybrid cricket formats—particularly a condensed version that blends the durability of Test cricket with the pacing of One Day Internationals.

This concept is not without historical precedent. Cricket's evolution has long been marked by format reinvention. The earliest ODIs in the 1970s were 60-over-a-side contests, as seen in the legendary Prudential World Cups of 1975, 1979, and 1983. Those tournaments provided a glimpse of Test match rigor within a limited time frame. Even domestic one-day matches in England, until the early 1990s, often featured 55 overs per side. The format accommodated both grind and aggression—factors that could serve as inspiration for a modern reboot of the game.

The proposed hybrid format would consist of two innings per team, each limited to 55 overs, resulting in a potential 220-over match over three days. Each day would feature up to 80 overs, allowing a total of 240 overs, giving a 20-over cushion for interruptions—an important safeguard considering the impact of rain on Test matches. Unlike ODIs or T20s, this format would incorporate many of Test cricket's rules: the option to declare, the possibility of enforcing a follow-on, white clothing, and red ball, along with no fielding restrictions.

The bowling limitations would also follow a modified pattern. In a 55-over innings, each bowler could be limited to a maximum of 15 overs, encouraging both strike bowling and workload distribution. There would be no restriction on the number of bowlers used, giving captains strategic flexibility to rotate between pace and spin.

In the proposed hybrid format, the equation of a draw would be eliminated entirely—unless external interruptions like persistent rain prevent a result. By design, the structure encourages results-oriented cricket, aligning with modern audience expectations and eliminating the safety net of playing for a draw.. A result—either a win or a loss—must be produced. This would align well with the fast-moving, result-oriented world of the future. While traditionalists may argue that draws are part of the sport's charm, modern audiences increasingly lean toward decisive outcomes. Test matches that end in dull stalemates often lose their narrative appeal, especially among younger fans.

This hybrid format can offer intensity, strategy, and spectacle, and potentially replace either failing format—whether that be Test cricket in countries with waning support, or ODIs in a landscape oversaturated with white-ball cricket. The aggressive nature of modern batting techniques also supports this structure. Teams today can score 300-plus runs in 55 overs with relative consistency, proving that a hybrid format would not be lacking in pace, excitement, or momentum swings. This isn't a hypothetical. In fact, as far back as 1992, just after their World Cup triumph, England piled on 363 runs in a 55-over ODI against Pakistan—a then-record total that showcased the scoring potential of the format even in a pre-T20 era. Fast forward to 2014, and Pakistan famously chased down 302 against Sri Lanka in just over 50 overs in Sharjah, leveling the series 1-1 in dramatic fashion. These matches underline that the 55-over structure is more than capable of delivering high-octane cricket, blending the endurance of the red-ball game with the explosiveness of modern batting.

That is why Ben Stokes' "Bazball" era stands as a truly transformative chapter in modern Test cricket. Under his leadership, England has rejected the passive safety-first mentality that often led to dull stalemates. Instead, Stokes has infused Test cricket with an unapologetic emphasis on *winning*—treating a draw not as a safe fallback, but as a failure to push the game forward. This mindset is more aligned with the expectations of the 21st-century audience, who demand intensity and outcome-oriented sport. In many ways, Bazball isn't just a tactic—it's a philosophical shift that mirrors the very evolution cricket must undergo if it's to survive into the next century. It signals that long-format cricket can still be bold, aggressive, and deeply compelling—if the intent is clear and the fear of failure is discarded.

Furthermore, three-day scheduling allows better flexibility in international calendars. With travel times reduced due to technological advancements and player workloads carefully managed via AI systems, these shorter matches can slot seamlessly into modern schedules. More importantly, the time demand on fans is significantly reduced—making in-person attendance and global viewership more viable. Broadcast networks would also find a 3-day, 2-innings contest easier to package and monetize than a 5-day marathon.

In a future where cricket seeks to balance heritage and innovation, hybrid formats could provide the solution. They respect the two-innings narrative of Test cricket while acknowledging the pressing reality of time constraints and attention spans in the AI-dominated digital age. For nations that cannot sustain five-day cricket or example Afghanistan and Ireland—either for financial or infrastructural reasons—this model offers a viable, competitive, and globally appealing alternative.

If implemented wisely, hybrid cricket could revive bilateral series, create new international rivalries, and serve as a platform for both red-ball specialists and white-ball aggressors to co-exist. This format could even function as a qualifying layer between traditional Test status and associate limited-overs status, giving emerging nations a stepping-stone format to play elite opposition in a fairer, more time-efficient setting.

While it may not yet be time to sound the death knell of Test or ODI cricket, preparing for future formats is essential. At least in the immediate future—through the 2030s—the current structure of international cricket, with its three-format ecosystem, remains relatively secure. Test matches still draw attention during marquee series, ODIs retain importance through the World Cup, and T20s continue to thrive globally. However, as attention spans shrink and scheduling pressures mount, the cricketing world must acknowledge the inevitability of structural innovation. By the 2040s and beyond, three-day hybrid matches—merging the strategic depth of Tests with the tempo of limited-overs cricket—may no longer be optional experiments, but a necessary evolution to preserve relevance across generations.

Much like the innovations introduced in 2007 with the inaugural T20 World Cup or the way IPL transformed the cricketing economy, hybrid formats may well define the sport's survival in the 22nd century.

Another pressing concern for the sport's future lies in the worsening political climate between India and Pakistan. Relations between the two cricketing giants further deteriorated following *Operation Sindhoor*, leading to an almost complete freeze in any form of cricket. The two nations haven't played a Test match since 2007—marking an 18-year gap—and bilateral series have been absent since the winter of 2012, over 13 years ago. While cricket has long been influenced by geopolitics—be it the isolation of apartheid-era South Africa or sporting sanctions during wartime—the stakes are higher today in a sport with limited global spread. With only a dozen or so Test nations, disruptions to key rivalries shrink the sport's reach and impact. Given the current volatility, it may be wise for both nations to pause bilateral ties in the near term. However, cricketing authorities must urgently draft a neutral, binding framework for future engagement—one that balances political realities with the health of the game. If left unresolved, the sport risks sacrificing one of its most watched and storied contests on the altar of nationalism.

13.3 Future Laws: Experimental Rules for 2050 and Beyond

Cricket in 2025 is at a pivotal crossroads. As the game continues to stretch across time zones, digital platforms, and evolving fan demands, the question is no longer just about formats — it's about laws. Are cricket's existing rules sufficient to carry the sport into the future, or do they require reimagining to suit a world defined by hyper-speed communication, synthetic environments, and algorithmic decision-making?

One area where serious debate has emerged is the imbalance between bat and ball. Modern bats, reduced boundary sizes, and ultra-flat pitches have turned bowlers into statistical pawns. Teams now routinely score 300+ even in T20s — a format designed originally for quick and modest totals. Such run-fests are entertaining in bursts, but they strip the game of its tension, nuance, and chess-like complexity.

Compounding this problem is the use of two new balls in ODIs. Introduced to maintain consistency across both innings, the dual-ball system has eliminated reverse swing — a hallmark of subcontinental cricket and a decisive skill that once separated the average from the great. In the name of visibility and ball integrity, artistry has been sacrificed. As cricket pushes deeper into a data-defined era, there's growing consensus that reintroducing a single ball per innings — paired with AI-monitored wear-and-tear alerts to prevent tampering — could restore this lost dimension without compromising fairness.

Powerplays too have become predictable. Fixed field restrictions produce near-automated run-scoring patterns. In the near future, we may see adaptive powerplays, where AI reads pitch behaviour, outfield speed, and dew data to suggest strategic fielding constraints in real time. This would allow teams to tactically modulate aggression rather than follow a template.

Technology must also address cricket's oldest lottery: the toss. In conditions like the Indian subcontinent or Southeast Asia, dew plays an outsized role. Batting second can provide an unfair advantage, with bowlers struggling to grip a damp ball. New-age solutions — like anti-dew outfields built with nano-fibres or under-soil heating — may be adopted by 2050. But until then, ICC could explore the idea of a Dew Index, where predicted moisture levels adjust target scores much like rain-affected matches are adjusted today.

On that note, one innovation already ahead of its time is the Duckworth-Lewis-Stern (DLS) method. Despite criticism from some fans, DLS has been a stabilising force. By combining probabilistic modelling with over-by-over scoring patterns, it provides remarkably fair recalculations during weather interruptions. It deserves credit not only for saving many matches from ambiguity but also for keeping the rhythm of ODI cricket alive. Looking ahead, the system could evolve to account for micro-weather shifts and drone-based cloud tracking — making it even more precise.

Bat size and regulation remain another touchpoint. Today's bats are veritable planks with broad spines and thick edges. Even mis-hits travel beyond the rope. While minor restrictions were enforced in 2017, compliance remains inconsistent. By mid-century, expect all bats to be 3D scanned and blockchain-certified before tournaments, with instant disqualification for unapproved dimensions. Similarly, boundary dimensions should be standardised globally. No elite sport allows such disparity between venues — a six in Delhi should be a six in Dunedin, not 12 metres shorter.

No-ball and wide counts have grown disproportionately. One potential reform is a penalty escalation — after a team concedes five no-balls or wides, the sixth onwards carries two-run penalties or a free hit, even in Tests. Similarly, over-rate delays may result in removing a fielder for the final overs — a method trialled with some success in The Hundred.

Looking further, match outcomes themselves may need restructuring. As the world moves faster, fans increasingly demand resolution. The traditional draw — a pillar of Test cricket — might become obsolete. Unless rain wipes out entire days, future matches may use AI-based algorithms to assign match outcomes based on metrics like wickets in hand, run rate, and overs remaining. Alternatively, predefined tiebreakers or fourth-innings run chases might be introduced in three-day Test variants. A draw becomes a no-result — only wins and losses stay.

The captain's role may be revolutionised as well. With the rise of real-time strategy and wearable tech, future captains could receive AI-fed inputs via discreet earpieces — not unlike what disgraced South African captain Hansie Cronje allegedly trialled with Bob Woolmer during the 1999 World Cup via an illicit earplug. In 2050, such tools may be legal, provided all teams have access and are ICC-approved. This would particularly help weaker teams navigate complex match situations with greater strategic depth.

Scientific advances will also enter the fray through bio-sensory uniforms that detect fatigue, hydration, and injury risk — allowing for substitutions or bowling restrictions based on player wellness. Data-driven umpiring might rely on AI systems capable of integrating UltraEdge, ball-tracking, thermal imaging, and biomechanics to deliver composite verdicts within seconds — without human appeal. While controversial, such automation may become necessary in an ultra-competitive age.

Even the notion of day-night Test matches could expand. Smart stadiums with adjustable UV filtration and climate-controlled domes could allow matches in hostile environments — deserts, monsoons, or even space stations on Mars. With fanbases turning more global than ever, cricket must be playable in any timezone, under any conditions, for any audience.

The goal of these experimental rules is not to tamper with the game's soul but to safeguard its future. Cricket's history is one of constant adaptation — from timeless Tests to coloured clothing, from wooden scoreboards to DRS. The laws must not be static in a dynamic world.

By embracing innovation and anticipating challenges, cricket can remain not just relevant but essential in the 22nd century. It need not lose its charm or tradition — it simply needs to evolve intelligently, with balance, fairness, and vision.

13.4 – Global Franchises and the Rise of Borderless Leagues

By the 2020s, franchise cricket had already rewritten the global cricketing calendar. But as the 21st century enters its second half, these leagues are not just shaping the sport — they are redefining its borders, loyalties, and power centers. The Indian Premier League (IPL) was merely the first wave. What began as a commercially driven domestic tournament has now transformed into a global blueprint. The key shift is no longer in how many leagues exist — but in how interconnected they've become.

Today, nearly every major cricketing country has its own franchise tournament: the Big Bash League in Australia, the Pakistan Super League, The Hundred in England, the Caribbean Premier League, the SA20 in South Africa, and the ILT20 in the UAE. But the striking development over the last few years is the cross-ownership model. Indian conglomerates now own teams across continents — Mumbai Indians have franchises in Cape Town and New York, while Knight Riders operate in the Caribbean and USA. These aren't just marketing alignments; they're full ecosystem strategies. Shared branding, analytics teams, scouting networks, and player rotation have created what are essentially transnational cricket enterprises.

This emerging model is reminiscent of football's City Football Group, where one parent company owns or partners with clubs across leagues and continents. In cricket, this means that a young player signed in New York could graduate to Cape Town, then find himself in Mumbai — all within the same corporate umbrella. This has wide-ranging implications for player development, global marketing, and fan base acquisition. Fans in New Jersey now support MI Cape Town, not because of local ties, but because they wear the same blue as Rohit Sharma's squad.

Crucially, this has begun to blur national lines in cricket economics. A Sri Lankan cricketer may now be financially dependent on an Indian franchise that owns a team in Canada. A promising Afghan teenager may spend more time in Dubai or Texas than in Kabul. With player contracts now spanning multiple leagues — and centralized across companies — we are witnessing the birth of borderless leagues, where allegiance is corporate rather than national.

This evolution has benefits. It provides a stable financial ecosystem in countries where cricket boards are weak or unstable. Players no longer need to rely solely on central contracts from their home boards — a crucial factor for nations like Zimbabwe, Afghanistan, or Ireland. It also brings in tech-driven scouting, health management, and high-performance infrastructure, which many national systems can't afford.

Yet, there are concerns. As leagues proliferate, scheduling overlaps have become inevitable. The 2023–2025 period saw top players skipping national duty for franchise commitments — a trend that may worsen. Boards struggle to enforce availability clauses, especially when their own revenues are dwarfed by the leagues. In response, some boards have considered partial league ownership or licensing models, seeking both control and a share of the profits.

Further, the idea of neutral league hubs is gaining traction. Dubai, Florida, and Singapore are positioning themselves as year-round franchise hosts — cities without traditional cricketing heritage but with infrastructure and commercial ambition. These could become permanent "cricket ports," hosting multi-franchise tournaments with players from all over the world, untethered to any national identity.

Looking ahead, there's even speculation about "World Club Cricket" — a Champions League-style tournament for the top franchises. While past attempts like the CLT20 failed due to scheduling, the modern calendar, AI-driven fixture optimization, and global viewership trends make it far more viable now. This could be cricket's version of the UEFA Champions League — a tournament that transcends geography and becomes the definitive stage for franchise glory.

For all its potential, this shift also presents governance challenges. Who regulates player movement? What happens when a player's league contract conflicts with national duty? Will the ICC establish a Franchise Governance Wing — or will a new, autonomous global body emerge, run by corporate stakeholders?

The romantic purity of cricket — of playing for flag and country — will always remain part of the sport's soul. But in the age of global leagues, economic gravity is pulling the game toward borderless cricketing capitalism. The shift is already underway — not just in contracts or fixtures, but in how fans consume, players train, and the sport is imagined.

As long as there are guardrails in place — to protect national cricket structures, to ensure young talent is nurtured ethically, and to prevent monopolization — borderless franchises can be the lifeblood of the sport's global future. They are not a threat to the game. If anything, they may be its next great evolution.

13.5 Algorithmic Governance and the "AI MCC"

The Marylebone Cricket Club (MCC), as the historical guardian of cricket's laws, has long embodied the spirit of custodianship and deliberation. But as cricket undergoes a seismic transformation in how it is played, consumed, and governed, the question looms: What does rule-making look like in a future where Artificial Intelligence is embedded in every aspect of the sport? Will the MCC — or an evolved entity akin to it — retain full human discretion? Or will it share its authority with intelligent systems capable of simulating millions of scenarios before framing a single law?

The notion of an "AI MCC" is not as far-fetched as it once seemed. Already, cricketing data is vast and deeply granular. From ball-by-ball simulations to heat maps, predictive analytics, and biomechanical insights, the volume of information available has outgrown traditional decision-making models. In the past, new rules emerged reactively — a controversial incident would prompt debate, followed by months of deliberation, trials, and eventual adoption. But in a data-saturated future, algorithms could preemptively model the potential fallout of experimental laws, simulating thousands of games in varied conditions before proposing tweaks.

This could revolutionize how we think about rule-making. For instance, an AI model could assess whether shortening the pitch to 20 yards in urban leagues would benefit batters disproportionately, or simulate the impact of reducing the number of fielders in the circle across hundreds of match contexts. It could even suggest rule variations by venue, format, or weather, tailored dynamically through machine learning systems. The idea isn't to replace cricket's soul with a cold machine, but rather to create an adaptive legal framework that is faster, fairer, and more context-aware.

That said, any attempt to shift authority from human lawmakers to AI systems must be navigated with caution. Cricket, unlike digital simulation games, is deeply tied to culture, tradition, and nuance. The moral and aesthetic dimensions of the game — sportsmanship, timing, momentum, crowd energy — are not easily quantifiable. An AI might recommend rules that maximize scoring, but do they honor the rhythm of a Test match? Can it truly appreciate the narrative arc of a five-day battle, or the psychological fragility of a collapsing side under twilight skies?

Moreover, bias in AI is a known concern. Algorithms are only as fair as the data they are trained on. If training datasets are drawn mostly from conditions in Australia, India, and England, then recommendations may inadvertently skew toward those conditions. To avoid this, the "AI MCC" must be governed by a diverse panel of human overseers — technologists, former players, ethicists, and statisticians — who can ensure that AI-generated insights serve the global game, not just the power centers.

Another issue is regulatory uniformity. Will all member nations be bound to adopt these AI-informed laws, or can they opt out based on tradition or logistical limitations? Cricket's future rule-making will likely become modular, allowing certain experimental formats to operate under "dynamic law protocols," while marquee Test series retain the classic rulebook. In essence, multiple playing environments may coexist — much like "red-ball" and "white-ball" formats do today — but with greater legal granularity, managed by AI systems and endorsed by human consensus.

It's not just about gameplay either. An AI MCC could oversee disciplinary procedures, scheduling fairness, player load monitoring, and even financial ethics. For example, it might detect algorithmic anomalies in player auction data, or suggest match timings optimized for player health based on sleep-cycle analytics. The rule of law in cricket, long regarded as conservative and slow-moving, may become more responsive, transparent, and rooted in probabilistic insight — provided that human judgement always retains the final word.

Ultimately, the MCC — or its successor — must evolve without surrendering its essence. Cricket's appeal lies in its tension between tradition and innovation, memory and momentum. The laws that govern it must reflect both.

The AI MCC is not a rejection of human wisdom. It is an augmentation. A tool to help the sport stay fair, stay modern, and stay meaningful, even in a world where the pace of change threatens to outstrip our capacity to respond. As long as the game remains human at heart, its laws — whether written by pens or algorithms — will continue to resonate.

13.6 AI Workload Management and Smart Scheduling

One of the most pressing challenges facing modern cricket is the ever-expanding calendar. With bilateral series, franchise leagues, ICC tournaments, and domestic obligations overlapping throughout the year, elite players now face unprecedented physical and mental strain. Managing player workload is no longer a luxury—it is a necessity for longevity, performance, and sustainability of careers. And as cricket prepares to stretch into new geographies, formats, and digital dimensions, it becomes clear: only intelligent automation and innovative scheduling can prevent long-term burnout.

In the past, international cricketers would rarely play more than 50 to 60 days of international cricket in a year. Today, especially for multi-format stars, 100+ match days per year is common, not counting training, travel, and recovery. The pressure is immense, and many players have started opting out of one format—usually Tests—to extend their T20 careers and reduce physical wear. Names like Ben Stokes (brief ODI retirement), Trent Boult (switch to freelancing), and Pat Cummins (rested from various formats) reflect a growing trend: the body can only carry so much.

This raises a deeper question: how can cricket preserve its formats without breaking its athletes?

Enter automation. Leveraging AI-powered tools, cricket boards are beginning to experiment with calendar algorithms that optimize tour durations, rest windows, and travel logistics. Machine learning models trained on historical injury data can now recommend when a player is nearing red zones of fatigue or mental overload. Some federations already deploy biofeedback sensors and load-tracking software that feeds real-time metrics into scheduling dashboards. These are no longer futuristic luxuries—they're becoming standard.

But automation alone isn't enough. Cricket must reimagine the formats themselves.

This is where the 3-day hybrid format—combining elements of ODI and Test cricket—emerges as a game-changer for workload balance. Composed of two innings of 55 overs per side, with a maximum of 80 overs bowled per day, this format reduces the mental grind and physical toll of five-day Tests while retaining the strategic depth and resilience-building features missing in T20s and ODIs.

By removing the possibility of draws (unless rain intervenes), matches will become more result-oriented and engaging, without dragging on. Crucially, players who have opted out of traditional Test cricket due to its demands may find the hybrid format a suitable compromise, allowing them to remain part of red-ball cricket in a condensed, dynamic version.

The shorter match window—just three days—makes it easier to slot into an already packed calendar, offering flexibility for boards and broadcasters alike. Such formats can also reduce travel burdens by allowing mini-tours between similarly ranked teams. For example, Pakistan vs West Indies or Sri Lanka vs Zimbabwe in four-match hybrid series could provide high-quality, meaningful cricket without exhausting players.

Moreover, AI-based calendar automation could personalize schedules based on player types. Fast bowlers may receive longer rest cycles, while spinners or top-order batters may rotate based on venue types and weather analytics. The goal is to maintain elite performance without crossing the fatigue threshold—something that caused dramatic form collapses in past players due to overwork.

As more data becomes available, AI systems can also optimize global coordination of league windows, Test series, and ICC events. Perhaps in the next decade, we'll see a global cricket calendar that is 3D mapped, fluid, and algorithmically balanced, where leagues and nations no longer operate in zero-sum competition but in coordinated symbiosis.

This would not only extend player careers but also allow newer teams to be scheduled based on developmental needs. Afghanistan, Ireland, and the USA, for instance, can be guided into tiered exposure without burning out or being neglected in scheduling congestion.

Ultimately, the future of cricket will depend as much on player wellness infrastructure as it does on bats and balls. AI-assisted rest planning, format reinvention through hybrid models, and equitable calendar distribution are not futuristic indulgences—they are essential guardrails for a sport rapidly expanding in speed, scale, and expectation.

The hybrid formats may not solve all structural inefficiencies, but they offer a compelling step forward, one that aligns with both athlete realities and audience demands in the decades ahead.

Reader's Notes

Three Centuries, Three Formats: *Cricket's evolution has been punctuated by major format shifts—Tests in the 19th century, ODIs in the 20th, and T20s in the 21st. The 22nd century may herald the rise of hybrid formats that balance tradition with speed.*

Hybrid Cricket Models: *The proposed 3-day, 55-over-per-innings format merges the tactical depth of Tests with the urgency of ODIs. It removes draws (except for weather-affected games) and limits bowling quotas, offering pace, intensity, and competitive balance.*

Ben Stokes & the Bazball Blueprint: *Stokes' aggressive Test captaincy has reimagined red-ball cricket. His refusal to settle for draws may reflect the kind of strategic mindset required to make hybrid cricket thrive.*

ODI's Identity Crisis: *Bilateral ODIs are facing dwindling interest. Only the World Cup remains relevant, prompting debate over whether a quadrennial ODI showcase is sufficient to keep the format alive.*

Test Cricket's Survival Depends on Depth: *With only the Big Three (India, England, Australia) consistently supporting Test cricket, the format's global survival hinges on revitalizing teams like Pakistan, West Indies, and Sri Lanka.*

AI-Driven Calendar Management: *Intelligent automation could soon power scheduling. AI models may optimize rest periods, injury prevention, and even suggest ideal series durations based on player workload data.*

Franchises Without Borders: *As T20 leagues evolve, the concept of geo-agnostic franchise teams—where players represent brands, not countries—is growing. This could alter national loyalties and reshape cricket economics.*

The AI MCC: *In future decades, rule-making may be guided by algorithmic models and predictive simulations. A digital "AI MCC" may oversee governance, fairness, and real-time adaptation of playing conditions.*

Player Burnout & Format Selection: *Modern players increasingly skip formats for longevity. Hybrid formats could attract players who've exited Tests due to five-day fatigue but still want to engage in multi-innings cricket.*

Governance Challenges: *The rise of AI, hybrid formats, and new markets necessitates new regulatory approaches. Cricket needs to rethink its structure to accommodate a digital-first, format-diverse future—without eroding its core essence.*

Chapter 14 – Metaverse, Web3, and Decentralized Cricket Economics

14.1 NFTs, Tokenized Tickets, and Digital Fan Ownership

By the mid-2020s, cricket began actively reshaping its economic and fan engagement models through blockchain-based innovations, with non-fungible tokens (NFTs) taking center stage. Initially seen as speculative digital collectibles, NFTs have evolved into powerful tools of micro-ownership, gamified loyalty, and decentralized community participation.

The earliest use of cricket NFTs emerged through platforms like Rario, FanCraze, and Sorare, offering digitally tokenized player cards, stadium scenes, and iconic moments—such as Tendulkar's effortless straight drive, Dhoni's historic six in the 2011 World Cup final, or Yuvraj Singh's six sixes off Stuart Broad in 2007. These were not just aesthetic assets but also became tradable commodities, often appreciating in value, and offering smart contract-based resale royalties to players, creators, and boards. For instance, FanCraze's Sachin Tendulkar NFTs reportedly sold for upwards of $25,000 USD, and the platform has secured partnerships with the ICC and Cricket Australia, giving NFTs institutional legitimacy.

However, the real breakthrough in Web3 cricket lies beyond collectibles—in functional, utility-based tokens that transform how fans interact with the game. The tokenization of match tickets has been one of the most revolutionary use cases. Tickets issued as NFTs are tamper-proof, non-replicable, and embedded with metadata tied to seat number, match location, date, and fan identity. Smart contracts ensure equitable revenue distribution—resale profits are split automatically between boards, stadiums, and even original buyers. The BCCI piloted this model at the 2025 ICC World Test Championship Final, showcasing both its technical scalability and potential to eliminate black-market ticketing.

Even more transformative is the emergence of digital fan ownership. Drawing inspiration from Socios.com's fan tokens and DAO (Decentralized Autonomous Organization) governance models in football, cricket franchises such as the Kolkata Knights DAO (a hypothetical future model) have begun offering tokenized "fan shares." These grant voting rights over non-strategic decisions like team jersey colors, stadium anthem choices, or locations for exhibition matches. While these tokens do not grant boardroom power, they represent a shift in fan involvement from passive consumers to active participants.

These tokens also unlock exclusive experiences: virtual meet-and-greets, early NFT drops, behind-the-scenes content, or access to "digital luxury boxes" inside the metaverse. Paired with loyalty staking models, fans earn rewards by simply holding or using these tokens—similar to frequent flyer miles, but blockchain-native.

Crucially, engagement in cricket's Web3 ecosystem is no longer measured merely by television ratings, social media impressions, or stadium turnouts. The new metrics of fan participation now include blockchain wallet holdings, voting behavior in governance polls, and involvement in NFT curation and community-led forums. A new type of fan economy is unfolding—one where participation is not just emotional or observational, but also financial, reputational, and deeply creative.

This decentralized model is also reshaping monetization from the bottom up. Increasingly, fans are minting their own NFTs—ranging from stylized digital art to short-form video edits and meme culture tributes. These creations, subject to community curation and DAO approval mechanisms, find their way into officially sanctioned marketplaces. The result is a merchandising landscape that no longer flows exclusively from team to supporter but allows fans to contribute directly to the economic and aesthetic ecosystem of cricket culture.

14.2 The Rise of Virtual Cricket Leagues in the Metaverse

During this modern era, the metaverse—defined as an always-on, immersive, and interconnected 3D digital ecosystem—began to reshape cricket in ways previously confined to science fiction. Leveraging advances in virtual reality (VR), artificial intelligence (AI), and blockchain infrastructure, cricket has entered a phase of virtual expansion that no longer depends on geographical limitations, physical stadiums, or even real-world weather.

Major technology firms, in collaboration with cricket boards and private franchises, launched the first generation of fully virtual cricket leagues by 2025 and 2026. These tournaments, hosted within expansive metaverse platforms such as Meta Horizon Worlds, The Sandbox, Decentraland, and new proprietary South Asian VR ecosystems, offer a wholly digitized version of the sport. Unlike earlier video games or simulations, these leagues combine AI-generated avatars, blockchain-verified performance stats, and interactive fan inputs to create a living, evolving league—one that functions beyond the constraints of real-world logistics.

Virtual cricket teams are made up of motion-captured avatars of real cricketers or entirely synthetic athletes powered by generative AI. These AI-driven players are not static codes; they evolve by ingesting data from real-life matches, past player behaviors, and even in-league simulations. Fan input adds another layer—viewers can suggest tactical changes, vote on training regimes, or contribute to a player's in-game decision-making through smart contracts. Over time, this interactivity generates unique team identities and strategic nuance far removed from traditional gaming.

Virtual stadiums amplify the immersive nature of the experience. Fans equipped with VR headsets or mobile AR interfaces can choose any vantage point—whether it's a drone cam hovering above the bowler's arm, or a digital VIP box with customizable surroundings. The user interface allows for tweaks to crowd size, weather conditions, commentary language, and even match aesthetics. In these arenas, the boundary between spectator and participant becomes increasingly fluid.

Monetization in the metaverse is radically different. Virtual ad placements—ranging from rotating holographic billboards to branded player skins—are auctioned to sponsors in real time. Players, whether AI or human-controlled, receive tokenized performance bonuses. Fans too are rewarded for their engagement—be it predicting match outcomes, managing virtual teams, or hosting digital watch parties in shared metaverse lounges. Brands like Coca-Cola and Paytm have already begun sponsoring virtual overlays and exclusive digital experiences within metaverse matches in pilot trials.

A prominent early example is the Metacricket Premier League (MPL), launched in 2024. Backed by a consortium of South Asian entertainment firms and blockchain-based DAOs, the MPL offered 10 franchises, each co-owned by a mix of token holders and institutional investors. Within its first season, MPL reported over two million concurrent users during its grand final—a virtual showdown between the Mumbai Meshers and the Lahore Lightnings, played in a floating, futuristic sky-stadium in the metaverse. Critics who initially dismissed it as a gimmick now acknowledge the MPL as a credible alternative format, especially during off-seasons or when geopolitical tensions make real-world cricket logistically challenging.

Importantly, metaverse leagues are proving to be a force for democratization. Aspiring cricketers from regions without strong domestic infrastructure—be it northeast India, rural Afghanistan, or interior Kenya—can now create avatars, upload video performances, and participate in open qualifiers. AI scouts analyze their data points—

bat speed, shot timing, reaction to spin—and assign performance ratings. Exceptional players are already being scouted by real-world franchises, inverting the traditional talent pipeline that previously flowed from elite academies downward.

As traditional cricket struggles with saturated schedules, declining bilateral viewership, and increasingly empty stadiums, the metaverse offers a new horizon. It is not a substitute for real cricket, but an extension—an alternative dimension where data, imagination, and fandom converge. In this space, cricket is untethered from climate, geopolitics, and physical wear-and-tear. It is experimental, inclusive, and potentially transformative.

The question is no longer *if* cricket will adapt to the metaverse—it is how soon fans, boards, and players will fully embrace this new format as a core part of the sport's identity.

14.3 Decentralized Web3 Investments and Franchise Ownership

The rise of Web3 has ushered in a quiet but foundational transformation in cricket's financial ecosystem, particularly in how franchises are funded, owned, and governed. The traditional model—where teams were owned by private investors or state-backed boards—is slowly giving way to decentralized finance (DeFi) frameworks, enabling distributed ownership, fractional investing, and tokenized governance through DAOs (Decentralized Autonomous Organizations).

By 2025, several Tier-2 leagues and emerging franchise ecosystems, particularly in South Asia and the Caribbean, began issuing tokenized equity instead of seeking venture capital or broadcast-heavy backing. Fans no longer sit at the periphery—they are now stakeholders. These franchise tokens function as tradable digital assets, granting holders a

273

real, verifiable stake in the team. With that stake comes access to shared revenue, early rights to merchandise and NFT drops, and participatory voting on non-core decisions like team branding, theme music, or friendly match locations.

Unlike traditional sports IPOs or equity crowdfunding—often opaque and centralized—Web3 models offer radical transparency. Smart contracts executed on public blockchains manage revenue sharing automatically. Every income stream—ticketing, merchandise, digital collectibles, streaming rights, or even metaverse licensing—is accounted for and distributed according to pre-coded logic. There's no waiting for dividends or royalty settlements; everything is automated, traceable, and trustless.

In India, the Telangana Titans, part of the Emerging India T20 Super League, became the first cricket team to experiment with DAO-led governance. Up to 40% of operational decisions—ranging from secondary jersey design to scheduling exhibition matches—were opened to token holders through mobile-based voting portals. A governance token, dubbed TITANX, tracks user engagement and grants tiered privileges. Fans with higher voting power can even propose new initiatives, while a multisig treasury wallet ensures transparency in fund allocation.

Internationally, the Caribbean Premier Cricket DAO (CPCD) set another precedent by launching a fully tokenized ownership model for its expansion team, the Kingston Krakens. Equity was issued via the Ethereum-based Polymesh network, attracting investors from over 30 countries. For the first time in cricket history, retail investors could trade team shares on decentralized exchanges (DEXs), bringing real-time liquidity to what was once an exclusive ownership model.

A more recent trend is the rise of athlete-led investment vehicles. Some professional cricketers—particularly younger internationals—have begun issuing performance tokens, where the value fluctuates based on real-life form, milestones, and match impact. Fans who hold these tokens gain access to exclusive content, voting rights on fan events, and rewards linked to on-field achievements. This direct-to-community financial model allows athletes to monetize their personal brand without relying solely on agents, sponsors, or boards.

These innovations are not without challenges. The regulatory landscape for tokenized sports assets remains unsettled in many jurisdictions. Token price volatility can deter risk-averse investors, and DAOs are still learning how to prevent governance deadlock when decision-making is distributed among thousands. Yet, despite these risks, the direction is clear: cricket's franchise economy is evolving.

Where the 20th century was dominated by boardroom decisions and billionaire ownership, the 2020s are revealing a future in which teams are community-owned, algorithmically managed, and transparently operated. Franchises are no longer gated empires; they are living, digital cooperatives powered by fans, investors, and smart infrastructure.

This shift doesn't just democratize investment—it redefines what it means to *belong* to a team. In a tokenized future, ownership is not symbolic—it is active, programmable, and accessible to anyone with a digital wallet and a stake in the game.

14.4 Nano-Tech Cricket: Programmable Pitches and Smart Balls

As cricket enters a new age of technological integration, the convergence of nanotechnology, smart materials, and real-time analytics is revolutionizing the sport's core mechanics—particularly its playing surfaces and the cricket ball itself. While previous innovations like drop-in pitches, pink balls, and LED stumps were seen as incremental, the developments post-2024 mark a paradigm shift. This is not just about tweaking the aesthetics or optics of cricket; this is about redesigning its very environment and equipment.

At the forefront of this transformation are programmable nano-surface pitches—engineered with smart polymeric layers embedded with nanosensors and microfluidic actuators. These surfaces can adjust their behavior dynamically, responding to environmental factors like temperature, humidity, wear, or even player footfall. Curators, using handheld devices or centralized AI dashboards, can modulate surface friction, bounce, seam movement, and abrasion patterns on demand. What once took nature and weather days to influence, can now be recalibrated between sessions—or even mid-match.

Pilot projects have already taken shape in stadiums across Dubai, Bengaluru, and Adelaide, where hybrid test beds are being used to simulate different pitch conditions across time. A match might begin on a surface mimicking dusty Chennai turners, then shift to a WACA-like bounce post-lunch. The implications for training camps, broadcast engagement, and multi-format tournament hosting are enormous. Such programmable surfaces also offer more equitable balancing of contests—ensuring no format, player type, or side of the ball (bat or ball) gains long-term dominance due to static pitch behavior.

Equally groundbreaking is the emergence of smart balls—cricket balls embedded with nanotech microchips and inertial sensors directly beneath the seam. Unlike traditional ball-tracking systems that depend on camera triangulation (e.g., Hawk-Eye), these balls emit live telemetry data through edge networks. Parameters such as rotational velocity, release angle, seam tilt, air turbulence, ball degradation, and impact force are transmitted in real-time.

This technology is not theoretical—it is being actively trialed in select training environments and franchise leagues with enhanced technical infrastructure. For bowlers, the data can be fed back via haptic feedback gloves or AI-driven dashboards, alerting them to minor flaws in wrist positioning or over-rotation. Coaches can overlay biometric data with ball analytics to predict injury risk, fatigue, or bowling efficiency. This could eventually lead to "smart coaching"—where real-time micro-adjustments replace traditional between-over instructions.

Perhaps most intriguing is the role these smart balls could play in regulatory enforcement. The debate around suspect bowling actions, particularly the interpretation of "chucking," has plagued cricket for decades. Smart balls paired with motion sensors in player jerseys could precisely measure angular elbow flexion, delivering automated biomechanical compliance in real time. Controversial calls could be replaced by data-verified thresholds, eliminating grey areas in legal delivery definitions.

There are, however, philosophical questions. Critics argue that cricket's allure lies in its imperfection, its reliance on instinct, and its organic variability. They worry that programmable pitches and AI-generated swing metrics might sterilize the game, leaving little to fate, intuition, or the art of improvisation. But proponents see this evolution as augmentation, not automation—similar to how DRS and ultra-edge didn't destroy cricket's essence but refined it.

The introduction of such high-precision tech could also reshape how fans interact with the game. Real-time graphics of spin RPMs, seam wobble, or reverse swing deviation could be layered into AR/VR broadcast feeds. Viewers might receive predictive insights into the next ball's expected trajectory or likelihood of inducing an edge—all powered by live sensor data from the field.

In this new nano-cricket era, the role of the curator, coach, umpire, and broadcaster is being redefined. The ground is no longer a passive canvas but a programmable interface. The ball is no longer just leather and cork but a data-generating instrument. And the game itself is transitioning from a purely physical contest to a hybrid theatre of human intuition and machine intelligence.

Importantly, cricket's governing bodies must ensure that such technologies are deployed in a way that preserves the sport's spirit, ensures equal access, and avoids the divide between tech-rich and tech-poor nations. Regulation must be proactive, not reactive—lest the gap between cricketing "haves" and "have-nots" becomes unbridgeable.

In the end, programmable pitches and intelligent balls do not aim to erase tradition; they seek to enhance it. They give curators control, provide athletes insight, and deliver fans immersion. For a sport that has always balanced heritage with reinvention, nano-tech cricket may be its most nuanced evolution yet.

14.5 Cross-Franchise NFTs and Virtual Cricket Merch Markets

As cricket's commercial ecosystem enters the age of decentralization, a new era of borderless fan ownership and cross-franchise merchandising is emerging—powered by interoperable blockchain ecosystems and Web3 standards. No longer confined by national boundaries or single-team loyalty, cricket fandom is being reimagined through cross-platform NFTs and virtual merchandise that transcend the silos of traditional leagues.

These next-generation cross-franchise NFTs serve as digital keys to a multi-layered cricketing metaverse. One such example is a limited-edition NFT titled *"Fastest Deliveries in T20 History"*, which might feature avatars or highlights of bowlers like Bumrah, Rauf, and Shaheen Afridi. But beyond its visual appeal, the NFT unlocks tangible benefits across different leagues: early ticket access for an IPL double-header, a draft advantage in the Caribbean Premier League (CPL), or voting rights on All-Star match-ups in The Hundred. These tokens are minted with standardized metadata on interoperable blockchains like Polygon, Flow, and Solana, making them usable across platforms—a practice borrowed from the gaming and decentralized finance (DeFi) sectors.

Virtual merchandising has followed this cross-platform logic. NFT-based caps, jerseys, holographic wristbands, and avatar gear are now traded as wearable assets in cricket-themed metaverses. A fan could, for instance, outfit their avatar in a Mumbai Indians jersey while attending a virtual Lahore Qalandars vs. Trinbago Knight Riders match inside a mixed-reality stadium. These wearables are not just cosmetic—they often serve as access tokens to loyalty programs, unlock fantasy league bonuses, or enable VIP entry into virtual lounges, press conferences, or live Q&A sessions with players.

Brands have quickly adapted to this shift. Joint NFT drops—such as a Dhoni-Pollard commemorative release celebrating iconic six-hitters of the 2020s—are co-launched by merch platforms and franchise stakeholders. Smart contracts govern the royalty distribution, ensuring that revenue is transparently and automatically split between players, NFT creators, and licensing boards. This model not only brings passive income to athletes but also creates sustainable revenue loops for fans and creators alike.

More significantly, the gates are now open for fan-generated content to be tokenized and legitimized. Platforms increasingly allow users to mint their own NFTs—whether it be stylized artwork, fanfiction, memes, or self-edited highlight reels. These assets undergo community curation through DAOs (Decentralized Autonomous Organizations), which vote on quality and authenticity. Approved NFTs enter curated marketplaces where fans can buy, trade, or display them, effectively blurring the line between consumer and creator.

Liquidity is another game-changer. Cricket NFTs—especially rare or utility-rich ones—are now accepted as collateral on Web3 lending platforms. A fan holding a rare "Virat Kohli Final-over Chase" NFT could potentially secure a micro-loan or swap tokens within a sports-focused DeFi pool. This is no longer just memorabilia; it is programmable digital property with economic leverage.

This evolving NFT economy is creating what many now call "metacultural fandom"—a form of fan identity that is fluid, participatory, and global. A supporter of Chennai Super Kings may also collect Big Bash League memorabilia or own governance tokens in a US-based startup T20 league. Allegiances are no longer confined by location, history, or even format. Instead, identity becomes modular, constructed from a mosaic of collectibles, virtual appearances, DAO participation, and social reputation within Web3 communities.

Much like how cricket evolved from a colonial pastime into South Asian mastery and global passion, its commercial arm is now evolving from proprietary to participatory. Where once fans were sold jerseys and posters, today they mint, trade, vote, and earn. The shift is not merely digital—it is philosophical. Fandom is no longer about being a passive recipient of culture; it is about being a co-author of cricket's economic and cultural narrative.

14.5.1 E-Sports Cricket: When the Game Leaves the Field

If cricket's expansion into the metaverse is about immersive fandom, then e-sports represents the moment when cricket itself detaches from the boundary ropes and re-emerges in a wholly digital arena. Competitive gaming—long dominated by titles like FIFA, NBA 2K, and League of Legends—has begun to shape the way traditional sports are consumed by younger generations. Cricket, though a late entrant into this space, is now experimenting with its own digital twin: professionalized e-cricket tournaments, streamed globally and attracting both gamers and fans who might never have played the sport in the physical world.

The first signs of this came in the early 21st century with titles such as *EA Sports Cricket* and *Don Bradman Cricket*, which introduced rudimentary commentary, player likenesses, and simulated stadiums. Though primitive by today's standards, these games laid the foundation for a generation comfortable with cricket as a digital experience. Fast forward to the 2020s, and e-cricket is no longer confined to console games in living rooms. Instead, international e-sports platforms now host competitive cricket tournaments, some backed by national boards and private franchises. ICC has tested formats for a possible "eCricket World Cup," while streaming giants such as Twitch and YouTube Gaming now broadcast simulated matches to audiences in the hundreds of thousands.

Unlike fantasy leagues, which simulate management, or metaverse cricket, which emphasizes immersion, e-sports cricket creates an entirely new category of competition. Professional players—gamers rather than athletes—train in reflexes, hand–eye coordination, and tactical decision-making within digital cricket ecosystems. Franchise owners see this as another layer of fan capture: a Delhi Capitals e-cricket side could exist alongside its IPL counterpart, tapping into sponsorships, NFT-driven rewards, and cross-promotions between digital and physical matchdays. For young audiences who consume more hours of gaming content than live sport, this is cricket re-engineered to match their habits.

Yet the rise of e-cricket is not without complications. Purists may see it as a dilution of the game's essence: a bat, a ball, and a contest in the sun reduced to pixels and algorithms. There are also questions of legitimacy—should e-cricket be treated as an extension of the sport, or as a parallel entertainment product like fantasy gaming? Further, the economics of e-sports can skew heavily toward streamers and platforms, raising concerns about whether cricket's governing bodies risk losing control of another revenue stream.

Still, the momentum is undeniable. As broadcasting becomes more personalized and digital economies expand, e-sports cricket is carving a niche not by replacing traditional cricket but by coexisting with it. For a teenager in Seoul, Berlin, or São Paulo, who may never have held a bat, the gateway to the sport could be through a digital league watched on a smartphone. In that sense, e-cricket does not diminish cricket's sovereignty—it expands it into entirely new demographics and geographies.

The question is whether administrators will embrace this evolution proactively or reluctantly. Because when cricket leaves the field and enters the console, the future of the game may no longer be shaped solely by boards, players, or fans—but by coders, platforms, and the communities of gamers who redefine competition in the digital century.

14.6 AI-Powered Fantasy Ownership Leagues

Fantasy cricket has long existed as a bridge between fan imagination and the unpredictability of real-world sport. But in the age of artificial intelligence, it has evolved from passive prediction into a live, dynamic, and participatory economy—where managing a team is no longer just a game, but a form of micro-ownership. What once relied on gut instinct and post-match analysis is now shaped by real-time machine learning, tokenized assets, and algorithmic curation. Welcome to the era of AI-powered fantasy ownership leagues.

Unlike traditional fantasy platforms that fix line-ups before matches and lock strategies into static weekly rounds, these new-age leagues operate like adaptive financial portfolios. Users no longer pick players and wait—they oversee constantly rebalanced teams, assisted by AI agents trained on a mosaic of data: historical performances, pitch conditions, weather predictions, injury reports, fitness data, even player sentiment extracted from social media. These intelligent assistants operate under selectable personas—some designed for aggressive optimization, others for conservative, value-focused strategy. The result is a layer of personalization rarely seen in conventional fantasy formats.

But the innovation goes far beyond gameplay mechanics. Fantasy teams themselves have become tokenized assets—blockchain-registered entities with unique IDs, historical records, and market value. In this economy, a well-managed team is a monetizable unit. Players can auction off successful squads, lease them for tournaments, or split ownership among a syndicate of fans. Cross-platform leagues have emerged, where teams perform in various formats—from mainstream international fixtures to under-19 domestic tournaments, women's cricket, and even virtual simulations.

The player tokens within these teams are also NFTs, their values fluctuating in real time with form, popularity, and scarcity. A rising young cricketer in a regional tournament can become a hot asset overnight—not because of broadcast exposure, but because their fantasy stock surges, driven by AI-analyzed performances and market speculation. Fantasy leagues are, in many ways, becoming early talent identification ecosystems, with some franchises and scouts now monitoring leaderboard analytics and AI heatmaps to detect emerging players or tactical innovations.

This entire economy is gamified with deep-learning mechanics. Fantasy participants can unlock exclusive NFT rewards based on rare in-game achievements: a bowler claiming a hat-trick across two innings, a last-over six from a wildcard captain, or a fielder earning a surprise run-out. These scenarios, run through millions of AI simulations, offer fans personalized challenges that enhance retention while blurring the lines between gameplay, fandom, and investment.

Yet, with complexity comes responsibility. Ethical AI governance has become a non-negotiable foundation. To prevent unfair advantages or exploitative monopolies, leading platforms have adopted open-source model audits, capped rewards, and transparent weightings for all AI decisions. Algorithmic behavior is version-controlled, and some platforms allow community-led peer reviews of the AI systems themselves—an emerging form of technological self-regulation in fantasy gaming.

Perhaps the most profound change lies in the nature of ownership. In older formats, fantasy leagues reset each season, and teams faded into irrelevance. Now, they carry legacy—each squad has a history, a performance curve, and a valuation. The best-managed franchises have become digital sports assets, bought, sold, co-owned, or borrowed like any equity. Sponsorships, ad impressions during simulated broadcasts, affiliate collaborations—all now flow back into these decentralized fantasy ecosystems, creating a parallel cricketing economy.

In a time where younger audiences are increasingly native to esports, streaming, and algorithmic interaction, AI fantasy leagues are doing more than just extending cricket's appeal. They are redefining it. Cricket is no longer only played by athletes on the field—it is now co-authored by fans and algorithms, run in real-time simulations, governed by smart contracts, and tracked across blockchain registries.

This is not merely a future imagined. It is a future being built—one fantasy team at a time.

14.7 Governance in a Tokenized Cricket World

As cricket enters its tokenized era—where fans participate through DAOs (Decentralized Autonomous Organizations), purchase governance tokens, and access digital voting rights—a fundamental question emerges: who governs this ecosystem when interests diverge?

The idea of shared governance through blockchain-based DAOs promises democratic participation, but it remains a technical and legal grey area. For instance, if a DAO-based cricket franchise votes for a branding decision that contradicts a board's commercial contract, which stakeholder has the final say? In most current implementations, token-based voting powers are largely symbolic—designed more for engagement than true decision-making. The result is often hybrid governance: legacy cricket boards retain core authority, while token holders are steered toward non-critical areas such as jersey design or exhibition venues.

This raises concerns about what some critics call "governance theatre"—where participatory optics mask the persistence of centralized power. True decentralization, as promised by Web3, would require clear legal frameworks to define the contractual authority of DAO resolutions, voting thresholds, dispute resolution protocols, and smart contract enforceability (i.e., whether blockchain-based decisions can be upheld in traditional courts).

Presently, most cricket DAOs are not legal entities under sports law, financial law, or even commercial code. The lack of legal personhood leaves them vulnerable in litigation, sponsorship disputes, or tax liability questions. Moreover, the global nature of these DAOs means participants operate across jurisdictions—creating complex regulatory challenges. If a DAO-based team has token holders from 30 countries, which country's laws apply when internal conflict arises?

To ensure meaningful governance, future DAO-cricket hybrids must consider multi-jurisdictional legal models, transparent tokenomics, and dual-board governance structures, where fan votes hold contractually binding power within clearly defined limits. Without legal and institutional innovation, tokenized cricket risks becoming participatory only in form—not in function.

As cricket evolves in digital spaces, governance must evolve too—not just in terms of who holds power, but how that power is recognized, constrained, and enforced.

Readers' Notes

Blockchain Match Tickets

Cricket boards now issue match tickets as digital tokens (NFTs), preventing counterfeiting and black-market sales. These smart tickets include details like seat number and buyer history—and resale profits are shared fairly between the organizers and original buyers.

Fan Ownership and Voting Rights

Fans can buy special tokens that allow them to vote on fun, non-strategic team decisions—like jersey colors, theme music, or friendly match venues. It's a small but symbolic way for supporters to co-own the teams they love.

VIP Digital Access for Fans

Owning certain cricket NFTs grants access to online "VIP areas"—like private interviews with players, virtual match lounges, or metaverse screening rooms. It's fandom with exclusive perks.

Cricket in the Metaverse (e.g., MPL 2024)

The Metacricket Premier League became the first all-digital cricket league played inside virtual worlds like Meta Horizon. Matches involved AI avatars of real players and were attended by fans using VR headsets.

Personalizing Your Virtual Match

Inside metaverse stadiums, fans can change their match experience—switch camera angles, mute or amplify crowd sounds, change weather conditions, or even decorate the stadium design virtually.

AI-Generated Cricketers

Some teams now use synthetic players—AI-generated avatars trained on data from real-world stars. These avatars learn, adapt, and compete in digital leagues like real athletes.

DAO-Controlled Teams (e.g., Telangana Titans)

Some teams are partially run by their fan community. Token holders vote on smaller operational decisions, making the team more democratic and less boardroom-only.

Owning a Piece of a Team

Instead of just watching cricket, fans can now invest directly in a team by buying tokens. These tokens may earn revenue from merchandise sales, ticket profits, or online streaming.

Player Tokens That Track Performance

Some cricketers release their own digital tokens. If they perform well in real matches, the value of their tokens rises—creating a direct link between player form and fan rewards.

Programmable Cricket Pitches

Advanced pitches now use nano-technology to change conditions between sessions—like turning slow and dusty before lunch, then bouncy and fast afterward—offering more variety in play.

Smart Cricket Balls with Built-in Sensors

Modern cricket balls now have chips that record things like speed, spin, and seam angle in real-time. This helps broadcasters, analysts, and fans get richer data.

Spotting Illegal Bowling Actions Automatically

These smart balls, paired with AI cameras, can detect if a bowler's action goes beyond the legal limits—providing accurate, unbiased decisions.

NFTs That Work Across Leagues

Imagine owning a Dhoni NFT that unlocks perks in both the IPL and CPL. Cross-franchise NFTs now allow fans to get bonuses, access, or merch across different tournaments.

Fan-Created Digital Merch

Fans can now design and sell their own digital cricket merchandise—jerseys, avatar gear, highlight art—and earn money through resale in verified NFT marketplaces.

Using Cricket NFTs for Loans

Rare digital collectibles—like an NFT of a famous cricket moment—can now be used as loan collateral in the world of decentralized finance (DeFi).

AI Fantasy Team Managers

Fans can pick an AI "persona" to manage their fantasy team live during matches. These AI managers make decisions based on data, trends, and even social media buzz.

Fantasy Teams With Real Value

Fantasy teams are now registered assets that can be traded, sold, or leased. A successful fantasy team could become a digital business in its own right.

Match Moments That Unlock Bonuses

AI systems track special in-game moments—like hat-tricks or final-ball sixes—and reward fans with digital badges, exclusive tokens, or in-game boosts.

Ethical AI in Fantasy Platforms

To ensure fairness, fantasy platforms limit AI advantages and review algorithms publicly to prevent cheating or manipulation.

Scouting Talent from Fantasy Leagues

Fantasy leagues are now so detailed that real-world scouts track top-performing users or teams for analytics and player insights. The fantasy world is becoming a pipeline into the real game.

Chapter 15 – Climate Change and Cricket's Survival

15.1 Scheduling in a Hotter World: Shifting Seasons and Indoor Stadiums

As global temperatures continue to rise, cricket faces mounting pressure to adapt to a climate-disrupted world. Historically considered a sport attuned to the seasons, cricket's traditional scheduling—aligned with dry summers and temperate evenings—is now being destabilized by extreme heatwaves, rising humidity, poor air quality, and increasingly erratic rainfall.

The first adaptation strategy is the reshaping of playing calendars. Many cricketing nations are reassessing their domestic and international schedules to avoid peak summer extremes. Boards in South Asia and Australia are considering pushing matches into colder seasons—late winter and early spring—to reduce heat stress. In England, county cricket authorities are evaluating fixture models that reduce play in high-summer heat and shift games to cooler months with modified turf care protocols.

A more radical change is the rise of indoor and hybrid stadiums. Traditionally reserved for sports like tennis or basketball, fully enclosed, climate-controlled cricket venues are now viewed as an infrastructural solution to worsening outdoor conditions. Concept proposals for such enclosed, solar-powered cricket stadiums have emerged in hot-weather nations like the UAE, where summer temperatures routinely exceed safe playing thresholds. While no official "Dubai Cricket Dome" project has been confirmed, the push for domed or partially covered venues is growing, offering potential solutions for year-round play and climate-controlled safety.

Yet challenges remain. Playing in the high humidity of the UAE, Sri Lanka, and coastal India continues to pose risks, even in early mornings or evenings. Humid conditions intensify heat stress, cause dehydration, and reduce recovery time. Stadium cooling systems and smart scheduling can only go so far. There is a growing need to develop regional heat management standards—such as enforced hydration breaks, mandatory rest periods, and match timing protocols based on heat indices, not just convenience.

Cricket boards are now turning to climate forecasting tools powered by AI to assist with these decisions. These tools integrate hyperlocal climate data, air quality indexes, and even biomechanical stress models to map when and where games should be held. Matches in high-risk zones are increasingly shifted to cooler time slots—early morning starts, twilight games, or night fixtures—combined with LED cooling systems and shaded seating.

Fan behavior, too, is shifting. Many stadiums report dwindling attendance during extreme weather conditions, even when ticket prices are reduced. In response, broadcasters and teams are amplifying digital engagement—investing in virtual stadiums, real-time commentary bots, and immersive second-screen experiences to maintain fan interest from the safety of their homes.

Finally, there is the ethical dimension: Can the game continue to justify frequent, carbon-heavy international tours? The ICC and leading boards are exploring regional tournament clustering, carbon offsetting strategies, and even digital-only tours as experimental models. The conversation around building a low-carbon, climate-aligned cricket economy is gaining traction.

Ultimately, the climate crisis is not a hypothetical future—it is an active, accelerating force already reshaping how, when, and where cricket is played. Cricket's survival in the 21st century second half will depend not only on technology and infrastructure but on cultural adaptability, ecological responsibility, and a willingness to rewrite the rules of the game in alignment with planetary realities.

15.2 Climate-Resilient Infrastructure: AI Pitches, Super-Soppers, and Cooling Tech

As the climate crisis accelerates, cricket infrastructure is being forced into a phase of rapid reinvention. What were once considered rare disruptions—monsoon downpours, intense heatwaves, unplayable humidity, or choking air pollution—are now increasingly part of the routine. To keep pace, cricket grounds around the world are undergoing a quiet revolution, reimagining their design, operations, and technologies to become climate-resilient and environmentally intelligent.

At the heart of this transformation is the emergence of AI-enhanced playing surfaces. Unlike traditional pitches that rely solely on human curatorship, the new generation of "smart" wickets integrates a network of underground sensors to monitor moisture levels, soil health, turf stress, and heat index in real time. These systems are linked to adaptive irrigation networks that activate automatically based on forecast data and in-play surface stress. In some pilot programs, satellite-linked AI models are being used to predict when cracks might form on a dry pitch, or when uneven bounce zones may appear due to rapid moisture loss.

While fully autonomous AI-managed pitches remain experimental, many international grounds are already laying the groundwork. Bengaluru's M. Chinnaswamy Stadium, long a leader in sustainable turf management, is exploring such systems as part of its climate-adaptive maintenance program. The aim is not just pitch preservation but optimization—ensuring surfaces remain safe, playable, and consistent even under hostile climatic shifts.

Rain management, too, is undergoing major innovation. Traditional super-soppers, once manually operated, are now evolving into autonomous, sensor-equipped drying units. These robotic systems can scan the field, detect saturation zones, and prioritize extraction in real time—cutting match resumption delays by nearly half. Beneath the surface, stadiums are reengineering their drainage architecture, using multi-layer permeable turf systems, underground bioswales, and even vertical water tanks that store excess rainfall for reuse. Such systems are particularly vital in rain-heavy geographies like Bangladesh, Sri Lanka, and India's east coast, where cloudbursts can swamp outfields within minutes.

As temperatures soar—often crossing 40°C in major cricketing cities—heat mitigation has become essential. Newer stadium designs now incorporate high-SRI (Solar Reflectance Index) roofing materials that reflect sunlight and reduce thermal load. In elite venues, player dugouts and dressing areas are being equipped with radiant cooling floors and smart ventilation systems that track carbon dioxide and humidity. For spectators, misting zones, shaded seating canopies, and heat index display boards are increasingly becoming the norm. Synthetic turf materials are also evolving—built to breathe, release heat, and reduce the risk of skin burns and injuries.

A more recent and alarming concern is air pollution. In urban centers like Delhi, Lahore, and Dhaka, air quality levels can spike into hazardous territory, especially after major festivals or during winter inversions. To counter this, stadiums have begun experimenting with temporary clean-air domes—portable structures built using HEPA-grade filtration, carbon dioxide regulation, and real-time PM2.5 and AQI monitoring. While these systems cannot cover the entire ground, they aim to create safe micro-environments for players, umpires, and support staff during high-risk events.

Simultaneously, sustainability is moving from peripheral CSR to a core operational priority. Stadiums are investing in solar panel installations across rooftops, advanced rainwater harvesting systems, and even kinetic walkways that generate small amounts of electricity from crowd movement. Some newer venues are deploying AI-powered facility management tools that control lighting, air conditioning, and even water usage based on real-time occupancy and environmental load, reducing energy waste without compromising comfort.

This convergence of smart technology, environmental sensitivity, and cricketing tradition is giving rise to a new model of stadium—one that doesn't just react to climate challenges but anticipates and manages them with agility. In many ways, these venues are becoming miniature prototypes of sustainable urban design. They demonstrate how legacy infrastructure can be updated, not just for survival, but for leadership in the age of climate volatility.

For cricket, this is more than a logistical upgrade. It is a cultural transformation—signaling the sport's willingness to evolve, to protect its players and fans, and to act as a responsible global citizen in the face of a planetary emergency. The stadiums of the future will not only host matches. They will embody climate intelligence, resilience, and renewal.

15.3 – Greening the Game: Towards a Carbon-Neutral Cricketing Future

As climate change continues to reshape global priorities, cricket is confronted with a question far deeper than where or when it can be played—it must now ask how the game can be played sustainably. Beyond adapting infrastructure or rescheduling matches to escape the worst impacts of heatwaves and rainfall, cricket's long-term survival may depend on its ability to contribute to the climate solution itself. The future of cricket is no longer just about mitigating damage—it is about mobilizing the game's cultural capital for environmental leadership.

One of the most urgent pathways is the implementation of carbon audits across tours and tournaments. From intercontinental air travel to diesel-run logistics, cricket's carbon footprint has remained largely unexamined. However, several forward-looking leagues are beginning to change that. England's Hundred and Australia's Big Bash League have piloted green initiatives such as using electric buses for team transport and encouraging public transit for fan movement. Some international series are even experimenting with "low-carbon bubbles," where team hotels, stadiums, and practice venues are chosen for walkability or renewable energy usage.

Carbon offsetting is also emerging as a serious option. Cricket boards and franchises are partnering with environmental NGOs to invest in reforestation projects, clean cooking initiatives, and solar energy programs. Smart contracts and blockchain tools are being tested to verify and tokenize these carbon offsets, allowing fans to trace their match tickets or NFTs to real-world environmental action. The concept of "green NFTs"—where revenue contributes directly to carbon mitigation—has seen traction in experimental campaigns in the Caribbean and New Zealand.

Fans themselves are being brought into the sustainability ecosystem. Stadiums are rolling out carbon-aware ticketing systems, where fans can opt for bike parking, electric shuttle services, or carbon-neutral packages that include offset costs. In metaverse environments, cricket leagues are rewarding fans who attend digital-only broadcasts with digital collectibles that support green causes. Some franchises are exploring "tree-per-ticket" models, in which every physical seat sold contributes to afforestation in climate-vulnerable regions.

There is also growing interest in cricket-themed climate events. South Asian countries, Pacific Island nations, and even African boards are considering the launch of a "Climate Cup"—a special series or tournament focused entirely on sustainability, hosted in vulnerable regions and aligned with the UN's climate agenda. These events would feature plastic-free zones, solar-powered pavilions, and mandatory green certification for all stakeholders involved. A partnership between the Maldives Cricket Board and a European climate NGO, for instance, has proposed a floating solar stadium as a flagship concept.

Perhaps the most powerful shift is taking place at the grassroots. Young cricketers across India, Bangladesh, and Kenya are participating in dual development programs that combine cricket training with climate education. NGOs and local academies have started "eco-clubs" within cricket training centers—organizing waste cleanups, awareness drives, and even installing solar nets and energy-efficient lighting for training grounds. This fusion of sport and sustainability nurtures both future athletes and future stewards of the environment.

The climate crisis poses existential risks—but also opens an unprecedented window for cricket to transform. The game has a long and complex history tied to colonial trade, industrialization, and global mobility. But in this era, it can become an unlikely ambassador for ecological harmony. From carbon-neutral World Cups to low-emission domestic leagues and green stadium innovations, cricket can redefine what it means to play responsibly on a planetary scale.

In doing so, it will not only survive—it will lead.

15.4 The Carbon Footprint of Streaming and Virtual Cricket

While cricket's transition toward digital infrastructure—streaming platforms, metaverse matches, NFTs, and VR experiences—reduces travel-related emissions, it introduces a less visible but equally important sustainability concern: the carbon footprint of digital systems themselves.

Contrary to the belief that "online equals green," digital cricket is energy-intensive. Every streamed match, NFT minting, or VR stadium experience draws on data centers that rely heavily on electricity. According to the International Energy Agency (2023), global data centers now account for approximately 1.5–2% of total electricity demand, with blockchain networks like Ethereum previously consuming energy on par with mid-sized countries before moving to Proof-of-Stake protocols.

Streaming platforms such as Disney+ Hotstar and YouTube, when broadcasting major tournaments like the ICC T20 World Cup or IPL, serve tens of millions of concurrent viewers. High-definition streams, cloud-based replays, and algorithmic highlights consume bandwidth and server resources that indirectly contribute to emissions. Even seemingly low-impact actions—like checking Cricinfo ball-by-ball coverage or fantasy cricket dashboards—draw on server infrastructures powered by fossil-fuel-heavy grids in regions like South Asia and the Middle East.

Furthermore, NFT minting and trading, integral to the Web3 cricket economy, also introduce energy costs—though platforms are increasingly moving to more sustainable, low-energy blockchain alternatives like Polygon or Flow. Nevertheless, a single NFT drop involving tens of thousands of assets still results in measurable environmental impact, especially if built on older Proof-of-Work protocols.

Cricket's climate strategy must account for its digital shadow. Potential solutions include carbon-offset partnerships for streaming services, sustainable NFT platforms, AI-optimized video compression, and pressure on hosting providers to transition to renewable energy. Broadcasting partners should also publish transparency reports detailing the ecological cost per streamed match—just as travel miles are tracked for touring teams.

Importantly, digital cricket is both a solution and a problem. As cricket moves deeper into the metaverse and digital immersion, it must not outsource its environmental responsibilities to invisible infrastructures. The carbon cost of going digital is real—and must be addressed with the same urgency as physical emissions.

Readers' Notes

AI-Augmented Pitches – *Conceptual smart pitches with embedded sensors, moisture controls, and turf adaptation models are being explored, though not yet widely implemented.*

Chinnaswamy Stadium's Eco-Leading Role – *Bengaluru's Chinnaswamy Stadium is a pioneer in water management, solar energy use, and sustainable drainage but has not trialed full AI pitch tech.*

Autonomous Super-Soppers – *New water-removal bots use saturation mapping to reduce post-rain downtime by up to 60%, improving match continuity in flood-prone venues.*

Radiant Cooling Systems – *Some stadiums are experimenting with cooled flooring, mist zones, and smart ventilation in response to rising pitch-side temperatures.*

High-SRI Roofing & Breathable Turf – *Reflective roofing materials and new turf blends help reduce surface heat and improve player comfort during matches.*

Air Quality Management – *Delhi and other urban venues are testing localized filtration domes and air quality monitoring to combat matchday smog conditions.*

Kinetic Energy Floors – *New stadiums are piloting concourse flooring that harvests energy from crowd movement, contributing to low-carbon power goals.*

Smart Infrastructure AI – *Algorithms manage lighting, cooling, and irrigation based on crowd size, ambient conditions, and power grid demand.*

Permeable Drainage Surfaces – *Instead of just sopping water, upgraded fields use bioswales and porous materials to absorb flash flooding efficiently.*

Green Stadium Movement – *Cricket venues are becoming early test beds for sustainable, smart-city-style infrastructure that balances tradition with climate adaptation.*

Climate Cup (Proposed): *A global, eco-certified cricket tournament could set new benchmarks for sustainability in international sport.*

Grassroots "Eco-Cricket": *Young cricketers are trained in both batting and climate literacy, preparing the next generation of green ambassadors.*

Carbon Audits & Offsets: *Some boards are calculating tour emissions and offsetting them through verified reforestation and clean energy projects.*

Tree-per-Ticket Campaigns: *Several leagues are planting trees for every ticket or NFT sold, turning attendance into an act of sustainability.*

Chapter 16 – Technology, Broadcasting, and Immersive Fan Experiences

16.1 Augmented Reality (AR) and Virtual Reality (VR) Matchday Spectacles

As cricket continues its transformation into a digitally immersive sport, Augmented Reality (AR) and Virtual Reality (VR) technologies are no longer speculative add-ons—they are becoming integral to how fans experience matches. By 2024, the ICC T20 World Cup held in the USA and West Indies served as the sport's first large-scale testbed for immersive tech deployment. Select matches allowed users to watch games through VR headsets, offering multiple angles, live stat overlays, and even virtual "stadium seating" where friends could sit next to each other as avatars, regardless of geography.

Following this success, all upcoming major ICC tournaments from 2025 onwards are expected to elevate these innovations even further. Several pilot programs—co-developed by local tech startups and international broadcasters—plan to introduce real-time AR overlays accessible through smartphones and wearables. These overlays will provide player biometrics, ball trajectories, and probability graphs during live play, allowing users in the stadium and at home to access tactical data previously reserved for commentators and analysts.

At the stadium level, AR glasses are being designed for in-person spectators. These will offer real-time captions, stats, and immersive 3D replays without taking eyes off the pitch. For fans watching at home or in VR lounges, "digital hospitality suites" are being launched—virtual boxes modeled after luxury skyboxes that fans can purchase access to. Within these virtual spaces, users can interact with friends, engage in live trivia, or even be joined by AI-generated holograms of cricket legends offering commentary in personalized languages and dialects.

Meanwhile, mixed reality (MR) is blurring the lines between physical and digital. Stadiums are now experimenting with MR fan zones, where digital avatars of fans from across the globe are projected live into the venue on holographic billboards or via drone displays. This fosters a new sense of transnational community engagement, especially for diaspora fans who can't attend games in person but still wish to "be present."

This convergence of sports and immersion is not limited to elite fans. Affordable AR experiences on mobile devices are being developed by regional boards like the PCB and BCCI, making interactive broadcasts accessible to millions in rural or economically underserved areas. From overlaying fielding positions on the phone screen to using local language voice bots for match commentary, the democratization of immersive tech is a key strategy for expanding the fan base.

The implications of this shift are cultural as well as technological. Cricket is evolving from a spectator sport into a participatory simulation, where fans don't just observe—they experience, interact, and even influence the narrative. As broadcasters increasingly compete with gaming platforms for attention, this blending of matchday spectacle with virtual interaction is emerging as cricket's most powerful tool for engaging younger, digital-first audiences.

As we move toward the end of this decade, innovations in AR and VR will likely become as essential as camera crews and commentary boxes once were. Whether through smart glasses, virtual stadiums, or interactive overlays, cricket is expanding its borders—not just geographically, but dimensionally.

16.2 Holograms, Stadium Drones, and Global Simulcasts

As the 2020s progress, cricket's evolution as a broadcast spectacle is being redefined—not by what happens on the field, but by how the game is delivered, visualized, and re-experienced around the world. From drone-assisted cinematography to holographic replays and transcontinental simulcasts, the line between stadium and screen is beginning to dissolve.

Stadium drones have already made their mark. Initially restricted to static overhead shots or security sweeps, drones are now increasingly integrated into broadcast packages. The 2024 ICC T20 World Cup, hosted jointly by the USA and the West Indies, saw licensed drones deliver sweeping in-play aerial visuals, enhancing angles unreachable by traditional fixed cameras. This innovation has expanded beyond spectacle; real-time drone feeds are being used by analysts to map player positioning, bowling angles, and boundary dynamics with a level of clarity previously impossible from ground-level perspectives.

In parallel, holographic technology is making its way into cricketing venues, training facilities, and public fan zones. Though still nascent, the fusion of 5G, projection mapping, and volumetric capture allows for the partial realization of holographic broadcasting. Pilot hologram screenings—such as virtual appearances of past legends like Shane Warne or Kapil Dev at global ICC fan parks—have hinted at the medium's potential. In the near future, it's entirely plausible that fans in Delhi, Birmingham, or Nairobi could attend real-time holographic match viewings, watching Virat Kohli or Babar Azam bat live as full-body projections in ultra-high fidelity, beamed in from another continent.

Such cross-border immersion is tied closely to the concept of global simulcasts—synchronized match screenings designed for transnational audiences. With cricket's growing popularity in non-traditional markets like the United States and the Middle East, boards are now experimenting with localized broadcast layering. For instance, a match aired live in Dubai may include Arabic commentary, region-specific overlays, fan sentiment heatmaps, and local sponsor integrations—all generated dynamically in real time.

This multilayered broadcast architecture is driven by AI-fed editing suites and cloud-based production workflows. Companies like Star Sports, Willow TV, and Sky Sports have begun adopting modular broadcast models, where a single match feed is customized into dozens of regional variants—tailored by language, camera angles, in-screen graphics, and even ad delivery based on viewer geolocation and profile data.

The immersive fan experience also extends to drone light shows, which have become a staple of high-profile matches, especially in India and the UAE. These coordinated aerial displays, powered by hundreds of programmable drones, animate cricketing motifs—balls crashing into stumps, flags waving in the sky, or portraits of retiring players—turning stadium airspace into a cinematic canvas.

These spectacles are not mere decoration; they reflect the sport's shift toward synesthetic engagement, where light, sound, and narrative choreography are as important as the scorecard. The younger generation of fans, raised on Fortnite, Marvel, and TikTok, demand more than passive viewing—they expect immersion, novelty, and story-driven presentation.

Technologically, these developments are enabled by improvements in low-latency 5G networks, volumetric video, and cloud-rendered graphics. India's rapid rollout of 5G infrastructure has already made low-delay streaming and real-time data layering more accessible for broadcasters and mobile users alike. In parallel, partnerships between cricket boards and spatial computing companies are being explored to push the boundaries of what a "matchday" experience entails—both for in-stadium attendees and remote viewers.

Importantly, this transition is not purely commercial. Global simulcasts, if implemented with care, offer a chance to democratize elite cricket access. A fan in Afghanistan, Namibia, or Nepal may never travel to a World Cup final—but with immersive tech and multi-market broadcasts, they can still feel connected to the moment.

Cricket's greatest strength has always been its adaptability—across colonies, continents, and centuries. In the age of holograms and drones, that spirit endures. The boundary ropes of the game are no longer physical; they are broadcast signals, holographic beams, and the synchronized pulse of a billion live streams.

16.3 Data-Driven Engagement: Fantasy Cricket 3.0 and Personalized Feeds

Cricket has always thrived on numbers—batting averages, strike rates, and session-by-session breakdowns. But in the era of algorithmic personalization, these numbers are no longer just for statisticians or armchair analysts. They are the currency of a new relationship between fan and game, driven by real-time data, machine learning, and behavioral analytics.

Fantasy cricket has moved far beyond its spreadsheet roots. The modern platforms, dubbed "Fantasy Cricket 3.0," operate as gamified, microeconomic ecosystems—where fans are not merely selecting players, but managing digital franchises augmented by artificial intelligence. These platforms draw on live biometric feeds, predictive performance models, and sentiment analytics to dynamically update player values during a match. The days of static teams and delayed scoring are over.

In India alone, the fantasy cricket industry crossed $3.7 billion in 2023, with over 180 million users participating across platforms like Dream11, MPL, and newer blockchain-native startups. These numbers have prompted boards and broadcasters to collaborate more closely with fantasy platforms—not just as sponsors, but as data co-creators. Matchday broadcasts now feature fantasy heatmaps, real-time player stock tickers, and AI-predicted "impact indices" that evolve as the game progresses.

For the fan, this convergence of sport and data delivers a far more interactive experience. Rather than passively watching a game, the user now toggles between multiple dashboards: one showing fielding positions, another tracking fantasy league standings, and a third streaming predictive win probabilities refreshed ball-by-ball. It's not uncommon for viewers to manage trades mid-match based on a bowler's live fitness telemetry or an unannounced change in pitch behavior.

The personalization doesn't stop at fantasy. Major broadcasters and sports tech firms have begun deploying AI-generated personalized feeds—where two viewers watching the same match receive entirely different visual narratives. One fan may prefer a data-heavy stream showing player efficiency charts, win expectancy graphs, and wagon wheels. Another might opt for a more cinematic feed with drone shots, replays from favorite angles, and crowd-focused storytelling.

This is made possible by real-time cloud rendering, edge-based video customization, and machine-learned viewer profiles. Platforms like Hotstar and FanCode are already experimenting with opt-in features that let users "train" their broadcast preferences. Eventually, the cricket feed becomes an algorithmic mirror of the viewer's identity—curated, responsive, and ever-evolving.

Such hyper-personalization has also made its way into commentary. AI co-commentators trained on regional languages and local cricket idioms now sit alongside human anchors, offering real-time player backstories, historical parallels, and sentiment-based insights tailored to each market. In Bangladesh, for instance, experimental pilots with Bengali-language AI commentators have achieved high engagement among younger fans, especially during domestic T20 leagues.

But these systems are not just about engagement—they are also economic engines. Every click, substitution, or scroll is data. This behavioral metadata is fed back into platform algorithms to optimize ad targeting, subscription models, and content pipelines. In many ways, the modern fan has become a co-designer of the game experience and a data resource in equal measure.

There are, of course, ethical questions. Concerns around algorithmic bias, data privacy, and the psychological toll of hyper-competition in fantasy ecosystems have begun surfacing. Responsible design—such as setting default cooling-off periods, transparency in recommendation algorithms, and age-based access limits—is now part of regulatory discussions across jurisdictions.

Yet despite the risks, the direction is clear: cricket is no longer just consumed—it is modeled, predicted, gamified, and adapted in real-time, based on who the viewer is and how they behave.

This isn't simply a new broadcast layer—it is a new layer of fandom. A real-time conversation between the viewer, the platform, and the game itself. And for a sport so deeply invested in narrative and nuance, this data-driven revolution is not the erosion of tradition—it is its next act.

16.4 Cricket in the Age of Brain-Computer Interfaces (BCIs)

As wearable technology evolves into neural technology, the future of cricket may be influenced not only by what players do—but by what they think. Brain-Computer Interfaces (BCIs), once the domain of neuroscience labs and speculative fiction, are inching closer to mainstream adoption. In the next two decades, they could radically reshape how cricket is played, coached, consumed, and even felt.

At its core, a BCI is a direct communication pathway between the human brain and an external device. Initially developed for clinical applications like assisting motor-impaired patients or restoring vision, BCIs are now being repurposed for elite sports performance and immersive fan engagement. The shift is being led by neurotech firms like Neuralink, Synchron, and NextMind, whose brain-signal decoding platforms are already undergoing real-world trials.

In cricket, BCIs could become the next frontier in cognitive analytics. Players might wear lightweight neural sensors embedded in helmets or headbands during training, capturing brainwave patterns associated with concentration, decision-making, and stress. These datasets, paired with biometric and video analytics, would offer coaches a more holistic performance profile—not just what a player does, but how their brain responds in high-pressure moments.

Imagine a batter being evaluated not just on footwork and timing, but on their split-second cognitive recognition of length and line. Or a bowler whose stress levels and mental fatigue are tracked after a long spell, triggering real-time substitutions or workload adjustments. Cognitive fatigue could become as measurable—and as actionable—as hamstring tightness or hydration levels.

In some experimental training academies in Australia and Japan, neurofeedback sessions are already being piloted. Players practice with EEG-equipped caps while AI systems interpret neural responses to deliveries. The goal is to increase "flow state" consistency—measured through patterns in theta and alpha brainwave frequencies. Early results indicate potential improvements in reaction time, mental resilience, and even shot selection under pressure.

For fans, BCIs open up unprecedented immersive possibilities. Passive neuro-sensing devices could allow viewers to interact with live broadcasts using only thought. Want to switch from camera angle A to B? Think it. Want replays of your favorite player's last over? Just concentrate on their avatar. Some prototypes already allow for such "neural shortcuts" in VR and AR environments.

Beyond control, there's the possibility of emotional co-spectating. Fan brainwaves could be aggregated in real-time to generate "neuro-atmosphere" metrics—showing the collective tension, joy, or shock of millions. These signals could influence ambient lighting in stadiums, audio dynamics in virtual arenas, or even be displayed as neural waveforms on screen during match climaxes.

BCI integration also hints at more participatory storytelling. In the long term, fans could experience historic matches "through the eyes" of legends—using recorded neuro-motor maps and gaze-tracking data to recreate what Dhoni saw in the 2011 World Cup final or how Muralitharan mapped out a wicket. It is cricket not just watched but cognitively relived.

Yet, ethical considerations loom large. The recording and interpretation of brain data raise complex questions around privacy, consent, and potential misuse. Could franchises mine players' mental patterns for psychological profiling? Might fans be nudged or manipulated through subtle neuro-feedback mechanisms? Sports regulators and tech developers will need to co-create robust frameworks for ethical neural engagement.

Nevertheless, as neural interfaces become more user-friendly, affordable, and integrated into consumer hardware, their arrival in cricket is not a matter of if—but when. And when it happens, the boundary between mind and match will blur in ways that redefine not only what we see—but how we experience the game.

In this vision, cricket becomes a truly multidimensional sport—one played not just with bat and ball, but with neurons and networks. Where focus, instinct, and emotion become quantifiable tools, and where the greatest contests may one day be fought as much in the brain as on the pitch.

16.4.1 Neuro-Cricket: The Psychology of Mind-Augmented Play

Cricket has always been a game of the mind as much as the body. From Dravid's patience under fire to Steven Waugh's calm in a crisis, mental resilience has often separated the good from the great. Brain-Computer Interfaces (BCIs) add a new dimension to this truth: they do not simply measure performance; they expose the psychology beneath it.

If the previous frontier of sports science was about physical optimization—bat speed, VO₂ max, recovery times—the next may be about cognitive mastery. In neuro-cricket, the contest extends to who can harness their focus most effectively, who can train their brain to enter a flow state on demand, and who can withstand psychological strain in environments of overwhelming pressure.

Consider the role of anticipation. A batter today relies on visual cues— reading a bowler's wrist position, release point, or length. With cognitive training, that anticipation could shift inward. Players might learn to recognize not just what their eyes see, but what their neural pathways predict before conscious recognition occurs. In effect, batting becomes a test not just of reflexes but of predictive cognition.

Bowling, too, could be transformed by neuro-augmented psychology. Beyond physical rhythm, a bowler might train to manipulate their own brain activity to mask predictability—essentially "bluffing" not through body language but through cognitive disguise. The mental duel between batter and bowler, already rich, could become layered with invisible psychological feints.

At the team level, neuro-cricket introduces the possibility of collective psychology. Squads might be trained not only for technical cohesion but for synchronized neural states—shared focus, calm under duress, or rapid adaptability in moments of crisis. A dressing room no longer prepares merely for tactics but for aligning mental rhythms, producing a form of psychological sovereignty that defines success.

For fans and analysts, this mental dimension could reshape how we talk about the game. Where once commentators admired "nerves of steel," in the future they might reference a player's ability to stabilize alpha waves under pressure, or to recover neural equilibrium after a setback. Concepts like temperament, clutch performance, and choking could be reframed in measurable, neuro-psychological terms.

Yet this raises deeper questions about authenticity. If a player's mind is trained, monitored, and optimized through external systems, does it still reflect natural instinct? Or does cricket risk becoming a contest of engineered concentration rather than human creativity? The very romance of unpredictability—that an underdog can summon inner reserves no model can predict—may one day collide with neuro-augmented preparation.

In this sense, neuro-cricket is not just about performance; it is about philosophy. It challenges how we define fairness, intuition, and the spirit of play. A six struck under duress is thrilling not just because of biomechanics, but because of the psychological courage behind it. As technology encroaches on this territory, cricket may be forced to decide whether mental sovereignty belongs to the player, the team, or the algorithms guiding them.

The future of cricket psychology, then, is unlikely to be a choice between tradition and augmentation. More plausibly, it will be a hybrid—where human resilience remains central, but is sharpened by neural insight. In such a future, the greatest players may not simply be those with flawless technique, but those who balance instinct and augmentation, emotion and analytics, the mind unassisted and the mind enhanced.

16.4.2 Controversies, Technology, and the Quest for Perfect Decisions

Few aspects of cricket provoke as much debate as decisions that seem to balance on the edge of human judgment. Umpiring controversies have shaped reputations, careers, and even entire series. From disputed catches to no-ball calls, cricket's rulebook has always depended on interpretation—and interpretation invites disagreement. Even in an era of Decision Review Systems (DRS) and slow-motion replays, the quest for "perfect decisions" continues to spark debate.

One of the most enduring controversies has been the legality of bowling actions. The so-called "15-degree rule," formalized by the ICC, sets a threshold for elbow extension during delivery. While designed as a scientific standard, it has long been criticized as arbitrary and inconsistently applied. Greats like Muttiah Muralitharan and Saeed Ajmal—bowlers who bewildered batters with unorthodox spin—found themselves under suspicion, with careers overshadowed by biomechanical scrutiny. Supporters hailed technology for clarifying legality, while critics argued it reduced artistry to laboratory measurements.

Catches, too, remain a fertile ground for disputes. Even with multiple camera angles, deciding whether a ball brushed the grass before being clasped in the fielder's hands is often inconclusive. Slow-motion replays sometimes create more confusion than clarity, with one angle suggesting a clean take and another hinting at a drop. Fans, commentators, and players alike are left dissatisfied, as technology that was meant to eliminate doubt instead magnifies it.

The Decision Review System itself, once heralded as cricket's great corrective, has not escaped controversy. Hawk-Eye ball-tracking, UltraEdge, and Snicko provide evidence-based judgments, yet captains and fans often remain unconvinced. Margins of error, predictive algorithms, and umpire's call provisions still leave room for frustration. Some argue that DRS restores fairness; others insist it shifts disputes from the field of play to the realm of technology's accuracy.

Looking ahead, one can imagine new layers of technological intervention. Quantum-based imaging and simulation systems may emerge, capable of reconstructing deliveries and dismissals at near-atomic precision. Captains might be granted the right to "challenge the DRS itself," demanding that a quantum model re-simulate the contested ball using trillions of data points—spin, seam, air currents, even micro-expressions of the batter. Such developments would offer the allure of certainty, but also raise the question of whether cricket risks becoming over-engineered, drowning its spirit in endless technical arbitration.

Ultimately, technology in cricket reflects the same paradox as elsewhere in society: it promises fairness yet introduces new forms of doubt. The 15-degree rule settled some arguments while igniting others; cameras resolved some catches while complicating others; DRS removed some umpiring errors while creating its own grey areas. Perhaps cricket will never find truly perfect decisions—only more sophisticated ways of negotiating imperfection.

The challenge, then, is not simply to pursue accuracy but to preserve trust. Cricket's beauty has always lain in its human margins—the possibility of error, drama, and debate. If future technologies can strike a balance between clarity and the game's spirit, they will not erase controversy but help cricket live with it more gracefully.

16.5 Cricket's Digital Lifeline: Platforms, Risks, and the Everyday Fan

While futuristic innovations dominate headlines, cricket's most vital technological transformation is far more familiar—and arguably more powerful. In a world defined by fragmented attention spans, time zone chaos, and multi-screen lives, cricket survives not because of stadium crowds or TV ratings, but because of digital continuity: apps, feeds, streams, and notifications. In short, cricket lives in your pocket.

Platforms like ESPNcricinfo, BBC's Test Match Special (TMS), The Guardian's Over-by-Over coverage, and even algorithm-driven social media snippets (Twitter/X, Instagram Reels, YouTube Shorts) have become the arteries of the global cricketing experience. When office meetings clash with match timings, it's the ball-by-ball ticker, not the broadcast, that keeps fans tethered to the game. When time zones make live viewing impossible, it's curated highlight reels, stat dashboards, and mobile notifications that carry the sport forward.

This "always-on" cricket ecosystem is especially critical for the corporate world and diaspora populations—fans in New York, Dubai, or Singapore who can't tune in at 3 AM for a Test match in Australia or an IPL evening fixture. For them, cricket isn't scheduled entertainment—it's ambient companionship, fed in micro-doses through apps, texts, and audio bites. The Guardian's literary coverage, Cricbuzz's instant updates, and BBC's radio commentary have preserved a deeply human connection to the game, even in an era of algorithmic overload.

However, this digital ubiquity comes with a darker undercurrent: the rise of unregulated gambling platforms and fantasy apps that now hover at the edge of legality and ethics. While regulated fantasy sports have become billion-dollar industries in India, the UK, and Australia, a growing shadow economy of crypto-fuelled betting apps—many hosted offshore or in loosely policed jurisdictions—poses real risks.

These platforms blur the line between casual engagement and predatory addiction, especially among younger or economically vulnerable users.

Additionally, the monetization logic of digital platforms risks reducing cricket to clickbait. Every dropped catch or sledging moment becomes an instant meme. AI-generated thumbnails, deceptive headlines, and algorithm-hunting content can erode the game's nuance, replacing analysis with outrage. Even legacy platforms face the temptation of sacrificing journalistic depth for engagement metrics.

Data privacy is another concern. Cricket apps collect vast quantities of user data—location, interests, spending patterns, and viewing history—which can be leveraged not just for personalized content but for behavioral targeting. In regions with weak data protections, this creates fertile ground for exploitation.

Still, the net effect remains deeply positive. Without digital platforms, cricket's post-COVID survival—particularly outside Test strongholds—would have faltered. Apps democratize access, broaden fandom, and ensure continuity even when stadiums go silent. For millions, the modern game isn't watched live—In many ways, these digital platforms have become the new home of cricket. They may not be as historic as a place like Lord's, but they are more accessible to people everywhere—and just as important in keeping the spirit of the game alive.

In many ways, these digital interfaces have become the modern pavilion. Less romantic than Lord's, perhaps, but more accessible—and just as sacred.

16.6 Cricket in Refugee and Stateless Communities

In today's uncertain world, shaped by displacement, migration, and political turbulence, cricket has quietly emerged as more than just a game of nations. It has also become a game of communities in exile. For those who have lost access to their homelands or stadiums, the sport has offered both continuity and hope.

Afghanistan provides perhaps the most striking example. Few national teams have faced such adversity: decades of conflict, foreign interventions, and social restrictions meant cricket had to grow in refugee camps and informal pitches in Pakistan rather than on Afghan soil. Yet, against these odds, Afghan players rose to international prominence. From refugee beginnings to World Cup appearances, their journey reflects not only sporting skill but also cricket's ability to give identity, pride, and structure to young people in difficult circumstances. Their story is a reminder that cricket can flourish even when infrastructure, security, and resources are scarce.

Pakistan, too, has experienced the pain of exile. After the 2009 attack on the Sri Lankan team in Lahore, international cricket disappeared from its soil for nearly a decade. During this period, Pakistan played its "home" matches in the UAE. The absence of crowds and familiar conditions was felt deeply, yet the team still found resilience, winning the 2009 T20 World Cup and the 2017 ICC Champions Trophy. This period of enforced displacement demonstrated that while the game thrives on home support, it can adapt and survive when circumstances demand.

History offers other examples. South Africa, isolated from international cricket during the apartheid era, endured over two decades of sporting separation. Its eventual return in the 1990s was strengthened by the robust domestic system it had preserved during exile. Similarly, smaller cricketing communities—be they migrant leagues in the Gulf, refugee tournaments in Europe, or diaspora clubs in North America—have shown how cricket can travel with people, providing stability and belonging wherever life takes them.

Looking ahead, the international cricket community must recognize that exile and displacement may remain part of the sport's reality. Political instability, sanctions, or even environmental crises could prevent nations from hosting matches at home. In such cases, the ICC and regional boards have a responsibility to ensure continuity. This might include offering neutral venues, guaranteeing fixtures, or channeling developmental support to ensure that exile does not become erasure.

Afghanistan's limited opportunities in Test cricket today illustrate this challenge. Without consistent five-day cricket, a generation of Afghan players risks being confined to the shorter formats, limiting their full development as cricketers. Structural support, thoughtful scheduling, and inclusive planning can prevent this and ensure that teams in exile are not left behind.

More fundamentally, cricket in exile invites us to rethink what makes a national team. Is it the home ground, the flag, the anthem? Or is it the community, the continuity, and the commitment to the game despite everything? The answer has implications for how the sport sees itself and who it includes in its future.

Cricket has always been a diplomatic language—whether in post-colonial contests or contemporary rivalries. But in the hands of refugees and stateless players, it becomes something even more potent: an act of defiance, a form of cultural survival. These teams do not demand recognition as much as they demonstrate it—simply by playing, by gathering, by enduring. Their matches may not always make the news, but their significance to cricket's moral imagination is profound.

If the future of cricket sees twenty or more Test nations by the century's end, some may never play consistently at home. Yet their journeys can still inspire, just as Afghanistan's has. In this way, cricket in exile should not be seen only as a loss, but as an opportunity for the game to show its inclusivity and adaptability—qualities that may prove decisive for its survival and growth in the 21st century.

16.7 The Sensory Stadium: Cricket Beyond Sight and Sound

For as long as it has been played, cricket has been experienced through the eyes and ears. The sight of a ball carving through the covers, the sound of leather striking willow, the rhythm of a commentator's voice, and the collective roar of a crowd have defined how the game is consumed. Yet advances in multisensory technology suggest a future where fans may not only see and hear cricket, but also feel, smell, and physically experience it in ways once confined to imagination.

Emerging haptic technologies already allow users to "feel" digital events—vibrations, pressures, or textures transmitted through wearable suits and gloves. Applied to cricket, such devices could let a remote fan experience the jolt of a bat striking a ball, or the shudder of a diving stop. Beyond touch, experimental scent diffusers are being trialed in immersive entertainment. A cricket broadcast might one day release the smell of cut grass, rain on turf, or the faint tang of leather and linseed oil, adding another layer of atmosphere to the spectacle. Vibration platforms, meanwhile, could transmit the swell of a crowd or the rumble of applause, creating a bodily resonance that connects viewers at home to the stadium's energy.

The rewards of such innovation are easy to imagine. For fans in countries where live cricket is rare, or for those unable to attend matches, sensory immersion could provide a powerful sense of presence. It could democratize access to the "feel" of cricket, narrowing the gap between watching and being there. For younger generations accustomed to immersive gaming and virtual worlds, it may offer an entirely new gateway into the sport.

Yet there are risks. Overuse of sensory cues could overwhelm rather than enhance, turning the subtle rhythms of cricket into an overstimulating spectacle. The commercialization of emotion also looms large. Will the smell of cut grass be genuine—or a branded scent package sponsored by a corporation? Could the physical "roar" of a crowd be artificially amplified to manipulate engagement, blurring the line between authentic atmosphere and engineered response? And will the game itself risk being overshadowed by its sensory packaging?

As with so many technological frontiers, balance will be key. If deployed with care, multisensory technologies could enrich cricket without compromising its essence, extending the intimacy of stadium experience to millions who may never step inside Lord's or Eden Gardens. But if pushed too far, they may risk commodifying the game's emotions, reducing authenticity to algorithm.

The sensory stadium, then, represents both opportunity and caution. It asks whether cricket, a game steeped in tradition, can embrace new ways of being felt as well as seen. And it challenges fans, players, and administrators alike to decide how much of the game's atmosphere should be delivered—and how much should remain the irreplaceable magic of being there in person.

16.8 Cricket and the Gig Economy of Sport

If the twentieth century made cricket a profession, the twenty-first century has turned it into a marketplace of gigs. Where once the sport revolved around players, coaches, and administrators on secure contracts, today an entire ecosystem of freelancers, content creators, and platform-driven workers sustains the game. This "gig economy of cricket" is reshaping not only how the sport is produced and consumed but also who holds power within it.

At one end of the spectrum are analysts, videographers, and performance consultants hired on short-term deals by franchises, often moving from league to league much like the players themselves. At the other end are independent commentators, podcasters, and digital influencers who build audiences on YouTube, TikTok, or Twitter, offering everything from tactical breakdowns to comedic match summaries. Some thrive on monetization through ads, others through sponsorships, but almost all operate outside the formal boundaries of cricket's governing bodies. Their voices may not carry official accreditation, yet they shape public narratives as much as legacy broadcasters once did.

The gig economy extends into the grassroots. Streaming platforms now allow small clubs to broadcast matches with a single camera and AI commentary overlays. Freelance scorers and data collectors provide live ball-by-ball feeds from remote grounds in Nepal, Nigeria, or Canada, feeding into global databases within seconds. Such micro-enterprises not only democratize cricket's visibility but also create precarious labor structures, where income is tied to clicks, views, and the volatile logics of algorithm-driven platforms.

For players too, gig dynamics have become unavoidable. The rise of franchise leagues across the world means that a journeyman cricketer can piece together an income by playing in four or five tournaments a year, often without the stability of a central contract. While this creates new opportunities for financial independence, it also raises questions of loyalty, burnout, and exploitation. The romantic notion of a cricketer representing "club and country" for decades has given way to careers shaped by auctions, drafts, and freelance availability.

The rewards are obvious: more voices, more entry points, and a decentralization of cricket's narrative power. But the risks mirror those of the wider gig economy: job insecurity, algorithmic dependence, and blurred lines between passion and precarious work. The sport increasingly relies on invisible labor—statisticians coding ball-tracking

318

data, part-time scorers updating apps, meme-creators driving engagement. They form the scaffolding on which cricket's digital empire rests, yet their sovereignty is fragile, contingent on clicks and contracts.

Cricket's gig economy thus poses a deeper question about the sport's future: who really owns its meaning? The boards and franchises who stage the matches, or the dispersed global workforce that interprets, broadcasts, and packages them for billions of fans? As the line between professional and amateur, insider and outsider, continues to blur, cricket is becoming less a game managed by institutions and more a cultural commons sustained by thousands of gig-driven contributors. Whether this enhances cricket's sovereignty or erodes it will depend on how fairly and sustainably this new workforce is recognized in the decades to come.

Readers' Notes

AR/VR Matchday Spectacles

Augmented and virtual reality technologies are being used to create immersive cricket experiences. Fans can now watch matches from virtual stadiums using VR headsets or see player stats and ball trajectories in real time using AR apps.

Holograms and Stadium Drones

Holographic projections of players and drones filming from new angles are changing how cricket is presented. These innovations allow fans to feel closer to the action, even from home.

Global Simulcasts and Multilingual Broadcasting

Matches are being streamed simultaneously in multiple languages and regions. AI-generated commentary and subtitles make cricket accessible to a much broader global audience.

Data-Driven Personalization

Platforms like Cricbuzz, Cricinfo, and The Guardian now offer custom notifications, player tracking, and real-time stats tailored to each user. Personalized match feeds and fantasy tips are common features.

Fantasy Cricket 3.0

Fantasy leagues have become smarter. AI suggests picks based on form, data, and injury updates. Newer platforms now feature dynamic pricing, mid-match transfers, and fan-led analytics.

Brain-Computer Interfaces (BCIs)

While still early in development, BCIs might one day allow users to control apps or games with their minds. Research is ongoing to explore how BCIs can enhance cricket gaming or immersive viewing.

Digital Apps and Time-Zone Flexibility

For fans in different parts of the world or those working corporate hours, apps like Hotstar, JioCinema, BBC TMS, and Cricinfo offer real-time updates, radio commentary, and highlights, allowing cricket to be followed on the go.

Cricket and Gambling Apps

Legal fantasy sports platforms have brought structured engagement, but unregulated gambling apps remain a concern. They risk promoting addiction, especially among younger fans.

Risks and Challenges

While technology enhances access and immersion, concerns exist around data privacy, algorithmic bias in personalization, and over-commercialization. Regulation, transparency, and ethical tech use are key to ensuring a healthy digital cricket ecosystem.

Chapter 17 – The Future of Power in Global Cricket

17.1 Economic Powerhouses and the Balance of Global Cricket

In the current geopolitical cricketing landscape, the Board of Control for Cricket in India (BCCI) stands as the undisputed economic superpower. With over 1.4 billion potential viewers, a mature domestic league in the IPL, and a firm grip on broadcast and sponsorship rights, the BCCI commands unparalleled influence over global scheduling, tournament hosting, and commercial negotiations. While this has helped elevate cricket's profile in the digital age, it has also raised serious questions about equity, sustainability, and the risks of centralizing too much power in one board.

To be fair, BCCI's financial strength has kept the global game afloat. Its commercial deals—especially with broadcasters, streaming giants, and tech sponsors—have enabled ICC tournaments to flourish and generated subsidies that support smaller cricketing nations. Just as major football clubs like Real Madrid, Manchester City or Barcelona help lift the commercial ecosystem of UEFA tournaments, BCCI's economic clout helps fund global cricketing operations.

However, history warns us against over-centralized control. Cricket thrives on healthy competition, narrative diversity, and multilateral participation. A single board dictating terms—whether in bilateral series, tournament windows, or franchise licensing—risks undermining the delicate balance needed for the game's global health. While the IPL is a cash machine, the growing practice of scheduling international windows around it has strained bilateral cricket and left smaller boards scrambling to retain relevance.

Boards like Pakistan's PCB offer an interesting case study. Despite not matching India's financial muscle, they have successfully hosted leagues like the PSL, upgraded domestic pathways, and continued to nurture world-class talent. But like competitive football clubs such as Juventus, Atlético Madrid, or Inter Milan—who depend heavily on UEFA Champions League qualification for revenue—the PCB's financial health is closely tied to its ability to stay competitive on the field. Qualification for top-tier tournaments, hosting rights, and marketable rivalries with India or England significantly affect their economic viability.

This logic extends to Sri Lanka, Bangladesh, Afghanistan, and other associate or emerging nations. Their financial sustainability relies on performance, exposure, and structural investment in youth systems. With cricket becoming more fragmented and franchise-driven, these boards face the dual challenge of keeping their national teams competitive while balancing the growing pull of private leagues. In some cases, participation in ICC events is akin to European football clubs making it to the Champions League knockout rounds—a critical driver of visibility, sponsorship, and long-term health.

Broadcast money and private investment will remain the lifeblood of the sport well into the 22nd century. Cricket's transition into a hybrid product—part sport, part digital entertainment—means financial modeling will dictate future viability. Whether through NFTs, tokenized fan economies, or AI-driven fan engagement, economics will increasingly determine who thrives and who survives. A scenario where only a few boards hoard resources, however, is unsustainable.

To avoid such imbalance, the ICC and regional confederations may eventually need to adopt a revenue-sharing model similar to global football. Investment in associate nations, equity-based tournament qualification, and a fairer distribution of media rights can create a more robust global structure. Cricket's next century demands an ecosystem where innovation, not just capital, drives power.

India's hegemony, then, is not inherently negative. But it must evolve from dominance to stewardship. If the game is to thrive from Dhaka to Dublin, from Karachi to Barbados, the future must be collaborative, economically diversified, and structurally inclusive. The rise of new markets, emerging technologies, and a shifting fanbase means no single board can own the game's destiny indefinitely.

17.2 The Rise of New Markets: USA, Canada and Africa

In the contemporary and future economic architecture of global cricket, the rise of new markets such as the United States, Canada and Africa represents not just regional diversification, but an essential strategy for financial sustainability and expansion. If the sport is to remain globally relevant deep into the 21st and 22nd centuries, the axis of growth must shift from legacy strongholds toward emergent financial ecosystems.

Cricket, unlike football, has historically been constrained by its post-colonial geographies. The market share was limited to nations of the Commonwealth, with broadcast revenues and player salaries concentrated in a narrow band of countries. However, in an era where sports and entertainment are increasingly dictated by venture capital, private equity, and tech-driven consumer engagement, remaining confined to a limited fan base is no longer viable.

The United States offers the most immediate economic opportunity. With its vast diaspora populations, media infrastructure, and appetite for sport-tech convergence, the U.S. is already being targeted by both ICC and private leagues for franchise-based T20 tournaments. The launch of Major League Cricket (MLC) in 2023 was not merely symbolic—it was an economic statement. Backed by venture capital, American broadcasters, and South Asian tech entrepreneurs, MLC represents the potential of cricket to tap into a trillion-dollar sports market, particularly in streaming, merchandising, fantasy leagues, and sponsorship. The American market is monetized by attention, data, and branding—and cricket must learn to operate within this framework. The United States successfully hosted several matches of the 2024 ICC T20 World Cup, including the marquee clash between India and Pakistan at the Nassau County International Cricket Stadium in New York—a sold-out spectacle that drew global attention and record digital viewership. While the event marked a breakthrough moment for cricket in North America, it is important to note that the U.S. is not entirely alien to the sport. As discussed earlier in this book, the world's first officially recorded international cricket match was played between the United States and Canada in 1844, held in Manhattan.

Despite this early start, cricket did not flourish in the U.S. for three key reasons: it lacked formal domestic structures and mass participation; it faced stiff competition from emerging American sports like baseball and American football; and it failed to develop a sustained media or commercial ecosystem to anchor it within mainstream U.S. sporting culture.

Canada remains an avenue worth reexploring — with its multicultural population, historic precedent of hosting bilateral ODIs, and established infrastructure, it presents a viable site for cricket's North American resurgence. In the mid-to-late 1990s, the Sahara Cup series brought the storied India–Pakistan rivalry to Toronto's Maple Leaf Cricket Club in King City, Ontario. Across three successive years — 1996, 1997, and 1998 — the two nations played five-match ODI series on neutral ground, drawing packed crowds that reflected both fierce loyalty and diaspora nostalgia. These matches were not mere exhibitions; they were high-stakes contests, often producing dramatic finishes and significant diplomatic undercurrents at a time when the two countries had suspended bilateral ties at home. The Sahara Cup era was marked by memorable individual performances — particularly the heroics of Sourav Ganguly, Inzamam-ul-Haq, Saqlain Mushtaq, and Anil Kumble — which elevated the stature of the Indo-Pak rivalry on Canadian soil. Despite the cold weather and unfamiliar terrain, the atmosphere in Canadian stadiums was electric — proof that cricket, when rooted in emotion and history, can transcend geography. Given Canada's growing South Asian population and its ongoing participation in global cricket events like the ICC T20 World Cup, revisiting Canada as a venue — whether for ICC tournaments, bilateral series, or franchise exhibition games — is a strategic and culturally resonant opportunity.

Africa, though currently undercapitalized in cricketing terms, represents a compelling long-tail investment opportunity. Several African nations—such as Namibia, Nigeria, Kenya, and Rwanda—are beginning to display cricketing enthusiasm and infrastructure ambition. Coupled with the continent's booming youth population and increasing digital connectivity, Africa may very well be home to the next billion cricket fans. However, meaningful commercial returns will depend on foundational investments in infrastructure, coaching academies, and localized broadcasting models. The economic case for Africa is not about short-term monetization, but about demographic foresight and strategic seeding.

Historically, African cricket suffered a major setback due to South Africa's 21-year ban from international cricket (1970–1991) during the apartheid era. In that vacuum, Zimbabwe carried the continent's international cricket presence, while Kenya briefly captured global attention with its impressive runs in the 1996 and 2003 ICC World Cups. Now, a new chapter is unfolding. The 2027 ICC Men's ODI World Cup—set to be co-hosted by South Africa, Zimbabwe, and Namibia—marks a symbolic and practical resurgence for African cricket. Much like the 2010 FIFA World Cup transformed perceptions of African sporting potential, the 2027 cricket event promises to catalyze interest, investment, and participation across the continent. It may prove to be cricket's most important developmental milestone in Africa since the sport first arrived on its shores.

Economically, the model is clear. Markets that generate eyeballs, subscriptions, and social media engagement are the lifeblood of modern sport. Cricket must operate like a global brand with regionally customized financial strategies. Broadcast rights in the U.S. must be bundled with streaming platforms and diaspora-targeted media. In the Middle East, commercial partnerships should tie cricket to tech, tourism, and ESG-aligned initiatives. In Africa, fintech and mobile-first platforms may offer the best route to monetization.

Ultimately, the expansion into these new regions is not about charity or even cultural exchange—it is about financial continuity. Without new markets and deeper wallets, cricket's over-reliance on a handful of dominant boards will become a liability. By 2050 and beyond, cricket's relevance will be measured not by its colonial legacy but by its adaptability to capital flows, platform economics, and its ability to become a sport of and for the global South and West simultaneously.

Money, in this context, is not a corruption of cricket—it is the condition of its survival. As broadcasting rights, sponsorship deals, and sovereign investments increasingly dictate the sport's direction, economic pragmatism must be balanced with cricket's core values. The future of the game, particularly in new and emerging markets, will hinge on the ability of administrators to convert capital into long-term infrastructure, competitive equity, and global accessibility. If stewarded wisely, the money flowing into cricket today could secure its place in the cultural and sporting imagination well into the 22nd century.

17.2.1 East Asia's Emerging Cricket Frontier: China, Japan, and South Korea

East Asia—particularly China, Japan, and South Korea—represents a potential frontier for cricket's long-term expansion. While grassroots engagement remains modest, the region's deep integration into global tech, esports, and digital entertainment makes it strategically relevant. China's market scale, Japan's Olympic legacy, and South Korea's broadcasting and gaming industries could, with the right cricketing formats and media partnerships, offer unique growth avenues. This chapter explores East Asia a region that has long stood at the periphery of cricket's global footprint but now presents significant long-term strategic potential. While sports like table tennis, football, baseball, and basketball dominate the region's cultural and athletic landscape, there remains meaningful room for cricket to develop over time—especially in a century that increasingly rewards sports with global digital traction, Olympic aspirations, and regional connectivity.

China represents both the greatest challenge and the greatest opportunity. With a population of over 1.4 billion, a rapidly advancing sports infrastructure, and deepening global influence, the Chinese market offers unmatched scale. Although cricket has yet to capture the public imagination in China, the International Cricket Council (ICC) has invested over $5 million toward its growth through grassroots initiatives, including youth programs and school-level competitions. The Chinese Cricket Association (CCA), an ICC member since 2004, has slowly expanded its footprint, but development remains modest when measured against the backdrop of China's sports ecosystem. One of the key hurdles is competition from dominant Olympic sports, alongside a lack of widespread exposure to cricketing culture. However, the inclusion of cricket in future Olympic Games—particularly the Los Angeles 2028 Olympics—could act as a gateway for China's deeper engagement.

Furthermore, China's ability to construct world-class stadiums at record speed, as demonstrated in the 2008 Beijing Olympics, gives the sport infrastructural room to grow. Climatic conditions across much of China are also suitable for both summer and indoor cricket. Beyond logistics, China's emergence as a future 22nd-century superpower— economically, militarily, and diplomatically—means cricket's long-term survival as a global sport may require some degree of traction in East Asia. Just as ping-pong diplomacy opened the door between China and the United States under President Nixon in the 1970s, sport-based soft diplomacy may help cricket find its place in a changing global order.

Japan and South Korea also offer long-view opportunities. These nations have already demonstrated their capacity for hosting global mega-events: the 2002 FIFA World Cup (co-hosted by both and won by Brazil) and the 2020 Tokyo Olympics showcased both countries' sporting competence and international appeal. While neither country has a deep cricketing tradition, both have small but growing domestic programs. Japan is a member of the ICC and has made strides in youth participation and female cricket. South Korea, with its tech-savvy population and robust university sports system, offers a unique context for experimental or short-format cricket—particularly through eSports tie-ins, augmented reality broadcasts, or cricket-as-content in digital streaming environments.

In both nations, cricket's appeal may not initially lie in traditional formats but in adapted versions—perhaps indoor cricket, T10, or urban street formats that align with the fast-paced nature of modern East Asian lifestyles.

Pakistan, with its historical, cultural, and strategic ties to China, could play a vital facilitative role. The longstanding politico-military friendship between Islamabad and Beijing gives Pakistan an opportunity to export cricketing expertise—through coaching exchanges, bilateral development camps, or hybrid franchise ventures that could promote cricket among Chinese youth. Pakistan could become to China what

England once was to South Asia—a transmitter of cricketing norms, narratives, and infrastructures.

How beautiful it would be — a crisp Beijing morning, where sunlight slants across a purpose-built stadium as two teams step out in pristine white kits for a new kind of contest: a three-day hybrid of Test and ODI, ancient and modern, played not just for runs, but for memory. In Osaka, the cherry blossoms might drift across a fast outfield, and in Seoul, the silent discipline of the crowd might meet the roar of a last-session surge. Imagine a T20 night in the cold winter of Shanghai — breath visible, floodlights glowing, cricket stitched into a new cultural fabric, bat meeting ball in the hush before history.

Cricket has long flourished in unexpected places. That spirit — of cricket adapting, migrating, and resonating beyond its traditional frontiers — remains alive. And perhaps, in Seoul or Shanghai, it will sing again.

Ultimately, cricket's journey into East Asia will be slow. It may take decades for it to move from novelty to institution. But the broader lesson of cricket's global expansion is that such journeys are always possible. Once confined to British colonies, cricket now belongs to a digital, interconnected world. If stewarded wisely, East Asia may yet emerge as an essential part of cricket's long horizon.

17.2.2 The Gulf's Ascendancy: From Sharjah to the Global Stage

The Middle East has rapidly positioned itself as cricket's emerging financial and infrastructural nerve center. Far from being a peripheral player, the region — particularly the United Arab Emirates (UAE), Saudi Arabia, and Qatar — now plays a pivotal role in shaping the sport's economic and logistical future. Petrodollar liquidity, coupled with visionary state-led investment strategies, has allowed Gulf nations to build a transnational hosting capacity supported by climate-controlled venues, advanced broadcast infrastructure, and tourism-oriented urban planning.

While the International League T20 (ILT20) has been a visible product of this transformation, the implications stretch further. Saudi Arabia's Public Investment Fund (PIF) has shown an appetite for global sports acquisitions, including cricket, as part of its Vision 2030 agenda. These investments are not philanthropic; they are geo-economic. In exchange for hosting rights and capital inflows, Gulf states acquire soft power, global visibility, and decision-making influence in the evolving architecture of international cricket governance.

Contrary to the perception of being newcomers, the UAE's involvement in global cricket dates back several decades. In the 1980s and 1990s, Sharjah's Cricket Stadium became an iconic venue by regularly hosting tournaments such as the Austral-Asia Cup, the Rothmans Cup, Sharjah Cups, and multiple Asia Cup editions. These events drew capacity crowds and featured top-tier international talent, becoming a staple of cricket broadcasting in the subcontinent. Beyond the statistics, Sharjah etched itself into cricketing folklore through unforgettable moments that remain deeply embedded in the collective memory of fans — Javed Miandad's last-ball six off Chetan Sharma in 1986, Wasim Akram's hat-trick against Australia in 1990, Waqar Younis uprooting Ian Bishop's stumps in 1991,Sachin Tendulkar's blistering "Desert Storm" innings against Australia in 1998 and Zahid Fazal's valiant yet often forgotten 98 against India in the 1991 Sharjah Cup final. Such moments elevated Sharjah from a neutral venue to an emotional crucible for South Asian cricketing drama. With the emergence of Dubai as a sporting and tourism hub in the 2000s, the UAE's role expanded dramatically. From 2009 to 2018, Dubai served as the de facto international home of Pakistan cricket — hosting all formats of bilateral series due to security concerns in Pakistan. This era solidified the UAE's image as a dependable, neutral venue.

The UAE has continued to solidify its position as a global cricketing hub. It successfully hosted the ICC Men's T20 World Cup in 2021 (alongside Oman), followed by the Asia Cup editions in both 2022 and 2025 — each demonstrating the country's capacity to organize high-profile, multi-nation tournaments with efficiency and flair. Most notably, the UAE staged key fixtures of the 2025 ICC Champions Trophy, including the Final, further reinforcing its stature in the international cricketing calendar. Beyond Dubai, both Abu Dhabi and Sharjah have consistently served as trusted venues for ICC-sanctioned events and franchise leagues. The presence of the ICC's global headquarters and the cutting-edge ICC Academy in Dubai underscores the UAE's central role in cricket's global governance and talent development infrastructure.

Looking ahead, the possibility of the UAE, Oman, and Saudi Arabia jointly hosting a main ICC ODI World Cup in the 2030s or 2040's is not only plausible — it is strategically desirable. The infrastructure is either already in place or rapidly developing. Dubai International Stadium has proven its capacity for hosting high-stakes events, while Abu Dhabi and Sharjah remain reliable secondary venues. Oman has experience hosting ICC fixtures, and Saudi Arabia, with its vast resources and commitment to sport as a diplomatic tool, is already confirmed to host the 2034 FIFA World Cup.

Why not then, envision Dubai — with its multicultural population, world-class hospitality sector, and growing reputation as a high-tech innovation hub — hosting the Final of a future ICC ODI World Cup? With over 100 nationalities residing in the UAE, the nation offers a truly global fan base and international atmosphere. The addition of purpose-built stadiums in Saudi Arabia, supported by AI-driven logistics, smart surveillance, and immersive fan technologies, could further redefine the experience of international cricket in the Middle East.

As cricket searches for new homes and fresh audiences, the Gulf presents not just a financial platform, but a culturally and technologically dynamic opportunity for the sport's next great expansion.

17.2.3 South America: A Dormant Frontier

Cricket has long struggled to gain a foothold in South America, where football dominates the cultural and sporting landscape with near-religious fervor. Structural challenges such as limited infrastructure, lack of public awareness, and minimal government or media support have inhibited the sport's growth across most of the continent. However, the picture is not entirely bleak. The presence of Guyana — geographically part of South America but culturally aligned with the Caribbean — offers a compelling case for cricket's potential in the region. Guyana has produced a line of outstanding cricketers, from Clive Lloyd, Carl Hooper to Shivnarine Chanderpaul, contributing significantly to West Indies cricket. This legacy provides a tangible example of how cricket can take root and flourish in South American soil under the right historical and cultural conditions. While it may be unrealistic to expect a cricketing revolution across the entire continent, targeted efforts in select nations — particularly those with large diasporic communities or Commonwealth links, such as Suriname or even Brazil and Argentina — may yet sow the seeds for future expansion.

17.2.4 Russia and Kazakhstan: Cricket's Eurasian Outpost

While cricket has found footholds in Asia, Africa, and the Middle East, its expansion into Russia has been anything but straightforward. Until 2019, cricket was not even officially recognized as a sport by Russian authorities. Yet, small groups of enthusiasts — largely expatriates from South Asia — kept the game alive, playing on football fields, disused patches of land, and indoor halls during harsh winters. Russia's cricketing community, though under-resourced, demonstrates resilience like how cricket first spread in unlikely colonial outposts.

The ICC's long-term vision requires looking beyond "comfort zones." If cricket could flourish in Afghanistan, Netherlands and Ireland, why not in Russia? Development is a slow process: it can take 30–40 years for a recreational pastime to mature into a structured national program. But planting seeds now matters. Moscow and Saint Petersburg already host informal leagues, often powered by South Asian diasporas. Over decades, these can grow into pipelines for local Russian players.

Climate change may unexpectedly make Russia and Central Asia more relevant for cricket. As traditional venues in South Asia face rising heatwaves, colder geographies such as Moscow, Saint Petersburg, or Almaty and Aktobe in Kazakhstan could emerge as practical alternatives for hosting summer tournaments. Kazakhstan, sitting at the crossroads of Europe and Asia, has the infrastructure of modern stadiums and a growing interest in positioning itself as a regional sports hub.

For the ICC, the case is not about immediate returns but strategic patience. Russia and Kazakhstan may never become cricket superpowers, but their inclusion matters for the sport's global identity. A cricket world that embraces both Melbourne and Moscow, Lahore and Almaty, signals that the game is truly planetary.

In the long horizon, introducing cricket in Russia and Kazakhstan is less about winning matches and more about winning minds: embedding the game in new cultures, creating curiosity among youth, and slowly building institutions that one day could surprise the cricketing world.

17.2.5 Cricket in the Olympics: Dream or Distraction?

Few announcements in recent years have generated as much buzz as the confirmation that cricket will return to the Olympics at the 2028 Los Angeles Games, nearly 128 years after its solitary appearance in Paris in 1900. The ICC, after years of lobbying, secured approval for a T20 format tournament beginning on July 12, 2028. For cricket's administrators, this is a milestone: Olympic inclusion promises exposure to billions of viewers worldwide, access to government funding for developing nations, and the symbolic legitimacy of being part of the "greatest show on Earth." For countries like the USA, where cricket is still niche, the Olympics could serve as an unprecedented marketing platform. For China, where state investment often follows Olympic sports, it might even spark interest that no bilateral series ever could.

Yet the decision is not without its skeptics. India, cricket's economic powerhouse, long dragged its feet, wary that Olympic participation might cede commercial control to the IOC and dilute the primacy of ICC events. The fear is not unfounded: football, despite being the world's biggest sport, has always been a secondary event at the Olympics. Restricted to under-23 players with a handful of senior stars, Olympic football has never rivaled the World Cup in prestige. Could cricket, in its rush for Olympic recognition, fall into the same trap— reduced to a truncated, second-tier version of itself, overshadowed by the ICC's own World Cup and the IPL juggernaut?

There are also practical concerns. With only six to eight teams likely to participate due to scheduling and logistics, the inclusivity of Olympic cricket may be more symbolic than real. Established powers like India, Australia, and England will almost certainly feature, but how many opportunities will there truly be for emerging nations? Will it be a catalyst for new growth, or a closed shop designed for spectacle?

The optimists argue that even symbolism matters. An Olympic gold medal in cricket, however contested, could become a cultural moment for countries like Nepal, the USA, or Germany, where cricket struggles for visibility. The very act of watching cricketers march in the opening ceremony alongside athletes of every discipline might inspire the next generation. The pessimists, however, caution that the sport's crowded calendar is already under strain, and squeezing in another global tournament risks over-saturation.

Ultimately, cricket's Olympic return is both dream and distraction. It offers visibility, legitimacy, and funding for expansion, but it also risks creating a diluted spectacle that cannot match the weight of a World Cup final at Lord's or an India–Pakistan clash at Eden Gardens. Much will depend on whether the ICC treats Olympic cricket as a sideshow for promotion, or as a genuine stage for its finest players. In either case, the 2028 Games will mark a turning point: for the first time in over a century, cricket will be judged not just in its own world, but on sport's biggest and most competitive stage.

For now, Olympic cricket remains both a promise and a puzzle — a chance to globalize the game but also a risk of diluting its essence. Yet even this debate underscores how far cricket has traveled from its colonial beginnings: no longer confined to empire or subcontinent, it now seeks legitimacy on the grandest of stages. And if cricket can find a place beneath the five Olympic rings, who is to say it cannot one day find its footing under alien skies?

17.3 The Long Horizon: Space Cricket and the Robo-Human Future

If someone had predicted in 1877—the year the first official Test match was played—that cricket would one day be played under floodlights, watched by billions on smartphones, or feature formats like T20 and The Hundred, most people would have laughed. But that's exactly what happened. Cricket has always evolved with the times, often in ways that seemed unimaginable just decades before.

So what happens next? As science and technology continue to push human life beyond Earth, could cricket follow us into space?

This may sound like science fiction—but many of today's real-world developments point in that direction. Companies like SpaceX, Blue Origin, and space agencies such as NASA, ISRO, and ESA are actively working on plans for human settlements on the Moon and Mars. Some scientists believe that by the 22nd century, human life could extend across the solar system. And where people go, sport inevitably follows. Just as cricket spread through imperial sea routes in the 19th century, it could one day travel via spacefaring vessels to orbital stations or Martian colonies.

Yet space cricket would look very different from the game we know today.

Take gravity: Mars has only about 38% of Earth's gravity, meaning a cricket ball could travel two or three times farther, and with unpredictable trajectories. Fast bowlers might struggle to generate bounce, while sixes could fly for hundreds of meters. On the Moon, where gravity is only one-sixth of Earth's, even a gentle nudge could send the ball into orbit—literally.

To accommodate this, the game might shift into giant domed habitats with artificial gravity, or perhaps even onto rotating space stations that simulate gravity through centrifugal force. These domes would require breathable air, climate control, and safe radiation shielding—meaning the pitch might feel more like an indoor arena fused with a space lab.

Equipment would also evolve. Players may wear lightweight, pressurized suits or modular exoskeletons to assist movement in low gravity. Bats might be made of carbon-fiber-lithium composites to suit new physics. Helmets could be augmented with heads-up displays showing trajectory predictions and ball spin analytics in real time.

The game formats themselves would likely change too. Long-form cricket may not be feasible in low-oxygen or high-radiation environments. Instead, we might see compressed formats—micro-matches of 5 overs per side, or even one-over showdowns, designed for high-energy, short-duration bursts. These versions could be optimized for colonist stamina, equipment limits, and entertainment schedules across time zones—perhaps with interplanetary time-delay broadcasting.

Technological enhancements would be extraordinary. Imagine fans on Earth watching Martian matches as immersive holograms—walking around the pitch in AR, viewing 360° replay footage with AI-generated commentary, or placing themselves virtually at silly point or third man. Drones, orbiting cameras, and satellite feeds would replace traditional broadcast vans. Martian Premier League? Why not.

By the 22nd century, the rise of quantum computing could revolutionize cricket analytics far beyond today's AI capabilities. Unlike classical computers, quantum processors can handle vast multivariable simulations at near-instant speed. This means entire matches could be simulated in real time, not just ball-by-ball prediction, but accounting for atmospheric changes on Mars, player fatigue in low-gravity environments, or micro-second biomechanical shifts in delivery actions. Coaches might use quantum models to optimize strategy across billions of permutations, while fantasy leagues could offer real-time quantum-driven outcome forecasts for in-game decisions. Umpiring, injury prevention, and performance prediction could become infinitely more precise, with every delivery analyzed against trillions of possible variables.

By the late 22nd century, as robotics and bioengineering reach extraordinary sophistication, cricket may witness the rise of hybrid leagues where humans and AI-powered humanoid robots compete side by side. These contests—perhaps branded as the Robo-Human Premier League—would blend athleticism with precision engineering, with robot players optimized for bowling accuracy, reflex fielding, or even wicketkeeping without fatigue. Human players, still admired for intuition, improvisation, and creativity, would captain these mixed teams, crafting strategies that combine emotion and algorithm. Though unlikely to be sanctioned as official international matches, such leagues could emerge as the ultimate test of man-machine synergy—part sport, part spectacle, part experiment in the limits of physical and artificial performance.

But let's pause and be clear: this is speculative fiction grounded in current trends—not a prediction. A century is a long time, and the path from here to there is full of unknowns—scientific, political, environmental, and ethical. Whether or not humanity even survives climate change, let alone builds cricket stadiums on Mars, remains uncertain.

Still, the thought experiment is valuable. It asks us to consider how far cricket's cultural gravity might extend. Just as cricket adapted to colonialism, commercialization, and digitization, it might one day adapt to off-world expansion. If it does, the game would serve not only as entertainment, but as a cultural thread connecting humans across planets—a sign of continuity amidst cosmic change.

In the 22nd century, cricket might be played under Martian skies, inside a translucent bio-dome, the red dust rising as a bowler runs in with slow, bounding strides. A batter steadies their stance in low gravity, adjusting their visor, the Earth glimmering faintly in the sky. And when bat meets ball, the sound—however muffled in the Martian air—might still carry the thrill that has lasted over 500 years.

Because no matter how far we go, some things—like cricket—go with us.

17.4 Robo-AI Commentary: The Optional Voice of the Future

The soundtrack of cricket has always been as much about the voices behind the microphone as the action on the field. From John Arlott and Jonathan Agnew's lyrical radio descriptions to Richie Benaud's dry wit, commentators have shaped the way generations experienced the game. Their words gave rhythm to matches, turning statistics into stories and silences into suspense. Yet even this tradition, deeply rooted in human intuition, is now encountering the possibilities of artificial intelligence.

The seeds of AI-assisted commentary were planted much earlier than many realize. As far back as the late 20th century, early cricket and football video games included basic, pre-recorded commentary that responded to in-game action. Though crude by today's standards—limited phrases stitched together mechanically—they hinted at a future where software could narrate play in real time. For their era, these systems were ahead of the curve, showing how even simulated sport felt incomplete without a guiding voice.

Fast forward to today, and AI-driven speech technologies are no longer novelties. Virtual assistants like Siri, Alexa, and Google Assistant already provide conversational interfaces for everyday tasks, from banking transactions to customer support. In finance and customer service, automated voices are often indistinguishable from human operators, delivering efficient, personalized responses. The leap from transactional dialogue to real-time sports narration is not as far as it once seemed.

In the latter half of this century, cricket broadcasting could integrate "Robo-AI commentary" as an optional layer of coverage. Unlike traditional commentary, which reflects the perspective and personality of individual broadcasters, AI systems would draw on vast datasets—player biometrics, quantum-processed analytics, real-time weather patterns, even historical archives—to provide a level of precision that no human can match. Imagine an AI voice explaining, mid-delivery, the exact probability of swing based on micro-climatic shifts or highlighting biomechanical variations in a bowler's action compared against millions of historical deliveries stored in a database.

Importantly, this would not replace human commentators. Just as audiences today can choose between commentary in English, Hindi, Tamil, or Urdu, the future may allow viewers to select from multiple panels: the classic human voices, or an AI-driven alternative that emphasizes pure data and probabilistic insights. For those weary of perceived bias or simply curious to experiment, an AI channel would provide a neutral, hyper-analytical option. It would also engage fans who currently mute broadcasts due to irritation with certain styles, giving them a fresh way to stay connected to the game.

The technology enabling this will likely be underpinned by advances in quantum computing. Where present-day AI can parse patterns, future systems will run complex simulations in real time, testing billions of outcomes for every ball bowled. Commentary could thus evolve into a fusion of narration and prediction, where audiences not only hear what has happened but also glimpse what might happen next with astonishing accuracy.

Yet, the essence of commentary—its poetry, humor, and ability to capture the intangible atmosphere of a match—remains uniquely human. Robo-AI commentary will not replace this but complement it, offering an alternative voice tailored for a certain type of audience. Just as cricket once embraced multi-camera broadcasts, stump microphones, and drone footage, it may one day embrace AI commentary as another choice in the viewer's toolkit.

In that sense, the commentary box of the future could be more diverse than ever: human broadcasters blending insight with personality, AI systems offering precision-driven perspectives, and audiences free to navigate between them. Far from ending the era of the commentator, this hybrid model could expand it, making cricket more inclusive, more adaptable, and more attuned to the varied ways fans wish to experience the game.

17.5 Women's Cricket as a Global Growth Engine

For much of cricket's long and storied history, the spotlight rested almost exclusively on men's cricket. The origins of women's cricket date as far back as the 18th century, with the first recorded match in 1745 in Surrey, England. However, organized women's cricket took shape much later, with the Women's Cricket Association formed in England in 1926 and the first women's Test match played between England and Australia in 1934. Despite these early developments, the women's game remained under-resourced, underpromoted, and underwatched for decades.

The turning point began in the late 20th century and gained real momentum in the 21st. The International Women's Cricket Council merged with the ICC in 2005, a decision that was instrumental in bringing women's cricket under a global governance structure with access to better funding, visibility, and international scheduling. Since then, the women's game has undergone a steady transformation— moving from the periphery of global sport to becoming one of cricket's most promising frontiers for expansion and innovation.

Historically, women's cricket has been shaped by the same cultural and societal forces that constrained female participation in many public spheres. The early decades saw fewer matches, little media coverage, and a significant pay disparity compared to male counterparts. However, landmark events slowly shifted public perception. The 2009 ICC Women's World Cup in Australia, for instance, introduced a broader international audience to the competitiveness and quality of women's cricket. England's victory and Charlotte Edwards' leadership brought a new level of attention.

But the true breakout moment came during the 2017 ICC Women's World Cup held in England. The final at Lord's, where India narrowly lost to England, drew a sold-out crowd and was watched by over 180 million people globally. This match catalyzed a wave of media coverage, corporate sponsorship, and governmental attention toward women's cricket. Players like Mithali Raj, Harmanpreet Kaur, Meg Lanning, and Ellyse Perry became household names, and the sport's image was no longer restricted to a niche demographic.

Credit must be given to the ICC for recognizing the potential of the women's game and gradually building its competitive architecture. Regular bilateral series, a revamped Women's Championship for World Cup qualification, and expanded participation in T20 formats have all provided momentum. The Women's T20 World Cup, in particular, has emerged as a crucial driver of interest, with the 2020 final between Australia and India at the Melbourne Cricket Ground drawing more than 86,000 spectators—the highest attendance ever for a women's cricket match and among the top ten for any women's sporting event globally.

Another major contributor to the rise of women's cricket has been the proliferation of domestic T20 leagues. The Women's Big Bash League (WBBL) in Australia set the gold standard early on. It showed that competitive women's cricket could be marketed successfully, televised widely, and supported by a dedicated fanbase. Following suit, India launched the Women's Premier League (WPL) in 2023, modeled after the IPL, with record-breaking bids for franchises and significant player salaries. In just its first season, WPL demonstrated the commercial and athletic potential of the women's game.

Beyond these top-tier nations, women's cricket is expanding its footprint into newer markets. Thailand's qualification for the 2020 Women's T20 World Cup was a landmark, showcasing how associate nations can be nurtured into competitive contenders with the right support. The ICC's role in funding grassroots programs, development tours, and coaching exchanges in regions like Southeast Asia, East Africa, and the Pacific is a key piece of the global puzzle.

Crucially, the rise of women's cricket is not just a story about growth—it's a story about change. The game is helping rewrite narratives around gender, athleticism, and national identity. Young girls in South Asia, once told cricket was not "for them," now grow up watching stars who look like them break records on television. Social media platforms and digital streaming services have further democratized access to women's cricket, allowing fans in rural and underserved regions to follow matches and players in real time. These platforms bypass traditional gatekeepers and give the women's game a direct line to its audience.

However, challenges remain. Pay equity is still a contentious issue. While countries like Australia and New Zealand have made strides in ensuring parity in match fees, the majority of women cricketers globally still earn a fraction of what male players do. Infrastructure remains uneven—many countries still lack dedicated academies, physiotherapy, and travel resources for women's teams. Cultural resistance in certain regions also slows participation rates and delays talent identification.

Despite these hurdles, the trajectory is undeniably upward. Women's cricket is now firmly embedded in the global cricket calendar, with more countries fielding professional teams, more tournaments being televised, and more corporate sponsors entering the space. It is not inconceivable that by the 2030s, women's cricket could rival men's cricket in terms of broadcast rights, advertising revenue, and global following—especially in the T20 format, which aligns well with contemporary viewing habits.

From a broader sports economics perspective, women's cricket represents an untapped market. Sponsors and broadcasters are discovering that women's sports offer better ROI in terms of engagement per dollar spent. As women's cricket continues to build loyalty among younger, more gender-conscious audiences, it will shape not only how the game is played but how it is perceived. This commercial opportunity must be nurtured with care, ensuring that commercialization does not come at the cost of inclusivity and development.

Looking ahead, the future of women's cricket is likely to be shaped by a few key trends: the rise of cross-border T20 leagues, increasing integration of performance analytics, improved athlete conditioning, and more robust pathways from grassroots to elite cricket. Technological integration will also play a major role—wearables, biometrics, and AI coaching assistants will help players optimize performance and prevent injury. As these tools become accessible, they will level the playing field between countries with high-performance budgets and those still catching up.

In conclusion, women's cricket is not just a growth engine—it is a redefinition of what the game stands for. It champions inclusivity, resilience, and evolution. It expands the audience base, diversifies cricket's future, and offers new narratives that the sport desperately needs in a fragmented, digital-first media landscape. If the 20th century belonged to the establishment of cricket's traditions, the 21st century may well belong to the transformation led by women. Their journey from invisibility to influence is already one of the most compelling stories in sport—and it's only just getting started.

17.6 The Ethical Horizon

As cricket crosses into new centuries of technological, geopolitical, and economic transformation, there emerges a quiet yet urgent question: not just where the game is going, but what kind of game it is becoming. In the rush toward innovation, monetization, and expansion, there is a risk that the very soul of cricket—the idea of fairness, dignity, and shared joy—might be lost unless actively protected. The future will not only be shaped by what is possible, but by what is permissible, and this distinction marks the ethical horizon of cricket.

The game has always operated with an unspoken moral grammar. Even in its earliest form, it carried embedded ideas of sportsmanship, restraint, and mutual respect. "The spirit of the game" was not merely a poetic abstraction but a form of cultural self-regulation. And yet, with each new decade, the foundational ideals have been tested—by money, power, politics, and now, by algorithms. What was once a contest between bat and ball is increasingly a contest between institutions, data systems, and corporate imperatives.

Cricket's increasing reliance on surveillance technologies—from player biometrics to ball-tracking, predictive analytics, and AI-based strategy engines—raises real ethical concerns. Players are now not just athletes but quantified bodies. Their muscle fatigue, reaction time, sleep cycles, and even emotional states are tracked, analyzed, and sold as insight. While these tools promise performance gains, they also risk turning players into datasets, stripping away agency and privacy. At what point does this datafication reduce the human complexity of the sport into a product optimized for screens and markets?

Another area of concern that warrants exploration is the use of BCI. Imagine a scenario where one captain is fitted with a BCI (Brain–Computer Interface), granting real-time access to predictive analytics, opponent tendencies, and AI-generated field strategies—while the opposing captain operates with an unaugmented human brain. While the former may have no direct control over the data stream, the enhancement creates an asymmetry in decision-making capacity. If cricket is to retain its soul as a contest of skill, wit, and intuition, the sport must develop clear guidelines about the role of neuro-augmentation. Will there be a 'baseline brain' policy for leadership roles? Or will the game embrace transhuman captains as the natural evolution of competitive advantage?

Equipment Ethics in the Age of Augmentation carry significant importance. The infamous 1979 incident where Dennis Lillee wielded an aluminium bat at the WACA — sparking protest from the English captain and umpires — marked a turning point in cricket's approach to equipment governance. That one act revealed how even minor technological deviations could provoke controversy over fairness and the spirit of the game. In the 22nd century, this concern will resurface in far more complex forms. Bats embedded with kinetic energy redistribution, invisible edge sensors, or neuro-responsive grip systems may appear identical to traditional equipment yet offer hidden advantages. Fielders might wear exoskeletal enhancements masked as apparel. Governing bodies will require not just sharper laws, but advanced forensic tools to verify material compliance and intent. The ethical challenge will not be mere detection — but deciding where innovation ends and unfair advantage begins.

Then there is the question of fairness across borders. The concentration of power, particularly economic and scheduling power, into a handful of national boards creates a deeply unequal cricketing economy. Smaller boards often play fewer games, generate less broadcast revenue, and face greater difficulty retaining top talent. Without structural interventions, these disparities will deepen, eroding the competitive ecosystem. There is no future for cricket that allows a dozen nations to dominate while the rest survive on scraps. Equity is not charity—it is sustainability. A fragmented cricketing world cannot inspire the next generation globally.

Fan data and monetization strategies are another pressure point. Fantasy cricket platforms, digital engagement trackers, NFT marketplaces, and betting-linked content engines are reshaping fan behavior, but often without sufficient safeguards. Consent, privacy, and fairness are frequently afterthoughts. In a digital cricket economy, fans are more than viewers—they are data points, consumers, and targets of behavioral manipulation. The sport must confront whether it is building communities or exploiting them.

The climate emergency adds another layer of responsibility. Cricket cannot remain untouched by the planetary crisis. Heatwaves, smog, rising sea levels, and resource scarcity are already impacting where and how the game is played. Yet most boards continue to operate with a short-term, event-driven logic. Hosting mega-tournaments in unsustainable venues, expanding international travel footprints, and neglecting climate adaptation protocols all run counter to the long-term health of the sport. Cricket must not be a bystander in this transformation—it should be a model of sustainable operations, ecological sensitivity, and local resilience.

And finally, there is the challenge of meaning. As cricket becomes increasingly immersive, algorithmic, and virtualized—from smart balls and programmable pitches to metaverse stadiums and synthetic players—what happens to the emotional, imperfect, human center of the game? Will the next generation of fans cheer for avatars optimized by neural networks? Will real-world rivalries become second to virtual simulations? These questions are not about resisting the future, but about ensuring that the future doesn't flatten the past. Technology should extend the magic of cricket, not sterilize it.

Ethics, then, is not a constraint on progress—it is the compass that ensures progress does not become destruction. The governing bodies of cricket, whether global or domestic, need to adopt long-term ethical charters. These would not be public relations gestures, but operational commitments to transparency, accountability, and inclusivity. Independent review panels could be established to evaluate new technologies, league models, and player data systems before adoption. Diversity of thought and representation—across gender, geography, and expertise—should be built into cricket's leadership structures.

Revenue-sharing mechanisms must evolve to reflect the realities of the 21st century, where digital platforms, not stadium gates, drive the sport's economy. A percentage of all global cricket revenue—whether from streaming, fantasy apps, or NFTs—could be routed into a global cricket development fund. This fund would support grassroots infrastructure, women's cricket, associate nations, and climate-resilient venues. Such a fund is not utopian—it is urgently practical. The game's financial architecture must match its moral ambition.

Players themselves will need new support structures. Ethics education, mental health services, digital literacy, and post-retirement transition programs must become the norm, not the exception. Cricketers are no longer just athletes—they are brand ambassadors, digital entrepreneurs, geopolitical figures, and social role models. They carry not just national hopes but algorithmic pressure, public scrutiny, and commercial contracts. Protecting their humanity is essential.

The same applies to fans. Digital fandom must not become digital addiction. Fantasy platforms and engagement apps should have limits—ethical nudges that prevent over-spending, real-time fatigue, and unhealthy competition. Algorithms must be transparent and accountable. Betting-linked content must be regulated with urgency. Cricket, unlike some other sports, still retains a large family audience. That trust cannot be betrayed for quarterly revenue.

In the end, the ethical horizon of cricket is not a final destination—it is a line that moves as the game moves. What matters is that we keep our eyes on it, that we ask hard questions before celebrating shiny answers. The decisions made now—on who governs, who profits, who plays, and who watches—will echo not just across seasons, but across generations.

Cricket's future must not only be fast and global—it must be just, inclusive, and wise. For a sport born in colonial privilege, and then reclaimed by post-colonial passion, there is a historic responsibility to do better than the world that birthed it. As we enter an age of climate stress, digital acceleration, and cultural fragmentation, cricket has the chance to be more than just a game. It can be a space of collective memory, ethical imagination, and human possibility.

This is not a sentimental hope. It is a call to act. Because if cricket is to be watched by billions, it must also be worthy of them.

Readers' Notes

Hegemony vs. Sustainability: *While one dominant board controls much of global cricket's economics and scheduling, this chapter emphasizes the need for balance between influence and fairness. Financial power can help smaller boards but must not come at the cost of competitive equality.*

Broadcasting Revenue is King: *Cricket's survival in the 21st and 22nd centuries is deeply tied to media rights, sponsorships, and digital streaming deals. Just like football clubs in Europe rely on Champions League income, cricket boards—especially smaller ones—must stay competitive to remain financially viable.*

New Markets Hold the Key: *The USA, Middle East, and Africa are positioned as the next big growth engines. The USA successfully co-hosted the 2024 T20 World Cup, and the Middle East continues to act as cricket's financial and logistical hub. Africa is a long-term bet, driven by youth demographics and digital access.*

Cricket in the Cosmos?: *Chapter 17.3 offers a speculative but intriguing look into "Space Cricket", imagining a future where the sport follows humanity into Mars colonies and beyond. It draws parallels to how unimaginable cricket's evolution would have been to those watching the first Test in 1877.*

Women's Cricket as a Catalyst: *Chapter 17.4 frames women's cricket not as a sideshow, but as a major force in expanding the game globally. Tournaments like the WPL and historic World Cup moments prove that the women's game is commercially viable, culturally impactful, and here to stay.*

Strategic Diplomacy, Not Just Sport: *Cricket's future governance will require careful balancing of interests—between mega-boards and emerging nations, between tradition and innovation, and between short-term revenue and long-term inclusivity.*

Human Resilience and Innovation: *Across its speculative and practical parts, the chapter makes a clear case: Cricket's survival depends on evolution—in technology, equality, broadcasting, and geopolitics. Money alone won't save it, but smart investments and shared power might.*

Robo-Human Premier League:

A speculative 22nd-century franchise cricket tournament featuring mixed teams of enhanced humans and AI-powered robots, blending biomechanics, machine learning, and sport-tech entertainment in post-Earth environments.

Robo-AI Commentary:

An optional late 21st and early 22nd century broadcast advanced innovation where artificial intelligence delivers real-time ball-by-ball narration, blending quantum-powered analytics, biometric data, and historical archives. Designed not to replace human commentators but to provide fans with a hyper-precise, neutral alternative alongside traditional voices.

Postscript – Beyond the Boundary: Sport, Sovereignty, and the Code to Come

As cricket journeys into its digital and decentralized future, the game finds itself at the intersection of sovereignty, identity, and code. This book has traced the evolution of cricket across empires, across borders, and now, across platforms. From its colonial roots in English aristocracy to its mass adoption in South Asia, and onward into the speculative terrains of blockchain, AI, and the metaverse, cricket has been more than a sport—it has been an evolving socio-political text.

Yet the final transformation we are witnessing in the first quarter of 21st century is perhaps the most profound. Cricket is no longer just a cultural artefact of empire or an economic product of broadcasting deals. It is becoming a programmable, participatory network. The locus of authority is shifting—from centralized boards to distributed fan communities, from administrators to token-holders, from physical stadiums to digital ecosystems. This transition demands a new conceptual framework.

What emerges from this analysis is the doctrine of post-imperial digital sovereignty through sport. This is a sovereignty defined not by territorial control, but by the architecture of participation and the logic of platforms. Cricket becomes a case study for how formerly colonized societies now exert cultural, technological, and even financial influence in a transnational, digitized world. This is not a metaphorical sovereignty—it is literal, if one examines the rise of DAOs, tokenized fan ownership, and digital franchises that defy traditional geopolitical borders.

The implications are threefold. First, sovereignty in the digital sports economy is increasingly relational. Legitimacy and power arise through participation—fans no longer consume cricket passively, but co-govern its formats, economics, and ethics through decentralized tools. Second, infrastructure itself is political. The blockchains on which digital cricket operates, the AI that curates feeds, and the algorithms that moderate behaviour all encode values and hierarchies. In a post-broadcast era, those who write the code effectively write the constitution. Third, the future of cricket—like the future of governance more broadly—is programmable. It can be simulated, iterated, and shaped not just by elites, but by crowds, protocols, and networks.

This shift does not guarantee a utopia. Without regulation, transparency, and digital ethics, the decentralised model could reproduce the very inequities it claims to solve. Yet cricket, by virtue of its hybrid heritage—colonial and anti-colonial, analog and digital—may be uniquely positioned to model a different kind of sovereignty. The game has always been about structure and improvisation, about rules and interpretation. These traits map surprisingly well onto the emerging world of decentralized governance and digital citizenship.

As questions of algorithmic fairness, biometric data ownership, cross-jurisdictional fan governance, and AI-augmented performance emerge, cricket may offer a surprisingly rigorous terrain to examine them. It is no longer merely a reflection of society—it is becoming a laboratory for it. The shift from stadium to server, from pitch to platform, is not a loss of authenticity. Rather, it is the next chapter in cricket's long evolution from a tool of empire to an arena of empowerment.

As such, the doctrine articulated here is not predictive dogma but a critical lens—a proposal that in the coming decades, sport, and particularly cricket, may serve as the medium through which digital sovereignty is contested, negotiated, and ultimately realized. As with all such propositions, time will determine its validity. But the evidence thus far—from tokenized teams to cross-platform fandoms, from metaverse tournaments to real-world decentralised governance experiments—suggests that this is no longer the realm of speculation. It is the boundary on which cricket now plays.

In the long view of history, perhaps cricket's greatest transformation is not its format or its rules, but its role. Once a symbol of imperial control, it is now a field on which new forms of global agency are being tested. And as empires dissolve and new networks form, cricket may well become a vanguard of digital democracy—its scoreboard reflecting not just runs and wickets, but values, choices, and shared futures.

The Sovereignty–Acceleration Theorem of Cricket

Cricket has never stood still. Its power has shifted across regions and its forms have shifted through innovations that were often mocked at first and later embraced as essential. What this suggests is that sovereignty in cricket and technological acceleration are not separate forces but intertwined cycles that have shaped the game across centuries. The Sovereignty–Acceleration Theorem proposes that cricket evolves through recurring patterns of power transfer and technological adoption, usually spanning thirty to fifty years, with each phase marked by resistance, transition, and eventual dominance.

In the eighteenth and nineteenth centuries, England exercised imperial sovereignty, codifying the laws and exporting the game across its empire. Even overarm bowling, initially condemned as illegitimate, became the norm. In the twentieth century, the sovereignty of cricket shifted to the colonial periphery, where the West Indies' golden era came to embody cultural resistance and sporting supremacy. During the same period, the idea of limited-overs cricket, once dismissed as artificial, accelerated into mainstream acceptance, culminating in the first World Cup in 1975. By the late twentieth and early twenty-first centuries, South Asia had taken command as cricket's commercial powerhouse. India's economic liberalization, the television revolution, and the IPL turned the region into the centre of the cricketing world. At the same time, T20 cricket—laughed at in its infancy—became the game's most dominant format within barely a decade.

The pattern is clear. Innovation appears, meets resistance, then gains acceptance, and ultimately achieves dominance. Sovereignty shifts toward whichever force is best placed to harness the new form. The next shift may not be national at all but digital and decentralized. Platforms, franchises, and technologies may well replace boards and states as cricket's sovereign agents. AI umpiring, e-sports cricket, and Olympic formats may follow the same trajectory of ridicule, normalization, and eventual supremacy.

The history of cricket suggests that its destiny is cyclical rather than linear, and that its future will be contested in code and commerce as much as in bat and ball. The Sovereignty–Acceleration Theorem is not a prediction but a recognition of a pattern that has repeated itself from the age of empire to the age of algorithms. It reminds us that cricket's essence lies not in resisting change, but in absorbing it until the new becomes tradition. The contest for sovereignty will continue, but the game will endure as it always has—at once ancient and ever-new, local and global, traditional and revolutionary.

Epilogue

This book began with a proposition: that cricket is more than a game. It is a living text—layered, mobile, and evolving—through which we can study the entanglements of empire, identity, innovation, and imagination. As the final page turns, that proposition feels not only reaffirmed, but also transformed.

Rather than compiling cricketing statistics or offering exhaustive biographical sketches—both of which are already widely available in the digital age—this book has sought to provide something rarer: a critical, future-facing case study of South Asian cricket and its global significance. It is an inquiry into how the sport intersects with wider social systems: migration, memory, geopolitics, platform capitalism, and emerging technology. It also probes how the game reflects back to us the aspirations and contradictions of a postcolonial world in motion.

The decision to forgo illustrations or photo inserts is a deliberate one. In an era where imagery and data are instantly retrievable, the true value lies in interpretation. This book privileges analysis over aesthetics—not to dismiss beauty, but to pursue clarity. It is a project of synthesis, reflection, and projection.

Across six sections, we have examined cricket's rise from imperial regulation to nationalist reinvention, and from grassroots resilience to billion-dollar digital ecosystems. We have traced the legacies of exile, the geographies of innovation, and the cultural currents shaping tomorrow's cricket—from Afghanistan to Silicon Valley, from Sharjah to Shanghai. We have dwelled on leadership, strategy, fandom, media, and market forces—not as side plots, but as essential scaffolding for understanding the game's evolution.

Crucially, this work has also made room for imaginative speculation. As sport increasingly overlaps with AI, biotechnology, and hybrid formats, cricket finds itself poised at the threshold of profound transformation. What might a three-day, pink-ball, floodlit Test look like in Seoul or Osaka? Can AI-coaches and predictive analytics coexist with the instinct of a Ben Stokes or the vision of an Imran Khan? Can cricket survive climate volatility, commercial saturation, and attention fatigue—and if so, in what form?

These are not rhetorical questions. They are provocations—meant to inspire further scholarship, debate, and curiosity. As readers, you are invited not just to absorb, but to contribute: to imagine cricket not as a finished product, but as a cultural process, perpetually shaped by its players, publics, and politics.

This book does not pretend to be the final word. Rather, it hopes to be a generative word—a point of departure for future dialogues between cricket and culture, empire and evolution, memory and innovation.

Because in the end, cricket's true power lies not in its preservation, but in its capacity for reinvention. And it is in that spirit—between the stumps and the stars—that the game, and this book, finds its resonance.

I will not be around by the dawn of the twenty-second century, but cricket almost certainly will—evolved, adapted, and still unfolding. If this book endures, let it serve not merely as a record of what has been, but as a synopsis of what may yet come, and a resource to be consulted by those shaping cricket's next frontier.

Bibliography

Birley, D. (1999). *A Social History of English Cricket*. London: Aurum Press.

Major, J. (2007). *More Than a Game: The Story of Cricket's Early Years*. London: HarperCollins.

Allen, D. (2010). *Cricket: An Illustrated History*. Oxford: Oxford University Press.

Underdown, D. (2000). *Start of Play: Cricket and Culture in Eighteenth-Century England*. London: Allen Lane.

Altham, H. S. & Swanton, E. W. (1962). *A History of Cricket: Volume 1 (to 1914)*. London: George Allen & Unwin.

Waghorn, H. T. (1899). *The Dawn of Cricket*. London: Electric Press.

Mangan, J. A. (1986). *The Games Ethic and Imperialism: Aspects of the Diffusion of an Ideal*. London: Viking.

Dirks, N. B. (2006). *The Scandal of Empire: India and the Creation of Imperial Britain*. Cambridge, MA: Harvard University Press.

Dalrymple, W. (2019). *The Anarchy: The East India Company, Corporate Violence, and the Pillage of an Empire*. London: Bloomsbury.

Chatterjee, P. (1993). *The Nation and Its Fragments: Colonial and Postcolonial Histories*. Princeton: Princeton University Press.

Bose, S. & Jalal, A. (2011). *Modern South Asia: History, Culture, Political Economy*. London: Routledge.

Washbrook, D. A. (2004). *South India 1770–1840: The Colonial Transition*. The Indian Economic and Social History Review, 41(4), pp. 447–473.

Metcalf, T. R. (2005). *Forging the Raj: Essays on British India in the Heyday of Empire*. New Delhi: Oxford University Press.

Gupta, A. (2007). *The East India Company and Cricket: Trade, Empire and Masculinity*. In *Sport in South Asian Society*, ed. Boria Majumdar and J. A. Mangan. London: Routledge.

Marshall, P. J. (1987). *The Making and Unmaking of Empires: Britain, India, and America c.1750–1783*. Oxford: Oxford University Press.

Guha, R. (2002). *A Corner of a Foreign Field: The Indian History of a British Sport*. London: Picador.

Majumdar, B. (2004). *Twenty-Two Yards to Freedom: A Social History of Indian Cricket*. New Delhi: Penguin.

Mills, J. H. (2001). *Subaltern Sports: Politics and Sport in South Asia*. London: Anthem Press.

Sandiford, K. A. P. (1994). *Cricket and the Victorians*. Aldershot: Scolar Press.

Stoddart, B. (1998). *Cricket, Social Formation and Cultural Continuity in the British West Indies*. In *The Cultural Bond: Sport, Empire, Society*, ed. J. A. Mangan. London: Frank Cass.

Cashman, R. (1980). *Patrons, Players and the Crowd: The Phenomenon of Indian Cricket*. New Delhi: Orient Longman.

Alter, J. S. (1994). *The Wrestler's Body: Identity and Ideology in North India*. Berkeley: University of California Press. *(for contextual comparison of colonial sports institutions)*

Guha, R. (2002). *A Corner of a Foreign Field: The Indian History of a British Sport*. London: Picador.

Majumdar, B. (2004). *Twenty-Two Yards to Freedom: A Social History of Indian Cricket*. New Delhi: Penguin.

Nandy, A. (2001). *The Tao of Cricket: On Games of Destiny and the Destiny of Games*. New Delhi: Oxford University Press.

Guptan, R. (2007). *Sachin Tendulkar: A Definitive Biography*. New Delhi: Rupa Publications.

Bandyopadhyay, K. (2007). *Cricket in India: Representative Playing Fields to the IPL*. London: Routledge.

Appadurai, A. (1996). *Modernity at Large: Cultural Dimensions of Globalization*. Minneapolis: University of Minnesota Press. *(chapter on cricket and nationalism)*

Ahmed, S. (2017). *Pakistan's Cricketing Exile: Identity, Politics and Survival*. London: Hurst.

Osman Samiuddin. (2014). *The Unquiet Ones: A History of Pakistan Cricket*. London: HarperCollins.

Shaharyar Khan. (2005). *Cricket: A Bridge of Peace*. Oxford University Press.

Haider, Z. (2009). *Between Bat and Ball: The Story of Cricket in Pakistan*. Lahore: Vanguard Books.

Lieven, A. (2011). *Pakistan: A Hard Country*. London: Penguin. *(chapters discussing cricket as soft power)*

Perera, S. (2015). *Cricket and National Identity in Sri Lanka*. London: Routledge.

de Mel, N. (2007). *Cricket, Nationalism and Masculinity in Sri Lanka: From Boys to Men to Warriors*. In *Sport in South Asian Society*, ed. B. Majumdar & J. A. Mangan. London: Routledge.

Ekanayake, E. (2006). *The Rise and Fall of Sri Lanka Cricket*. Colombo: Sarasavi Publishers.

Peiris, G. (2012). *Ethnicity, Conflict and the 1996 Cricket World Cup*. South Asia: Journal of South Asian Studies, 35(2), 195–212.

Rashid, M. (2015). *Bangladesh Cricket: From Struggles to Triumph*. Dhaka: The University Press Limited.

Hossain, M. (2018). *The Tigers Roar: Bangladesh Cricket's Journey to the World Stage*. Dhaka: Daily Star Books.

Ahmed, N. (2021). *Batting for Bangladesh: Politics, Pride, and the BPL*. Journal of Sport and Social Issues, 45(3), 237–255.

Karim, N. (2004). *Cricket and Nationalism in Bangladesh*. In *Cricketing Cultures in Conflict*, ed. B. Majumdar & M. J. King. London: Routledge.

Akbarzai, F. & Latif, A. (2018). *Out of the Dust: The Story of Afghan Cricket*. London: Hurst.

Bezhan, F. (2019). *From Refugee Camps to World Cup Fields: The Afghan Cricket Dream*. RFE/RL Reports.

Murtaza, S. (2015). *Afghanistan's Rise in International Cricket*. The Diplomat.

Subramanian, S. (2015). *Cricket in the Warzone: Afghanistan's Journey to the World Stage*. ESPNcricinfo Longform.

Rashid Khan. (2022). *From Kabul to Lords: My Story*. London: HarperSport.

Gupta, A. (2011). *The IPL and Indian Cricket: Globalization, Commercialization and the Cricketing Nation*. Journal of Sport and Social Issues, 35(3), 208–228.

Majumdar, B., & Mangan, J. A. (2005). *Sport in South Asian Society: Past and Present*. London: Routledge.

Bose, M. (2012). *The Magic of IPL: Cricketainment*. New Delhi: Rupa.

Osman Samiuddin. (2022). *Pakistan Super League: Revolution in Exile*. The Cricket Monthly.

Ahmed, S. (2020). *Cricket's New Cartographies: The Franchise Model and the End of the Nation-State Team?* Sport in Society, 23(8), 1309–1325.

Wagg, S. (2017). *Cricket and Commercialization: IPL and Beyond*. London: Palgrave Macmillan.

Hutchins, B., & Rowe, D. (2012). *Digital Media Sport: Technology, Power and Culture in the Network Society*. London: Routledge.

Mehta, N. (2019). *Cricket and the Digital Turn: Streaming, Hashtags, and Hyperlocal Fandoms*. Journal of Sport and Media Studies, 41(2), 100–122.

Sen, R. (2020). *Beyond the Boundary: Cricket and the Age of Clickbait*. New Delhi: Context.

Nielsen Sports. (2021). *Global Sports Media Consumption Report*. [Industry Report]

Disney Star India. (2023). *Inside the Numbers: IPL Viewership Metrics*. [Internal White Paper]

Wilson, M., & Suh, A. (2022). *Blockchain, Tokens and Sport: Exploring Web3 Fan Economies.* Sport Innovation Journal, 4(1), 67–84.

Deloitte. (2023). *Web3 and Sport: Opportunities for Fan Engagement.* SportsTech Insights Series.

Ali, H. (2022). *Cricket on the Blockchain: The NFTification of Fandom.* The Wire.

ICC (2022). *Future of Cricket: Digital Vision 2030.* [Strategic Report]

Sorare Cricket. (2023). *Whitepaper: Fantasy Leagues in the Web3 Era.* Sorare Labs.

IBM. (2021). *AI in Sports: Performance, Strategy, and Experience.* IBM Research Brief.

Rao, A. & Ghosh, P. (2020). *The Rise of AI in Cricket: Analytics, Strategy, and Coaching.* ESPNcricinfo Analytics.

Microsoft Sports AI Division. (2022). *Smart Stadiums, Player Insights, and Predictive Models.* [White Paper]

VRSE (2023). *Virtual Reality and Augmented Reality in Live Cricket.* VRSE Tech Journal.

BatSense. (2021). *Smarter Bats and Real-Time Biometric Feedback.* BatSense Technologies.

WWF. (2020). *Playing Against the Clock: Sport and Climate Change.*

ICC. (2022). *Sustainable Cricket Strategy: Resilience in the Age of Climate Change.*

Bateman, G. (2021). *The Heat Is On: Climate Stress and Global Sport Scheduling.* The Guardian.

Hulme, M. (2009). *Why We Disagree About Climate Change.* Cambridge University Press.

Collins, T. (2021). *Cricket in the Anthropocene: Heatwaves, Floods and the Fragile Future of the Game.* Sport, Ethics and Society, 10(1), 55–78.

UNEP (2023). *Carbon Emissions of Digital Streaming and the Future of Eco-Sport.*

Ahmed, Sara. *The Cultural Politics of Emotion.* Edinburgh University Press, 2014.

Andrews, David L., and Ben Carrington. *A Companion to Sport.* Wiley-Blackwell, 2013.

Bostrom, Nick. *Superintelligence: Paths, Dangers, Strategies.* Oxford University Press, 2014.

Campbell, Howard. "Cricket in the Camps: The Role of Sport in Refugee Identity." *Journal of Refugee Studies*, vol. 31, no. 2, 2018, pp. 222–239.

Clark, Andy. *Natural-Born Cyborgs: Minds, Technologies, and the Future of Human Intelligence.* Oxford University Press, 2003.

Crabbe, Tim. "A Sporting Chance? Using Sport to Tackle Drug Use and Crime." *Drugs: Education, Prevention and Policy*, vol. 7, no. 4, 2000, pp. 381–391.

Fukuyama, Francis. *Our Posthuman Future: Consequences of the Biotechnology Revolution.* Picador, 2002.

Gleeson, Brendan. *The Urban Condition.* Routledge, 2014.

Hassan, David. *Managing Sport and Leisure in the Digital Era.* Routledge, 2018.

Hoberman, John. *Mortal Engines: The Science of Performance and the Dehumanization of Sport.* Free Press, 1992.

Kennedy, David. "Sport, Refugees, and Asylum Seekers: The Role of Sport in Fostering Integration." *International Review for the Sociology of Sport*, vol. 44, no. 2-3, 2009, pp. 151–167.

Miah, Andy. *Genetically Modified Athletes: Biomedical Ethics, Gene Doping and Sport.* Routledge, 2004.

Nixon, Rob. *Slow Violence and the Environmentalism of the Poor.* Harvard University Press, 2011.

Oates, Thomas. *Football and the Boundaries of History.* Palgrave Macmillan, 2015.

Patel, Reena. "Cricket, Technology, and the Ethics of AI." *Sport, Ethics and Philosophy*, vol. 16, no. 1, 2022, pp. 34–52.

Roden, David. *Posthuman Life: Philosophy at the Edge of the Human.* Routledge, 2014.

Schwab, Klaus. *The Fourth Industrial Revolution.* World Economic Forum, 2016.

Sen, Amartya. *Identity and Violence: The Illusion of Destiny.* W. W. Norton, 2007.

Silk, Michael, and David L. Andrews. *Sport and Neoliberalism: Politics, Consumption, and Culture.* Temple University Press, 2012.

Swyngedouw, Erik. *Depoliticized Environments: The End of Nature, Climate Change and the Post-Political Condition*. Royal Holloway University Press, 2015.

Taylor, Matthew. *The Association Game: A History of British Football*. Routledge, 2008.

Tufekci, Zeynep. *Twitter and Tear Gas: The Power and Fragility of Networked Protest*. Yale University Press, 2017.

Zuboff, Shoshana. *The Age of Surveillance Capitalism*. PublicAffairs, 2019.

Bashir, O. (2022). *Afghan Cricket and the Politics of Exile*. The Diplomat.

UNHCR. (2021). *Sport in Refugee Contexts: Resilience and Belonging*.

Gilmour, H. (2018). *Stateless Athletes: Cricket in Camps and Diaspora*. International Journal of Sport and Society, 13(3), 133–148.

Butt, A. (2020). *Pakistan's Decade of Exile: Home Games in the UAE*. Cricbuzz Archives.

Dimeo, P. (2002). *Colonial Bodies, Colonial Sport: 'Martial Races' and South Asian Cricket*. Sport in History, 22(2), 44–64.

Nye, J. S. (2004). *Soft Power: The Means to Success in World Politics*. PublicAffairs.

Sen, R. (2021). *Beyond Boundaries: Cricket, Nationhood, and the Performance of Identity*. New Delhi: Aleph Book Company.

Sugden, J., & Tomlinson, A. (2002). *Power Games: A Critical Sociology of Sport*. London: Routledge.

ICC. (2023). *Cricket Diplomacy: The Role of the Game in Peace and Conflict*. ICC Reports.

Subramanian, N. (2019). *Cricket as Nation-Builder: The Sri Lankan Case Study*. Asian Journal of Sports Policy, 11(1), 22–39.

Anwar, M. (2020). *Diasporic Cricket Leagues and Transnational Belonging*. Sport and Migration Studies, 8(4), 144–162.

Szymanski, S. & Zimbalist, A. (2005). *National Pastime: How Americans Play Baseball and the Rest of the World Plays Soccer*. Brookings Institution Press.

Gupta, A. (2020). *The Political Economy of Cricket in India*. Contemporary South Asia, 28(4), 441–456.

ICC. (2024). *Global Expansion Strategy: New Markets and Growth Potential*. ICC Economic Reports.

Kshetri, N. (2022). *Digital Infrastructure and Soft Power: Middle East Investment in Global Sports*. Journal of Political Economy of Sport, 13(2), 201–218.

Dasgupta, R. (2023). *Streaming, Sovereigns, and Soft Power: Cricket in the Gulf*. Middle East Journal of Sport Studies, 8(1), 55–72.

USA Cricket. (2023). *Major League Cricket Launch Whitepaper*. [Internal Document]

FIFA. (2011). *2010 World Cup Legacy in Africa*. FIFA Technical Reports.

Musk, E. (2021). *Making Life Multi-Planetary*. New Space, 9(2), 51–61.

Arthur, C. (2022). *Gravity Games: Rethinking Sport on Mars*. Journal of Futurism and Sport, 5(4), 111–137.

Dvorsky, G. (2020). *Bioethics of Augmented Athletes*. Future Human Journal, 14(1), 23–36.

MIT Media Lab. (2023). *Mixed Reality Sport Simulations and Fan Immersion*. [Conference Proceedings]

WADA. (2022). *Gene Editing, Ethics, and the Future of Fair Play*. World Anti-Doping Agency Whitepaper.

Harari, Y. N. (2015). *Homo Deus: A Brief History of Tomorrow*. London: Vintage.

The Economist. (2024). *AI Coaches and Neural Analytics in Modern Sport*. The Future of Sport Report.

Velija, P. (2015). *Women's Cricket and Global Processes: The Emergence and Development of Women's Cricket as a Global Game*. Palgrave Macmillan.

ICC. (2022). *Women's Cricket Development Roadmap*. ICC Strategic Reports.

Goswami, J. (2019). *From Margin to Mainstream: The Rise of Women's Cricket in South Asia*. Sport and Gender Quarterly, 12(3), 76–94.

ESPNcricinfo. (2023). *Women's Premier League (WPL): Structural Overview and Growth.*

Chakrabarty, R. (2021). *Cricket, Capital, and the Women's Game in India.* The Wire.

Taylor, M. (2016). *The Globalization of Women's Sport: Perspectives and Policies.* London: Routledge.

Sandel, M. (2009). *Justice: What's the Right Thing to Do?* Harvard University Press.

Rawls, J. (1971). *A Theory of Justice.* Harvard University Press.

Zuboff, S. (2019). *The Age of Surveillance Capitalism.* PublicAffairs.

ICC. (2023). *Ethics in Emerging Cricket Economies.* ICC Governance Papers.

Brin, D. (2018). *The Transparent Society: Will Technology Force Us to Choose Between Privacy and Freedom?* Basic Books.

Millington, B. (2025). *Sport and the Promise of Artificial Intelligence.* Social Sport Journal.

Valerio, J. et al. (2012). *Ethical Implications of Neuroimaging in Sports Concussion.* Journal of Neurotrauma.

Musat, C. L. et al. (2024). *A Comprehensive Review of Injury Risk Prediction Methods.* Sports Medicine & Rehabilitation.

Kim, J. H. et al. (2025). *Ethical Concerns and Perceptions of Artificial Intelligence in Sport.* Science & Ethics in Sport.

Pietraszewski, P. et al. (2025). *The Role of Artificial Intelligence in Sports Analytics.* Applied Sciences, 15(13), 7254.

Ishida, S. et al. (2023). *A Comparative Review on Neuroethical Issues in Neuroscience and Neuroethics Journals.* Frontiers in Neuroscience.

Ienca, M. et al. (2017). *Towards New Human Rights in the Age of Neuroscience and Neurotechnology.* Life Sciences, Society and Policy.

Parsons, M. V. et al. (2025). *Ethical Implications of Neurotechnology in Industry.* Journal of Applied Ethics in Technology.

Glebova, E. et al. (2024). *Artificial Intelligence Development and Dissemination in the Sports Industry.* Sports Technology & Society.

Savulescu, J. et al. (2020). *The Ethics of Motivational Neuro-Doping in Sport: Praiseworthiness and Prizeworthiness.* Neuroethics.

World Economic Forum. (2025). *Artificial Intelligence in Media, Entertainment and Sport 2025.* WEF Reports.

IEEE Brain. (2023). *Neuroethics Framework: Sports & Competitions.* IEEE Publications.

Zhu-Tian, C. et al. (2022). *Sporthesia: Augmenting Sports Videos Using Natural Language.* ArXiv Preprint.

Jha, D. et al. (2022). *Video Analytics in Elite Soccer: A Distributed Computing Perspective.* ArXiv Preprint.

Li, L. et al. (2021). *Neural Efficiency in Athletes: A Systematic Review.* Frontiers in Behavioral Neuroscience.

Erden, Y. J. et al. (2023). *Ethical Issues of Neurotechnology.* Artificial Organs.

Midha, S. et al. (2022). *Ethical Concerns and Perceptions of Consumer Neurotechnology.* ACM Transactions on Human-Computer Interaction.

Rahmani, M., Majedi, N., Hemmatinejad, M., & Jamshidi, M. (2024). *Application of Artificial Intelligence in the Sports Industry: A Review Article.* AI and Technology in Behavioral & Social Sciences.

Li, W. et al. (2025). *Artificial Intelligence for Sports: Technologies, Ethics, and Legal Frameworks.* Sport and Technology Review.

UNESCO International Bioethics Committee. (2023). *Ethical Principles of Neurotechnology: Report of the International Bioethics Committee.* UNESCO Reports.

International Cricket Council (ICC) (2022). *Future of Cricket: Digital Vision 2030.* ICC.org. Available at: https://www.icc-cricket.com/news/icc-future-of-cricket-digital-vision-2030 [Accessed 22 September 2025].

International Cricket Council (ICC) (2023). *Global Expansion Strategy: New Markets and Growth Potential.* ICC.org. Available at: https://www.icc-cricket.com/media-releases/icc-global-growth-strategy-2023 [Accessed 22 September 2025].

ESPNcricinfo (2023). *Women's Premier League: A new era for women's cricket.* ESPNcricinfo. Available at: https://www.espncricinfo.com/story/women-s-premier-league-a-new-era-for-women-s-cricket-1368321 [Accessed 22 September 2025].

BBC Sport (2021). *How climate change threatens cricket's future.* BBC Sport. Available at: https://www.bbc.com/sport/cricket/56537845 [Accessed 22 September 2025].

The Guardian (2022). *Cricket and climate crisis: Can the game adapt in time?.* The Guardian. Available at:

https://www.theguardian.com/sport/2022/sep/03/cricket-and-climate-crisis [Accessed 22 September 2025].

Reuters (2022). *Cricket looks to the USA and beyond in global push.* Reuters. Available at: https://www.reuters.com/lifestyle/sports/cricket-looks-usa-and-beyond-global-push-2022-07-21/ [Accessed 22 September 2025].

Wisden (2021). *Cricket in Russia: From obscurity to recognition.* Wisden Almanack Online. Available at: https://wisden.com/stories/cricket-in-russia-from-obscurity-to-recognition [Accessed 22 September 2025].

The Economist (2024). *AI, algorithms, and the future of sport strategy.* The Economist. Available at: https://www.economist.com/sport/2024/07/18/ai-algorithms-and-the-future-of-sport-strategy [Accessed 22 September 2025].

Forbes (2023). *Blockchain, NFTs and the new era of fan engagement in sports.* Forbes. Available at: https://www.forbes.com/sites/blockchain-sports-nfts [Accessed 22 September 2025].

Malcolm, D. (2013). *Globalizing cricket: Englishness, empire and identity.*

Rumford, C. (2007). *More than a game: Globalization and the post-Westernization of cricket.*

Mitra, R. (2010). *The IPL and the Indian cricket fan: Following the spectacle.*

Mills, J. (2014). *Cricket, politics and empire: The colonial game in a decolonizing world.*

Dimeo, P. (2002). Colonial bodies, colonial sport: 'Martial races' and South Asian cricket. *Sport in History*, 22(2), pp. 44–64.

Williams, J. (2001). Cricket and race. *Ethnic and Racial Studies*, 24(4), pp. 634–652.

Gupta, A. (2011). The Indian Premier League and the making of a new cricketing order. *Sport in Society*, 14(10), pp. 1316–1335.

Senne, J. (2016). Gender equity in cricket: Progress and challenges. *International Journal of Sport Policy and Politics*, 8(4), pp. 627–642.

Raghavan, R. (2015). Cricket, cinema and nation: Cultural intersections in South Asia. *South Asian Popular Culture*, 13(3), pp. 213–229.

Hindley, D. (2020). Cricket and migration: Diaspora identities and sport in the UK. *Journal of Ethnic and Migration Studies*, 46(13), pp. 2771–2789.

Index

Index – Part II (Chapters 3–4)

Parsis
first Indian community to embrace cricket, 75

Partition (1947)
disruption of cricketing nations and legacies, 87

Azharuddin, Mohammad
captaincy in the 1990s, 100
embroiled in match-fixing scandal, 139

Bangalore (Chinnaswamy Stadium)
1996 World Cup quarter-final vs. Pakistan, 100

BCCI (Board of Control for Cricket in India)
liberalization era and financial rise, 100
dominance in ICC governance, 139
creation of IPL, 11

Calcutta (Eden Gardens)
1996 World Cup semi-final vs. Sri Lanka, crowd trouble, 100

Champions Trophy (ICC)
Indian heartbreaks (2013–2023), 11
Pakistan's 2017 triumph over India, 139
Sri Lanka's participation, 187

Coca-Cola Cup (Sharjah, 1999)
Pakistan defeating India in final, 139

Dhoni, Mahendra Singh
2007 World T20 captaincy breakthrough, 11
2011 World Cup-winning six, 11
2013 Champions Trophy win, 11

Dravid, Rahul
"The Wall," partnerships with Ganguly and Laxman, 11
key role in 2001 Kolkata Test vs. Australia, 11

Ganguly, Sourav
aggressive leadership style, 11
NatWest Trophy final win (2002), 11

Algorithmic governance
"AI MCC" proposals, 260; rule simulation & scenario testing, 254–255, 260–261; transparency & accountability, 238–240, 260–261; appeals & audit trails, 260–261.

Artificial intelligence (AI)
in umpiring & DRS, 230–233; predictive models (win probability, next-ball events), 231–233; selection & strategy (clustering, RL, Bayesian models), 233–237; injury risk & workload, 263–265; explainability (XAI) & bias, 238–240; governance & ethics, 238–240, 260–261.

Augmented reality (AR)
live overlays & smart lenses, 297–299; player POV & field maps, 297–299; training applications, 233–235, 303–306.

Bazball (England Test philosophy)
tactical profile & limits, 244–246; data-risk trade-offs, 244–246.

BCIs (Brain–Computer Interfaces)
broadcast interactivity & neural controls, 303–306; training & flow-state protocols, 303–306; cognitive metrics & consent, 303–306; controversies & safeguards, 308–309.

Ben Stokes
leadership & risk posture, 244–246; innovation within tradition, 244–246.

Blockchain
ticketing & authentication, 267–269; fan tokens & governance, 271–272, 282; royalties & smart contracts, 271–272; cross-league portability, 276–278.

Broadcasters (future stack)
cloud-first, edge distribution, 297–302; holographic & volumetric feeds, 299–301; multilingual "Robo-AI" commentary, 337–339.

Carbon accounting (cricket)
events & travel budgeting, 287–293; streaming emissions (codecs, CDNs, renewables), 294–295.

Climate change (impact on cricket)
heat, storms & rescheduling, 287–289; indoor/covered venues & cooling tech,

www.ingramcontent.com/pod-product-compliance
Lightning Source LLC
Chambersburg PA
CBHW041624140626
46547CB00030B/748